5A

FOCUS

ON

GRAMMAR

AN INTEGRATED SKILLS APPROACH

FOCUS

ON

GRAMMAR

AN INTEGRATED SKILLS APPROACH

THIRD EDITION

JAY MAURER

PEARSON
Longman

FOCUS ON GRAMMAR 5A: An Integrated Skills Approach

Pearson Education, 10 Bank Street, White Plains, NY 10606

Vice president, multimedia and skills: Sherry Preiss
Executive editor: Laura Le Dréan
Development editor: John Barnes
Production supervisor: Christine Edmonds
Production editor: Diana P. George
Art director: Ann France
Marketing manager: Timothy Benell
Senior manufacturing manager: Nancy Flaggman
Photo research: Aerin Csigay
Cover design: Rhea Banker
Cover images: Large shell, Nick Koudis, RF; background, Comstock Images, RF
Text design: Quorum Creative Services, Rhea Banker
Text composition: ElectraGraphics, Inc.
Text font: 11/13 Sabon, 10/13 Myriad Roman

Illustrators: Chris Gash pp. 2, 70, 99, 244; Burmar Technical Corporation pp. 11, 241;
Brian Hughes p. 51; A. J. Garces pp. 221, 259; David Klug p. 321; Jock MacRae p. 320;
Suzanne Mogensen pp. 175, 176; Andy Myer p. 349; Thomas Newsom pp. 110, 111,
393, 401, 402, 414, 415, 442; Dusan Petricic pp. 9, 28, 86, 141, 216, 335, 336; Susan
Scott pp. 52, 207, 253, 254, 293, 351; Meryl Treatner pp. 73, 81.

Photo credits: p. 16 AP/Wide World Photos; p. 26 Keri Pickett/Getty Images; p. 30 Printed by permission of the Norman Rockwell Family
Agency. Copyright © 1930 the Norman Rockwell Family Entities; p. 33 Getty Images; p. 56 Jack Hollingsworth/Getty Images; p. 57
Ron Chapple/Getty Images; p. 68 China Tourism Press/Getty Images; p. 89 Getty Images; p. 90 Steve Wood/Getty Images; p. 101 Hugh
Sitton/Getty Images; p. 114 Getty Images; p. 128 Art Wolfe/Getty Images; p. 139 SuperStock, Inc./SuperStock; p. 153 AP/Wide World Photos;
p. 165 Bettmann/Corbis; p. 180 (left) Martin Ruegner/Getty Images, (right) Joel Creed/Ecoscene/Corbis; p. 195 Photofest; p. 196 (top)
Photofest, (middle) New Line Cinema/The Kobal Collection, (bottom) Photofest; p. 231 AP/Wide World Photos; p. 233 (left) Dale
O'Dell/SuperStock, (right) AP/Wide World Photos; p. 235 (left) Wolfgang Kaehler/Corbis, (right) Royalty-Free/Corbis; p. 246 (left) Eric
Schaal/Getty Images, (left) ARPL/HIP/The Image Works; p. 247 (left) David Turnley/Corbis, (right) Gianni Dagli Orti/Corbis; p. 272 2002 Rick
London and Rich Diesslin; p. 285 Julian Hirshowitz/Corbis; p. 296 Pearson Education; p. 308 Pearson Education; p. 310 Syracuse
Newspapers/Dick Blum/The Image Works; p. 311 David Young-Wolff/PhotoEdit; p. 324 AP/Wide World Photos; p. 326 AP/Wide World Photos;
p. 326 AP/Wide World Photos; p. 340 Digital Vision/Getty Images; p. 352 Bonnie Kamin/PhotoEdit; p. 353 The Art Archive/Kunsthistorisches
Museum Vienna; p. 378 Bettmann/Corbis; p. 406 SuperStock, Inc./SuperStock; p. 422 Erik Dreyer/Getty Images.

Library of Congress Cataloging-in-Publication Data

Focus on grammar. An integrated skills approach — 3rd ed.
   p. cm.
  ISBN 0-13-147466-9 (v. 1 : student book : alk. paper) — ISBN 0-13-189971-6 (v. 2 : student
book : alk. paper) — ISBN 0-13-189984-8 (v. 3 : student book : alk. paper) — ISBN
0-13-190008-0 (v. 4 : student book : alk. paper) — ISBN 0-13-191273-9 (v. 5 : student book :
alk. paper)
  1. English language—Textbooks for foreign speakers. 2. English language—Grammar—
Problems, exercises, etc.
PE1128.F555 2005
428.2'4—dc22

2005007655

Printed in the United States of America

ISBN: 0-13-191281-X (Student Book A)
3 4 5 6 7 8 9 10—WC—12 11 10 09 08 07 06

ISBN: 0-13-193919-X (Student Book A with Audio CD)
3 4 5 6 7 8 9 10—WC—12 11 10 09 08 07 06

LONGMAN ON THE **WEB**

Longman.com offers online resources for
teachers and students. Access our Companion
Websites, our online catalog, and our local
offices around the world.

Visit us at **longman.com.**

CONTENTS

PART III   NOUNS

PART IV   ADJECTIVE CLAUSES

APPENDICES

GLOSSARY OF GRAMMAR TERMS

REVIEW TESTS ANSWER KEY

INDEX

ABOUT THE AUTHOR

Jay Maurer has taught English in binational centers, colleges, and universities in Portugal, Spain, Mexico, the Somali Republic, and the United States; and intensive English at Columbia University's American Language Program. In addition, he has been a teacher of college composition and literature at Santa Fe Community College and Northern New Mexico Community College. Mr. Maurer holds M.A. and M.Ed. degrees in Applied Linguistics and a Ph.D. degree in The Teaching of English, all from Columbia University. He is the co-author of the three-level *Structure Practice in Context* series; co-author with Irene Schoenberg of the five-level *True Colors* series and *Focus on Grammar 1: An Integrated Skills Approach*; co-author of the *True Voices* video series; co-author of *Teen Zone II*; and author of *Focus on Grammar 5: An Integrated Skills Approach*. Currently he writes and teaches in Seattle, Washington. *Focus on Grammar 5: An Integrated Skills Approach*, Third Edition, has grown out of the author's experiences as a practicing teacher of both ESL and college writing.

INTRODUCTION

The *Focus on Grammar* series

Written by ESL/EFL professionals, *Focus on Grammar: An Integrated Skills Approach* helps students to understand and practice English grammar. The primary aim of the course is for students to gain confidence in their ability to speak and write English accurately and fluently.

The **third edition** retains this popular series' focus on English grammar through lively listening, speaking, reading, and writing activities. The new *Focus on Grammar* also maintains the same five-level progression as the second edition:

- Level 1 (Beginning, formerly Introductory)
- Level 2 (High-Beginning, formerly Basic)
- Level 3 (Intermediate)
- Level 4 (High-Intermediate)
- Level 5 (Advanced)

What is the *Focus on Grammar* methodology?

Both controlled and communicative practice

While students expect and need to learn the formal rules of a language, it is crucial that they also practice new structures in a variety of contexts in order to internalize and master them. To this end, *Focus on Grammar* provides an abundance of both controlled and communicative exercises so that students can bridge the gap between knowing grammatical structures and using them. The many communicative activities in each Student Book unit provide opportunity for critical thinking while enabling students to personalize what they have learned in order to talk to one another with ease about hundreds of everyday issues.

A unique four-step approach

The series follows a four-step approach:

Step 1: Grammar in Context shows the new structures in natural context, such as articles and conversations.

Step 2: Grammar Presentation presents the structures in clear and accessible grammar charts, notes, and examples.

Step 3: Focused Practice of both form and meaning of the new structures is provided in numerous and varied controlled exercises.

Step 4: Communication Practice allows students to use the new structures freely and creatively in motivating, open-ended activities.

Thorough recycling

Underpinning the scope and sequence of the *Focus on Grammar* series is the belief that students need to use target structures many times, in different contexts, and at increasing levels of difficulty. For this reason, new grammar is constantly recycled throughout the book so that students have maximum exposure to the target forms and become comfortable using them in speech and in writing.

A complete classroom text and reference guide

A major goal in the development of *Focus on Grammar* has been to provide students with books that serve not only as vehicles for classroom instruction but also as resources for reference and self-study. In each Student Book, the combination of grammar charts, grammar notes, a glossary of grammar terms, and extensive appendices provides a complete and invaluable reference guide for students.

Ongoing assessment

Review Tests at the end of each part of the Student Book allow for continual self-assessment. In addition, the tests in the new *Focus on Grammar* Assessment Package provide teachers with a valid, reliable, and practical means of determining students' appropriate levels of placement in the course and of assessing students' achievement throughout the course. At Levels 4 (High-Intermediate) and 5 (Advanced), Proficiency Tests give teachers an overview of their students' general grammar knowledge.

What are the components of each level of *Focus on Grammar*?

Student Book

The Student Book is divided into eight or more parts, depending on the level. Each part contains grammatically related units, with each unit focusing on specific grammatical structures; where appropriate, units present contrasting forms. The exercises in each unit are thematically related to one another, and all units have the same clear, easy-to-follow format.

Teacher's Manual

The Teacher's Manual contains a variety of suggestions and information to enrich the material in the Student Book. It includes general teaching suggestions for each section of a typical unit, answers to frequently asked questions, unit-by-unit teaching tips with ideas for further communicative practice, and a supplementary activity section. Answers to the Student Book exercises and audioscripts of the listening activities are found at the back of the Teacher's Manual. Also included in the Teacher's Manual is a CD-ROM of teaching tools, including PowerPoint presentations that offer alternative ways of presenting selected grammar structures.

Workbook

The Workbook accompanying each level of *Focus on Grammar* provides additional exercises appropriate for self-study of the target grammar for each Student Book unit. Tests included in each Workbook provide students with additional opportunities for self-assessment.

Audio Program

All of the listening exercises from the Student Book, as well as the Grammar in Context passages and other appropriate exercises, are included on the program's CDs. In the book, the symbol ∩ appears next to the listening exercises. Another symbol ∩, indicating that listening is optional, appears next to the Grammar in Context passages and some exercises. All of these scripts appear in the Teacher's Manual and may be used as an alternative way of presenting the activities.

Some Student Books are packaged with a separate Student Audio CD. This CD includes the listening exercise from each unit and any other exercises that have an essential listening component.

CD-ROM

The *Focus on Grammar* CD-ROM provides students with individualized practice and immediate feedback. Fully contextualized and interactive, the activities broaden and extend practice of the grammatical structures in the reading, writing, speaking, and listening skills areas. The CD-ROM includes grammar review, review tests, score-based remedial practice, games, and all relevant reference material from the Student Book. It can also be used in conjunction with the *Longman Interactive American Dictionary* CD-ROM.

Assessment Package (NEW)

An extensive, comprehensive Assessment Package has been developed for each level of the third edition of *Focus on Grammar*. The components of the Assessment Package are:

1. Placement, Diagnostic, and Achievement Tests

- a Placement Test to screen students and place them into the correct level
- Diagnostic Tests for each part of the Student Book
- Unit Achievement Tests for each unit of the Student Book
- Part Achievement Tests for each part of the Student Book

2. General Proficiency Tests

- two Proficiency Tests at Level 4 (High-Intermediate)
- two Proficiency Tests at Level 5 (Advanced)

These tests can be administered at any point in the course.

3. Audio CD

The listening portions of the Placement, Diagnostic, and Achievement Tests are recorded on CDs. The scripts appear in the Assessment Package.

4. Test-Generating Software

The test-bank software provides thousands of questions from which teachers can create class-appropriate tests. All items are labeled according to the grammar structure they are testing, so teachers can easily select relevant items; they can also design their own items to add to the tests.

Transparencies (NEW)

Transparencies of all the grammar charts in the Student Book are also available. These transparencies are a classroom visual aid that will help instructors point out important patterns and structures of grammar.

Companion Website

The companion website contains a wealth of information and activities for both teachers and students. In addition to general information about the course pedagogy, the website provides extensive practice exercises for the classroom, a language lab, or at home.

What's new in the third edition of the Student Book?

In response to users' requests, this edition has:

- a new four-color design
- easy-to-read color coding for the four steps
- new and updated reading texts for Grammar in Context
- post-reading activities (in addition to the pre-reading questions)
- more exercise items
- an editing (error analysis) exercise in each unit
- an Internet activity in each unit
- a Glossary of Grammar Terms
- expanded Appendices

References

Alexander, L. G. (1988). *Longman English Grammar*. White Plains: Longman.

Biber, D., S. Conrad, E. Finegan, S. Johansson, and G. Leech (1999). *Longman Grammar of Spoken and Written English*. White Plains: Longman.

Celce-Murcia, M., and D. Freeman (1999). *The Grammar Book*. Boston: Heinle and Heinle.

Celce-Murcia, M., and S. Hilles (1988). *Techniques and Resources in Teaching Grammar*. New York: Oxford University Press.

Firsten, R. (2002). *The ELT Grammar Book*. Burlingame, CA: Alta Book Center Publishers.

Garner, B. (2003). *Garner's Modern American Usage*. New York: Oxford University Press.

Greenbaum, S. (1996). *The Oxford English Grammar*. New York: Oxford University Press.

Leech, G. (2004). *Meaning and the English Verb*. Harlow, UK: Pearson.

Lewis, M. (1997). *Implementing the Lexical Approach*. Hove East Sussex, UK: Language Teaching Publications.

Longman (2002). *Longman Dictionary of English Language and Culture*. Harlow, UK: Longman.

Willis, D. (2003). *Rules, Patterns and Words*. New York: Cambridge University Press.

TOUR OF A UNIT

Each unit in the *Focus on Grammar* series presents a specific grammar structure (or two, in the case of a contrast) and develops a major theme, which is set by the opening text. All units follow the same unique **four-step approach**.

Step 1: Grammar in Context

The **conversation** or **reading** in this section shows the grammar structure in a natural context. The high-interest text presents authentic language in a variety of real-life formats: magazine articles, web pages, questionnaires, and more. Students can listen to the text on an audio CD to get accustomed to the sound of the grammar structure in a natural context.

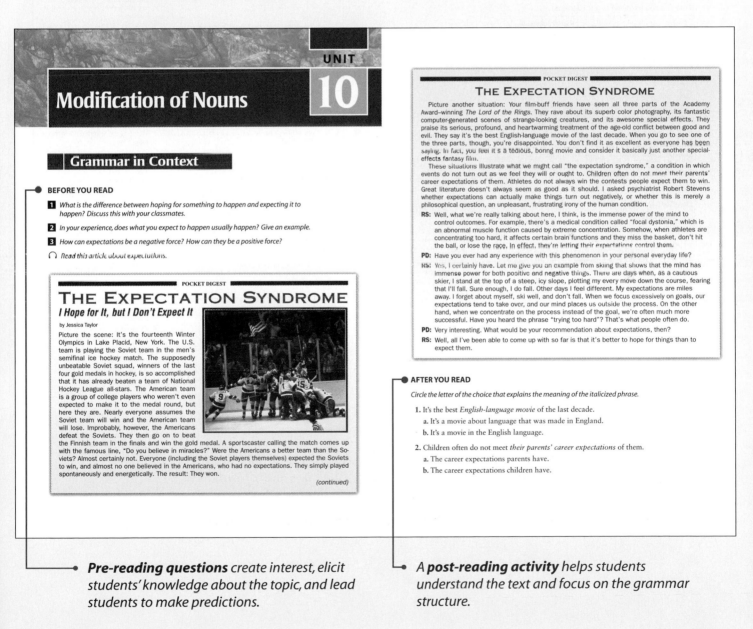

Pre-reading questions *create interest, elicit students' knowledge about the topic, and lead students to make predictions.*

A **post-reading activity** *helps students understand the text and focus on the grammar structure.*

Step 2: Grammar Presentation

This section is made up of grammar charts, notes, and examples. The **grammar charts** focus on the forms of the grammar structure. The **grammar notes** and **examples** focus on the meanings and uses of the structure.

*Clear and easy-to-read **grammar charts** present the grammar structure in all its forms and combinations.*

*Each **grammar note** gives a short, simple explanation of one use of the structure. The accompanying **examples** ensure students' understanding of the point.*

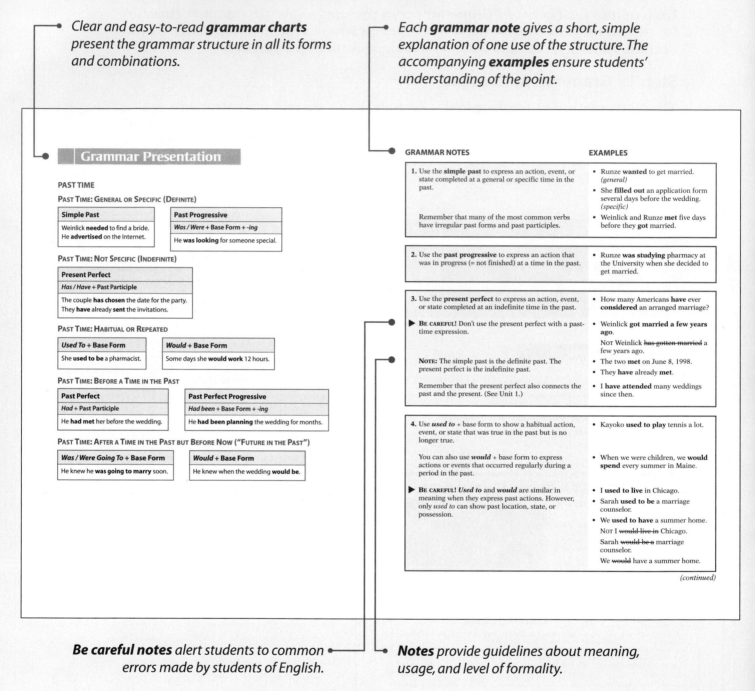

Be careful notes alert students to common errors made by students of English.

Notes provide guidelines about meaning, usage, and level of formality.

Step 3: Focused Practice

This section provides students with a variety of contextualized **controlled exercises** to practice both the forms and the uses of the grammar structure.

● Focused Practice *always begins with a "for recognition only" exercise called* **Discover the Grammar.**

Exercises are **cross-referenced** *to the appropriate grammar notes to provide a quick review.* ●

Focused Practice

1 | DISCOVER THE GRAMMAR

A *Look again at the opening reading. Find an example of each of the following changes from direct to indirect speech. Write the examples on the lines provided.*

1. _That . . . is less troubling / this was less troubling_
   (a present form of *be* changes to a past form of *be*)
2. _____
   (present progressive changes to past progressive)
3. _____
   (simple present changes to simple past)
4. _____
   (present perfect changes to past perfect)
5. _____
   (*will* changes to *would*)
6. _____
   (*ago* changes to another expression)

B *Read these statements in direct speech. Is the suggested change to indirect speech correct (**C**) or incorrect (**I**)?*

_C_ 1. Direct: That's a 5 percent change.

   Indirect: The reporter said that was a 5 percent change.

____ 2. Direct: In the latest GGG poll, Candidate A leads Candidate B by five points.

   Indirect: The reporter said that in the latest GGG poll, Candidate A had led Candidate B by five points.

____ 3. Direct: Candidate Q has gained two points on Candidate R.

   Indirect: The reporter said that Candidate Q gained two points on Candidate R.

____ 4. Direct: This suggests that Candidate Q is gaining momentum and that Candidate R is losing ground

   Indirect: The reporter said this suggested that Candidate Q was gaining momentum and that Candidate R was losing ground.

____ 5. Direct: That means that the Blues have to win 7 seats to take control.

   Indirect: The reporter said that meant that the Blues must have won 7 seats to take control.

____ 6. Direct: Recent estimates by experts on pollution show that more than 100 million Americans breathe polluted air.

   Indirect: The reporter said recent estimates by experts on pollution showed that more than 100 million Americans breathe polluted air.

● *A* **variety of exercise types** *guide students from recognition to accurate production of the grammar structure.*

5 | A PERSONAL INVENTORY *Grammar Notes 5–6*

Compare your life now to your life five years ago. Write eight sentences, using each of the quantifiers in the box.

a few	a little	a lot	fewer
less	many	more	much

Example: I have more friends now than I did five years ago.

6 | EDITING

Read this excerpt from a president's speech. There are 12 mistakes in the use of quantifiers. The first one is already corrected. Find and correct 11 more.

My fellow citizens: We are at a time in our history when we need to make some real
                                                     a great many
sacrifices. Recent presidents have made a great deal of promises they didn't keep. You may
not like everything I tell you tonight, but you deserve to hear the truth. On the economy,
we've made little progress, but we still have a great many work to do, so there are several
measures I'm proposing. First, I want to raise taxes on the very wealthy because a few of
them are really paying their share. Second, many of members of the middle class are
carrying an unfair tax burden, so I'm asking for a tax cut for the middle class. If I'm
successful, most of you in the middle class will be paying 10 percent less in taxes next year,
though few of you in the higher income group may see your taxes rise little.

How do I intend to make up the lost revenue? The problem with the national income
tax is that there are much loopholes in the current law which allow any people to avoid
paying any taxes at all; I want to close these loopholes. My additional plan is to replace the
lost revenue with a national sales tax, which is fairer because it applies to every people
equally. Third, we have no money to finance health care reform, and we've made a little
progress in reducing pollution and meeting clean air standards. Therefore, I am asking for
a 50-cent-a-gallon tax on gasoline, which will result in many more people using public
transportation and will create additional revenue. Thus, we will have enough of money to
finance our new health care program and will help the environment at the same time.

● Focused Practice *always ends with an* **editing** *exercise to teach students to find and correct typical mistakes.*

Step 4: Communication Practice

This section provides open-ended **communicative activities** giving students the opportunity to use the grammar structure appropriately and fluently.

A **listening** activity gives students the opportunity to check their aural comprehension.

Many exercises and activities are **art-based** to provide visual cues and an interesting context and springboard for meaningful conversations.

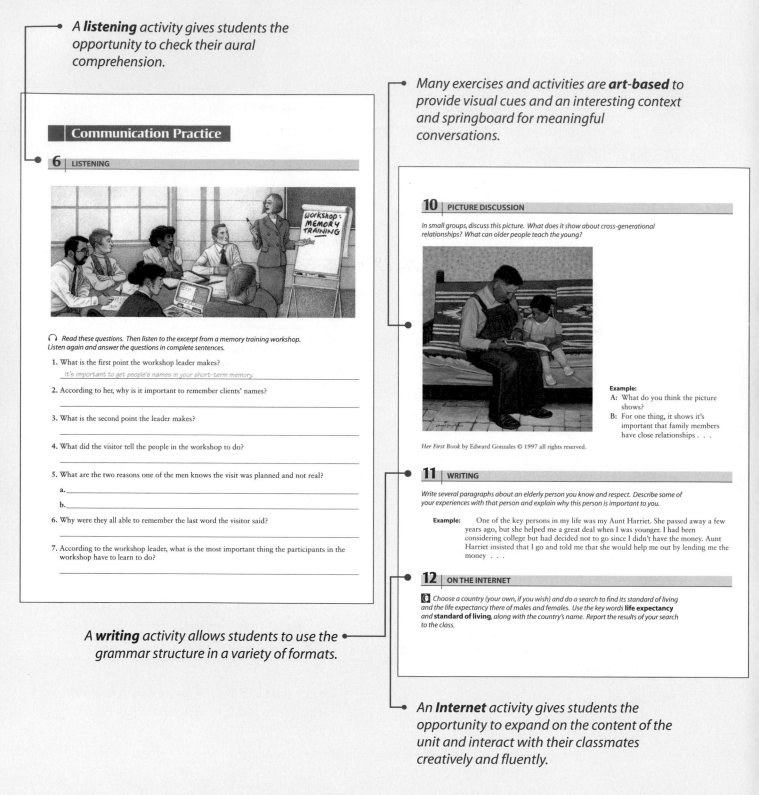

Communication Practice

6 LISTENING

🎧 *Read these questions. Then listen to the excerpt from a memory training workshop. Listen again and answer the questions in complete sentences.*

1. What is the first point the workshop leader makes?

   It's important to get people's names in your short-term memory.

2. According to her, why is it important to remember clients' names?

3. What is the second point the leader makes?

4. What did the visitor tell the people in the workshop to do?

5. What are the two reasons one of the men knows the visit was planned and not real?

   a.

   b.

6. Why were they all able to remember the last word the visitor said?

7. According to the workshop leader, what is the most important thing the participants in the workshop have to learn to do?

10 PICTURE DISCUSSION

In small groups, discuss this picture. What does it show about cross-generational relationships? What can older people teach the young?

Example:
A: What do you think the picture shows?
B: For one thing, it shows it's important that family members have close relationships . . .

Her First Book by Edward Gonzales © 1997 all rights reserved.

11 WRITING

Write several paragraphs about an elderly person you know and respect. Describe some of your experiences with that person and explain why this person is important to you.

Example: One of the key persons in my life was my Aunt Harriet. She passed away a few years ago, but she helped me a great deal when I was younger. I had been considering college but had decided not to go since I didn't have the money. Aunt Harriet insisted that I go and told me that she would help me out by lending me the money . . .

12 ON THE INTERNET

🖥 *Choose a country (your own, if you wish) and do a search to find its standard of living and the life expectancy there of males and females. Use the key words* **life expectancy** *and* **standard of living**, *along with the country's name. Report the results of your search to the class.*

A **writing** activity allows students to use the grammar structure in a variety of formats.

An **Internet** activity gives students the opportunity to expand on the content of the unit and interact with their classmates creatively and fluently.

TOUR BEYOND THE UNIT

In the *Focus on Grammar* series, the grammatically related units are grouped into parts, and each part concludes with a section called **From Grammar to Writing** and a **Review Test** section.

From Grammar to Writing

This section presents a point which applies specifically to writing, for example, combining sentences with time words. Students are guided to practice the point in **a piece of extended writing**.

● Activities focus on issues **important for successful writing**.

● Activities focus on issues **important for successful writing**.

PART

II

From **Grammar** to Writing
Topic Sentences

A common way of organizing a composition or other piece of writing in English is to begin with a **topic sentence**. A topic sentence is a general sentence that covers the content of the entire paragraph. All the supporting examples and details of the paragraph must fit under this sentence. It is usually the first sentence in the paragraph. Look at this paragraph from an essay.

> For me, a dog is a better pet than a cat. When I come home from work, for example, my dog comes to meet me at the door. He is always glad to see me. My cat, on the other hand, couldn't care less whether I'm at home or not, as long as I keep filling her food dish. Another good thing about a dog is that you can teach him tricks. Cats, however, can't be bothered to learn anything new. The best thing about a dog, though, is that he's a great companion. I can take my dog on hikes and walks. He goes everywhere with me. As we all know, you can't take a cat for a walk.

The topic sentence for this paragraph is "For me, a dog is a better pet than a cat." This sentence tells the reader what to expect in the paragraph: some reasons why the writer considers a dog a superior pet.

1 | *This paragraph contains many supporting details but no topic sentence. Read the paragraph. Then circle the letter of the best topic sentence for the paragraph.*

> For one thing, you should always remove your shoes when you enter a Japanese home, and you should leave them pointing toward the door. Another suggestion is to make sure that you bring a gift for your Japanese hosts, and to be sure to wrap it. A third recommendation is to be appreciative of things in a Japanese house, but not too appreciative. Finally, remember that when you sit down to eat, you do not have to accept every kind of food that you are offered, but you are expected to finish whatever you do put on your plate.

Choices

a. Visiting a Japanese home is very enjoyable.

b. Taking a gift is very important when you visit a Japanese home.

c. There are a number of things to keep in mind when you visit a Japanese home.

d. When you visit a Japanese home, be sure not to eat too much.

103

---

4 | *Look at the following sets of supporting details. For each set, write an appropriate topic sentence.*

1. _____
   a. For one thing, there's almost always a traffic jam I get stuck in, and I'm often late to work.
   b. Also, there's not always a parking place when I do get to work.
   c. Worst of all, I'm spending more money on gas and car maintenance than I would if I took public transportation.

2. _____
   a. One is that I often fall asleep when watching the TV screen, no matter how interesting the video is.
   b. Another is that watching movies is basically a social experience, and I'm usually alone when I watch videos.
   c. The main reason is that the TV screen, no matter how large it is, diminishes the impact that you get when watching a movie on the big screen.

3. _____
   a. Nothing spontaneous usually happens on a guided tour, but I've had lots of spontaneous experiences when I planned my own vacation.
   b. Tour guides present you with what *they* think is interesting, but when you are in charge of your own vacation, you do what *you* think is interesting.
   c. Individually planned vacations can often be less expensive than guided tours.

4. _____
   a. Cats don't bark and wake up the neighbors or bite the letter carrier.
   b. Dogs have to be walked at least two times a day, but cats handle their own exercise.
   c. Cats eat a lot less than dogs.

5 | *Write a paragraph of several sentences about one of the following topics, a similar topic that interests you, or a topic suggested by your teacher. Make sure that your paragraph has a topic sentence. Then share your work with three or four other students. Read each other's paragraphs. Identify topic sentences. Make sure that each one is not a fragment and that it is appropriate for the paragraph.*

Topics

- An annoying habit
- The best part of the day
- Night owls versus early birds
- The ideal vacation
- A problem in society
- Expectation versus reality

● **Writing formats** include business letters, personal letters, notes, instructions, paragraphs, reports, and essays.

● The section ends with **peer review** and **editing** of the students' writing.

Review Test

This review section, covering all the grammar structures presented in the part, can be used as a test. An **Answer Key** is provided at the back of the book.

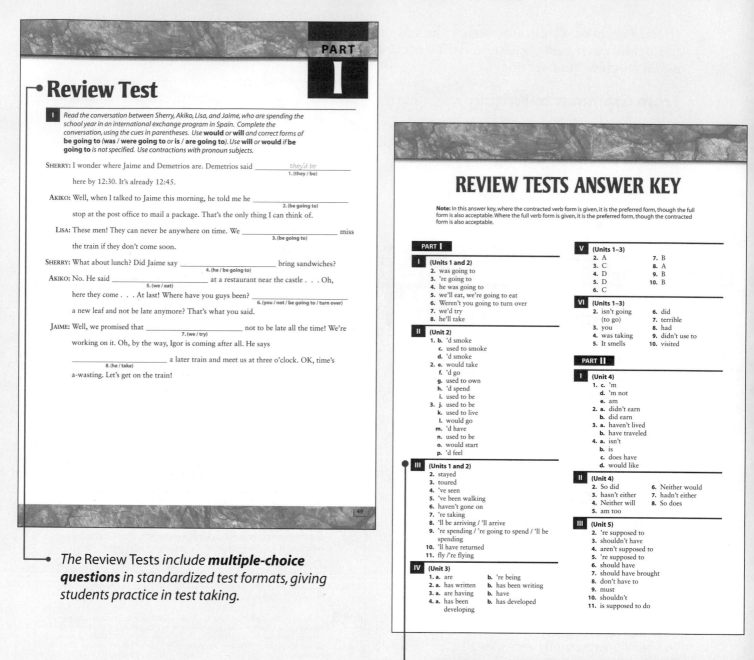

The Review Tests *include **multiple-choice questions** in standardized test formats, giving students practice in test taking.*

The Answer Key to the Review Tests *provides **cross-references** to the appropriate unit(s) for easy review.*

ACKNOWLEDGMENTS

Writing the Third Edition of *Focus on Grammar 5* has been even more interesting and challenging than the first two times. I'm indebted to many people who helped me in different ways. Specifically, though, I want to express my appreciation and gratitude to:

- My students over the years.

- Françoise Leffler, for her excellent editing work in the early stages of the project.

- Marjorie Fuchs, Margo Bonner, Miriam Westheimer, and Irene Schoenberg—the other members of the FOG author team—for their support and encouragement.

- That genius, whoever he or she is, who created the joke about the parrot that has been floating around in cyberspace for some time now. The same for the unknown authors of the bumper stickers.

- Nancy Blodgett and Kathleen Silloway for their expertise in moving the project along.

- Jane Curtis, whose experience and many excellent comments were invaluable in reframing the grammar charts and notes and the From Grammar to Writing exercises. Many thanks.

- Laura Le Dréan, for her confidence and excellent direction of the entire project. Thanks very much.

- John Barnes, my editor, for his patience with me, his excellent eye for detail, and his overall vision. He has been instrumental in making this a better book.

Above all I am grateful to:

- My friends at West Side who have encouraged me.

- My wife Priscilla for her love and wonderful support.

- My best friend.

I am also grateful to the following reviewers:

Mary Ann Archbold, South Bay Adult School, Redondo Beach, CA; **Sheila Badanic,** Douglas College, New Westminister, BC; **John T. Campbell,** Southeast Missouri State University, MO; **Tony Carnerie,** Allaint International University–San Diego, CA; **Amelia Chávez Ruiz,** Lake Forest School, Mexico State, Mexico; **Elizabeth Clemente,** Instituto Tecnológico de Estudios Superiores de Monterrey, Atizapan, Mexico State; **Susanna Eguren,** Instituto Cultural Peruano Norteamericano, Lima, Peru; **Shirley Freeden,** University of Saskatchewan, Saskatoon, Saskatchewan; **Stegan Haag,** Langara College, Vancouver, BC; **Martha Hall,** The New England School of English, Cambridge, MA; **Molly Hashman,** Calgary, AB; **Vicki L. Holmes,** University of Nevada, Las Vegas, NV; **Silvia Icela**

Espinoza Galvez, Colegio Lux, Hermosillo, Sonora; **Elena Lattarulo,** Cuesta College, San Luis Obispo, CA; **Louise Mavalankar,** Truman College, Chicago, IL; **Brian McDonald,** English Language Program, Grossmont College; **Martha McGaughey,** Language Training Institute, NJ; **Myo Myint,** Mission College, Santa Clara, CA; **Georgina Orozco,** Instituto Cumbre, Ciudad Obregón, Sonora; **Kathleen Pierce,** Bell Language School, Brooklyn, NY; **Rhonda Ramirez,** Garland High School, TX; **Ernesto Romo,** Lake Forest School, Mexico State, Mexico; **Fiorilla Ruggiero,** Penn Valley Community College, MO; **Fernando Rujeles,** Centro Colombo Americano, Bogotá, Colombia; **René Sandoval,** Martin Luther King, Jr. School, Guadalajara, Jalisco; **Rusten Seven,** Dokuz Eylul University School of Languages, Izmir, Turkey; **María Elena Vera de la Rosa,** Lake Forest School, Mexico State, Mexico; **Magneli Villanueva Morales,** Universidad Regiomontana, Monterrey, Nuevo León; **Carolyn Vizcaya,** Colegio Villa Rica, Boca del Río, Mexico

CREDITS

Pages 2–3: Based on Rich Beattie, "How to Bargain for Anything . . . Anywhere," *Travel Holiday,* September 1998, pp. 56, 58, 60.

Pages 9–10: David Holmstrom, "This Man's Been Nearly Everywhere." John Clouse. *Christian Science Monitor,* March 10, 1998, p. 1. Copyright 1998. The Christian Science Publishing Society. Reproduced with permission. All rights reserved. For permission to reprint, fax your request to 617-450-2031 or e-mail to copyrt@cps.com.

Pages 16–17: Based on information in "A Match Made in the Mall: Minnesota Anthropology Student Weds Bride Chosen by Family and Friends," *Dallas Morning News,* June 14, 1998, p. 7A, copyright: The Associated Press; "Here Come the Bridal Candidates: Society: Friends of 28-year-old will vote to select his mate. As election day nears, Dad is not so sure of the plan," Home Edition; *Los Angeles Times,* June 8, 1998, p. A-19.

Page 26: Adapted from Phil McCombs, *Washington Post.* In *Lakes Area News.* brainerddispatch.com. Web posted February 24, 2001.

Pages 56–57: Based on "Born First or Last: Does It Matter?" by Carol Kramer, Internet. OCP General Research, http://www.eisa.net.au/-santeri/fbol.html.

Pages 69–70: John Rosemond, "Asian Parents Differ on Childrearing." *Albuquerque Journal,* July 1, 1993. Family psychologist John Rosemond is the author of eight best-selling parenting books and is one of America's most popular speakers. For more information, see his website at www.rosemond.com.

Pages 72–74: Based on information in Rex Shelley, *Culture Shock: Japan* (Portland, OR: Graphic Arts Publishing, 1993).

Page 81: Based on information in Norine Dressler, *Multicultural Manners: New Rules of Etiquette for a Changing Society* (New York: John Wiley & Sons, 1996), pp. 94, 98–99.

Pages 89–90: Based on information in "St. Brendan's Isle," www.castletown.com/brendan.htm and "Who the Heck Did 'Discover' the New World?" by Donald Dale Jackson. *Smithsonian,* September 1991, pp. 76–85.

Pages 98–99: Based on information in David Feldman, *Imponderables: The Solution to the Mysteries of Everyday Life.* (New York: William Morrow, 1986, 1987).

Page 100: For riddle 1: Eric Elfman, *Almanac of the Gross, Disgusting, and Totally Repulsive* (New York: Random House, 1994); for riddles 2 and 3: Louis G. Cowan, *The Quiz Kids, Questions and Answers* (Akron, Ohio: Saalfield Publishing, 1941); for riddle 4: Ann Elwood and Carol Orsag Madigan, *The Macmillan Book of Fascinating Facts* (New York: Macmillan, 1989).

Pages 114–115: Based on Emma Duncan, "A Survey of Food," *The Economist,* December 13, 2003.

Page 121: Charlyn Fargo, "Fusion Cooking Melds Cultures and Tastes," Copley News Service (San Diego, CA), August 5, 1998, p. F5.

Pages 128–129: Based on Jared Diamond, "Twilight at Easter," *The New York Review of Books,* Volume 51, Number 5, March 25, 2004.

Page 134: Some information taken from *The World Almanac and Book of Facts 2004* (New York: World Almanac Education Group, Inc., 2004), pp. 183, 192.

Page 135: Excerpted from "Earthweek: A Diary of the Planet," by Steve Newman, ©Chronicle Features 2004. In *The Seattle Times*, February 27, 2004, p. A3.

Page 149: *The World Almanac and Book of Facts, 2004* (New York: World Almanac Education Group, Inc., 2004), p. 13.

Page 164: Adapted from the introduction to *Appointment in Samarra*, by John O'Hara. New York: Harcourt, Brace, and Company, 1934. Story originally written by W. Somerset Maugham in his play *Sheppey*.

Pages 180–181: Adapted from "What's Your Personality Type?" *New Woman*, August 1998, pp. 68–71, by Barbara Barron-Tieger and Paul D. Tieger, authors of *Do What You Are, Nurture by Nature*, and *The Art of SpeedReading People*.

Pages 206 and 209: *A Beautiful Mind*, copyright © 2002 by Leonard Maltin, from *LEONARD MALTIN'S 2003 MOVIE & VIDEO GUIDE*, by Leonard Maltin. Used by permission of Dutton Signet, a division of Penguin Putnam, Inc.

Pages 220–221: Based on information in Mark McGwire, "15 Minutes of Fame," *Biography Magazine*, September 1998; and Richard Severn, "D. B. Cooper: Perfect Crime or Perfect Folly?" *Seattle Times*, November 17, 1996.

Pages 235–236: Adapted from Patricia Hughes, "The Sacred Rac," in *Focusing on Global Poverty and Development* by Jayne C. Millar (Washington, D.C.: Overseas Development Council, 1974).

Page 250: Adapted from E. Randall Floyd, *Great American Mysteries* (Little Rock: August House Publishers, 1990).

Pages 252: Adapted from Kenneth C. Davis's *Don't Know Much About History?* (New York: Avon Books, 1990), pp. 13–14.

Pages 258–259: Based on Judith Viorst's essay "Friends, Good Friends, and Such Good Friends." in Alfred Rosa and Paul Eschholz, eds., *Models for Writers: Short Essays for Composition*, 3rd ed. New York: St. Martin's Press, 1989.

Pages 317–318: Based on information in Tamim Ansary, "What Makes a Sport Olympic?" www.encnet/features/column/?page=tamimhome.

Page 318, Exercise 4: Alex Salkever, Special to *The Christian Science Monitor*, "When Sports Become Too Extreme," *The Christian Science Monitor*, March 24, 1998, p. 1. Reprinted by permission of the author.

Pages 326–327: Based on information in Brad Darrach, "Journey: A Brave Family Changes Horror into Healing after a Child Dies," *Life*, October 1, 1995, pp. 42+.

Page 333: Sutapa Mukerjee, "A Caring Elephant That Died of Grief," *The Seattle Post-Intelligencer*, May 6, 1999, Copyright: The Associated Press.

Pages 340–341: Based on information in Emily Yoffe, "How Quickly We Forget," *U. S. News & World Report*, October 13, 1997, p. 52.

Pages 364–365: Author unknown. The story is adapted from one that has been circulating on the Internet for a number of years.

Page 372: Includes material adapted from "Humor," *The World Book Encyclopedia*, Volume H. (Chicago: World Book, 1998), pp. 435–436; and "Humour and Wit," *Encyclopedia Britannica*, Macropaedia (Chicago: Encyclopedia, 1998), p. 686.

Page 373: Some items from *Funny Bumper Stickers. The Canonical List of Bumper Stickers*. www.ruighaver.net/bumperstickers/list.htm.

Page 376: David Field, "They Do Have a Sense of Humor," *USA Today*, September 22, 1998. Reprinted with permission.

Pages 378–379: Adapted from Project for Excellence in Journalism, *Five Common Mistakes Journalists Make with Numbers*. Washington, D. C. journalism.org. Web posted October 2002.

PART

I

Past, Present, and Future

Grammar in Context

BEFORE YOU READ

1 *Where do you like to travel?*

2 *Look at the picture. When you travel, do you ever bargain to get a better price?*

3 *Is it fair to try to get a lower price for an item, or is it better to pay the price the seller wants?*

🎧 *Read this article about learning how to bargain.*

WORLD TRAVELER

It's a Bargain!

by Tammy Samuelson

ONE THOUSAND

SIX HUNDRED

$1,000.00

In an open-air market in Turkey, a tourist is admiring the beautiful oriental rugs on display. She finds one she likes and asks the price. "One thousand dollars," the vendor says. Knowing she shouldn't pay the full price, she says, "Six hundred!" "Nine hundred!" the vendor counters. The woman throws up her hands in mock frustration and walks away. The vendor goes after her. Not long afterwards, both vendor and buyer agree on eight hundred dollars, a 20 percent reduction. Both vendor and customer are smiling and happy. They've just participated in a ritual that has existed worldwide for centuries.

So you're visiting another country this year? You already have your tickets, and you leave next Tuesday at 4 P.M. A week from now you'll be relaxing in the sunshine or visiting famous landmarks. By the end of the summer, of course, you'll have been traveling for several weeks, and it'll be time to think about bringing back some souvenirs for friends and family. Souvenirs cost money, though, so maybe if you do some bargaining, you'll be able to get some good buys. . . . What? You don't know how to bargain? You're afraid to? Relax. In my capacity as the *Times* travel editor, I've been making trips abroad since 1997, and I've visited 38 countries. I take a trip every year, so bargaining is one thing I've learned to do. In this week's column I'm going to give you some tips on how to perform this most enjoyable activity. Once you learn to bargain, I think you'll like it.

Many people are used to paying fixed prices for items and are reluctant to bargain. Some may be afraid to hurt the vendor's feelings by offering too low a price. Others are afraid of being assertive. Some may even avoid bargaining because they want to give the impression they can afford anything. Bargaining is not too big a deal in some countries, but even in North America a certain kind of bargaining goes on whenever someone goes to a yard or garage sale and tries to get the seller to lower the price. Vendors in much of the world expect you to bargain and will be disappointed if you don't. So here are some bargaining tips.

FIRST TIP Find out how much something is worth. When you bargain with someone, the object of the game is not to beat the vendor. It's to pay a fair price for whatever you want to buy. So do some research. Get a good idea of the general price range for an item. That way you'll be able to bargain with confidence.

OK. You've done your research. You know how much things cost, so you can go shopping.

SECOND TIP Never accept the first offer. You'll make a counter-offer when the vendor says the price. Remember: The vendor expects this.

THIRD TIP Treat the vendor with respect. Keep in mind that the bargaining experience should not be a competition; it should be a game. Stick to your guns, but have fun with the process. If the vendor insists it's impossible to go any lower on the price, show her how much money you have. But be polite.

FOURTH TIP Be prepared to walk away if you don't get a fair price. Don't get angry. Just make it clear you're not going to buy if the vendor doesn't come down. If he doesn't, start to walk away. As soon as you do this, he will most likely come running after you.

THE FINAL TIP Be sure to wear sunglasses. For centuries people of many cultures have regarded the eyes as "the windows of the soul." If you're nervous or intimidated, this will show in your eyes. Wear dark glasses to conceal your anxiety. You'll feel more confident if you do.

Well, have I persuaded you? Do you feel a little more confident, or at least a little less nervous? By the time you get home, you'll have seen a lot of wonderful things. If you haven't bargained, though, you'll have missed out on one of life's most interesting experiences. Give it a try. Have a great trip, and have no fear!

AFTER YOU READ

What does each sentence mean or imply? Circle the correct answer.

1. So you're visiting another country this year?
   a. You're already visiting another country.
   b. You're going to visit another country in the near future.

2. I've been making trips abroad since 1997.
   a. The author certainly won't make any more trips abroad.
   b. The author may make some more trips abroad.

3. When you make it clear you're not going to buy, the vendor will lower the price.
   a. Neither action is in the future.
   b. Both actions are in the future.

Grammar Presentation

PRESENT AND FUTURE TIME

PRESENT TIME: IN GENERAL OR NOW

Simple Present
Tourists often **spend** a lot of money.

Present Progressive
Be + Base Form + *-ing*
A tourist **is looking** for a souvenir.

PRESENT TIME: FROM A TIME IN THE PAST UNTIL NOW

Present Perfect
Have + Past Participle
We **have visited** 11 countries so far.

Present Perfect Progressive
Have been + Base Form + *-ing*
We**'ve been traveling** for three weeks.

FUTURE TIME: A TIME IN THE FUTURE

Simple Future
Will / Be going to + Base Form
You**'ll like** the hotel. You**'re going to like** the hotel.

Future Progressive
Will be + Base Form + *-ing*
A week from now, you**'ll be relaxing** in the sun.

Simple Present
The tour **starts** tomorrow at 4:00 P.M.

Present Progressive
Be + Base Form + *-ing*
We**'re visiting** our friends later this summer.

Two Actions in the Future
I**'ll call** you as soon as we **land.**

Future Perfect
Will have + Past Participle
We**'ll have arrived** by 4:00 P.M.

Future Perfect Progressive
Will have been + Base Form + *-ing*
We **will have been flying** for hours by then.

GRAMMAR NOTES

EXAMPLES

1. Use the **simple present** to show actions, events, or states that are true in general or happen habitually.

   We also use the simple present to narrate events in sequence.

   - Vendors **work** long hours. *(true in general)*
   - We **spend** every August at the beach. *(habitual)*
   - A tourist **finds** a beautiful dress and **asks** how much it costs.

2. Use the **present progressive** to show actions or events that are in progress at the moment (not finished).

   ▶ BE CAREFUL! Don't use the progressive with non-action verbs.

   - A tourist **is admiring** the rugs. *(right now)*
   - She **likes** that rug.
     NOT She's liking that rug.

3. The **present perfect** and the **present perfect progressive** connect the past and the present. Use them to show actions and states that began in the past and continue until now.

   Note that they are often used with *for* + a length of time and *since* + a starting point.

   ▶ BE CAREFUL! Don't use the simple present for actions or events that began in the past and are continuing now.

   - Bargaining **has existed for** centuries.
   - She's **been writing** her travel column **since** 1997.
   - I've **been** here for three months now.
     NOT I'm here for three months now.

4. Use the **present perfect**, not the present perfect progressive, to describe completed actions with a connection to the present.

   - I've **visited** Italy four times.
     NOT I've been visiting Italy four times.

(continued)

<table>
<tr>
<td>

5. Use the **present perfect progressive** to show that an action with a connection to the present is unfinished or temporary.

</td>
<td>

- They**'ve been touring** Italy. *(They're still touring.)*
- He**'s been studying** in Boston but will soon return home.

</td>
</tr>
<tr>
<td>

6. Use *will* or *be going to* to say what you think will happen in the future.

▶ **BE CAREFUL!** Use *will*, not *be going to*, to express an unplanned future action.

▶ **BE CAREFUL!** Use *be going to*, not *will*, to talk about a future situation that is planned or already developing.

</td>
<td>

- I think I**'ll enjoy** the trip.

OR

- I think I**'m going to enjoy** the trip.
- Call me next week. Maybe I**'ll be** free.

 NOT Maybe ~~I'm going to~~ be free.
- We**'re going to take** our vacation in June this year.

 NOT ~~We'll take~~ our vacation in June this year.

</td>
</tr>
<tr>
<td>

7. Use *will* in the **progressive** to describe an action that will be in progress at a certain time in the future.

USAGE NOTE: We often use the **future progressive** informally to talk about a **future intention**.

</td>
<td>

- Next week at this time we**'ll be climbing** Kilimanjaro.
- We**'ll be visiting** Florence on our Italy trip.

</td>
</tr>
<tr>
<td>

8. You can use the **present progressive** to talk about a future action or event that has already been arranged.

</td>
<td>

- We**'re traveling** to Japan in August. We already have our tickets.

</td>
</tr>
<tr>
<td>

9. You can use the **simple present** to talk about a future action, state, or event that is part of a schedule or timetable.

</td>
<td>

- We **leave** on Saturday at 8:00 P.M.
- The plane **arrives** in Rome at 8:30 A.M.

</td>
</tr>
<tr>
<td>

10. To talk about two separate actions in the future, use *will* or *be going to* in the independent clause and the simple present in the dependent clause.

</td>
<td>

independent clause   dependent clause
- We**'ll rent** a car when we **get** to Italy.

 NOT We'll rent a car when we ~~will get~~ to Italy.

</td>
</tr>
</table>

> **11.** Use the **future perfect** to show an action, state, or event that will happen before a certain time in the future.
>
> You can also use the future perfect in the **progressive**.
>
> **NOTE:** We often use the future perfect with *by* and *by the time*.

> - By the end of our trip, we**'ll have seen** a lot of wonderful things.
>
> - By the end of the summer, we**'ll have been traveling** for several weeks.
> - ***By the time*** we finish our trip, we**'ll have visited** 18 countries.

Reference Notes
For definitions and examples of **grammar terms**, see Glossary on page G-1.
For a list of **non-action verbs**, see Appendix 2 on page A-2.
For a list of **non-action verbs sometimes used in the progressive**, see Appendix 3 on page A-3.
For a list of **words that begin dependent clauses**, see Appendix 20 on page A-9.

Focused Practice

1 | DISCOVER THE GRAMMAR

A *Refer to the article and follow the instructions.*

1. Read the first paragraph of the opening reading. Which verbs are used to:
   a. narrate events in sequence?
   b. show an action in progress?

2. In the last line of paragraph 1, what form is the verb phrase "has existed"? Why does the author use that form here?

3. In paragraph 2, the future is expressed in several different ways. Underline the verbs and label the ways.

B *Look at these sentences. Does the underlined verb refer to present time or future time?*

1. A tourist <u>is admiring</u> the beautiful oriental rugs. ___*present*___

2. A tourist <u>finds</u> a rug she likes. _____

3. She <u>asks</u> the price. _____

4. So <u>you're visiting</u> another country this year. _____

5. You <u>leave</u> next Tuesday at 4:00 P.M. _____

6. When you <u>do</u> some bargaining, you'll get some good buys. _____

7. You'll make a counter-offer when the vendor <u>announces</u> the price. _____

8. After you <u>make</u> it clear you're not going to buy, the vendor will come down. _____

2 | A LETTER HOME

Nancy Osborne is traveling in Europe. Complete her letter to her friend Evelyn with the correct forms of the verbs in the box. Use only the forms presented in this unit. Use a verb more than once if necessary.

be	get	go	love	shine	stay	visit

Sunday, July 19
Hi Evelyn,

    Well, I _____'ve been_____ in London for a week now,
1.

and the sun _____ every day since I got here.
2.

What a surprise! I _____ my favorite
3.

museums and all the usual attractions—went to the British Museum yesterday

and had such a good time that I _____ again today. Also went
4.

to the Tower of London. I really _____ a kick out of those
5.

guides in their funny hats.

    I _____ in a bed and breakfast that is really nice, but it's
6.

also pretty expensive, so I _____ to a hostel tonight. I don't
7.

think I'll mind staying there, since I don't need luxury.

    The British people _____ so friendly and helpful! And I
8.

really _____ the accent.
9.

    That's it for now. Hope things _____ OK with you. I'll write
10.

again soon.

Best,
Nancy

3 | **A WORLD TRAVELER**   *Grammar Notes 1–3, 6, 8*

Read this article about John Clouse. At the time the article was written, Clouse had visited more countries than anyone else in the world. Complete the passage by circling the correct verb forms.

This Man's Been Nearly Everywhere

John Clouse (has) / is having the thickest, most dog-eared passport in the world. Turn
1.

to page 16 of the 1996 *Guiness Book of World Records* and you are going to find / 'll find
2.

the reason. He will hold / holds the record for traveling to all 192 of the globe's inde-
3.

pendent countries, and to all but a few of the other territories that existed in early 1996.

Clouse, who has spent about $1.25 million roaming from A to Z in the past 40 years,

says he travels for the love of it, not to outrun anybody else who may be keeping a list. He

is now down to just three remote islands to visit.

Clouse has continued / continued his journeys since making the record book, and not
4.

only has he visited every country in the world, but some two or three times. Now he

focuses / is focusing on the remaining three islands.
5.

"Yeah, I 've been trying / try to get to three places: one is the Paracel Islands, owned
6.

by China in the South China Sea," he says. "And on two occasions the weather

has kept / has been keeping me from reaching Bouvet, an island in Norwegian Antarctica.
7.

No. 3 is Clipperton, a French island about 700 miles west of Acapulco."

After all his traveling he says / will say, "I don't believe there are evil empires and evil
8.

people. Yes, there are some bad leaders in the world, but seeing people as individuals has

taught me that they are all basically alike. You can be in some terrible place and someone

will extend hospitality to you."

Clouse is traveling / travels light, with a small suitcase, and seldom goes / will go
9.   **10.**

first class. His collection of *National Geographic* magazines is his source for research.

(continued)

Years ago he stopped taking photos and now has kept / keeps a journal of his travels.
11.

He has crossed the Atlantic Ocean at least 100 times, and the Pacific Ocean

40 or 50 times.

Clouse concludes / will conclude that the right attitude is synonymous with the
12.

lightness of his suitcase. "Travel without a lot of mental baggage," he says. "Try not to go

with preconceived notions that the place will be dirty or hostile, and if it is, go with the

flow and make the best of it."

"Learn a few words like *please* and *thank you*," he suggests. "That really

is going to please / pleases people."
13.

---

4 | **A TRIP TO EAST AFRICA**   *Grammar Notes 4–6, 8–10*

*Study the Lamonts' itinerary for their trip to East Africa. Then complete the sentences with
the correct present or future form of the verbs in parentheses.*

East Africa Trip Itinerary

Date	Destination
June 5	Land in Nairobi, Kenya, at 12 noon
June 5–6	Stay in Nairobi; tour the city
June 7	Visit Treetops resort in Kenya; stay the night there
June 8–9	Take the train to Dar Es Salaam, Tanzania; tour the city; travel to Mombasa on the afternoon of June 9; stay there that night
June 10	Tour Mombasa; take the boat to Zanzibar; stay there that night
June 11	Tour Zanzibar; return to Mombasa late afternoon; take the bus to Moshi at 5 P.M.; stay in Moshi that night
June 12–16	Climb Kilimanjaro
June 16	Take the bus to Ngorongoro Crater; stay there that night
June 17	Tour Ngorongoro Crater in a land rover until mid-afternoon
June 17	Stay in Arusha that night
June 18	Take the bus to Nairobi; arrive Nairobi 4 P.M.
June 18	Fly to New York, 9 P.M.

This book contains a printing error on page 11. Please use this corrected page as a substitute. We apologize for the inconvenience.

Present and Future Time | 11

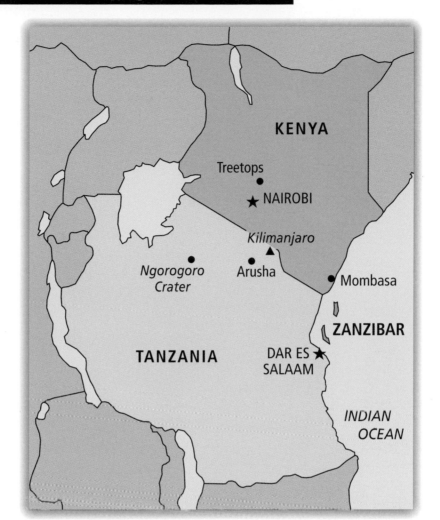

It is Tuesday, June 11, about 6 P.M. So far, the Lamonts _____*have visited*_____ three

                                                 1. (visit)

large cities: Nairobi, Dar Es Salaam, and Mombasa. They _____ at a

                       2. (also stay)

world-famous resort, Treetops, and _____ Zanzibar, the "Island of

                       3. (tour)

Cloves." Right now a bus is taking them to Moshi, Tanzania; they _____

                       4. (spend)

the night there. Tomorrow they _____ climbing Kilimanjaro,

                       5. (start)

which they will be climbing for a total of five days. After they _____ the

                       6. (finish)

climb, they _____ to Ngorongoro Crater, which they

                       7. (travel)

_____ on the following day before leaving for Arusha, Tanzania. They

8. (tour)

_____ in Arusha by early evening and _____ the

9. (arrive)   **10. (spend)**

night there. The bus for Nairobi _____ at 10 A.M. the next morning. The

                       11. (leave)

Lamonts _____ back in Nairobi by 4 P.M. on June 18, in time for their 9 P.M.

        12. (be)

departure for New York City.

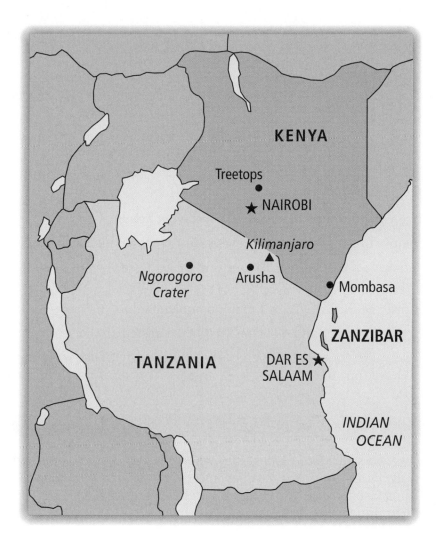

have visited

It is Tuesday, June 11, about 6 P.M. So far, the

Lamonts _____ three large cities:
                    1. (visit)

Nairobi, Dar Es Salaam, and Mombasa.

They _____ at a
              2. (also stay)

5 | THE FLEA MARKET
Grammar Notes 6, 10, 11

Read this dialogue. Number the sentences in the correct order. Then work with a partner to decide which sentences Student A and Student B say. Mark the sentences **A** *or* **B**. *Read the dialogue aloud with your partner.*

_____ Take it easy. We'll be there in a few minutes—as soon as we cross the big bridge coming up. See it?

_____ I'll have a splitting headache by the time we get there if you don't stop complaining. There'll still be some bargains!

_____ Next time you go to the flea market, I'm staying home!

_____ Yes, you are. You're making me nervous. Just stop making all that noise!

_1/A_ Can't you drive a little faster? By the time we get to the flea market, they'll have sold all the best items. Those antique vases I love will be all gone.

_____ Well, excuse me for living! But I'm not complaining!

_____ Yes. But we're *already* an hour late. We'll have missed all the best bargains.

_____ Next time, we're going to leave home two hours earlier. That way, even if we get lost, we'll still have time to get some good bargains. You know how I love to bargain.

6 | BY THIS TIME NEXT YEAR . . .
Grammar Notes 10–11

Write three sentences about your future plans, using **when** *or* **after**. *Use the simple present and future in these sentences. Then write three sentences about what you will have accomplished by this time next year. Use the future perfect in these three sentences. Share your sentences with a partner.*

Examples: When / After I **graduate** from college, I'll **apply** for a job.

By this time next year, I'll **have traveled** to India.

1. _____

2. _____

3. _____

4. _____

5. _____

6. _____

7 | EDITING

Read this travel log. There are 14 mistakes in the use of present and future verbs. The first mistake is already corrected. Find and correct 13 more.

Travel Log

I am writing these words in English because I need the practice. At this moment I am on an airplane over the Pacific Ocean, on my way to a year of study at Columbia University in the United States. I am looking forward to being there, but I am also a little afraid. What ~~do~~ *will* I find when I will get to America? Will the Americans be arrogant and violent? Will I make any friends? Am I happy?

These were the words I wrote in my diary on the airplane last month. But I'm here for a month now, and I've found that things are a lot different from what I expected. I've found that the majority of people here are friendly. They are going out of their way to help you if you need it.

On television, the news programs are speaking a lot about bad events like accidents, murders, diseases, and fights. But I don't see as much violence in my life as I do on television. I have not been mugged, and I don't worry all the time about my safety.

Two of the ideas I had about the United States, however, will seem to be true. One is that Americans aren't paying much attention to rules. One of my best American friends says, in fact, "Rules are made to be broken." The other idea I had is about the American family. In Asia the family is very important, but some Asian people are thinking that the family is meaning nothing in the United States. I'm not knowing if this is true or not. But I think it might be true, since my American friends almost never are mentioning their parents or their brothers and sisters. Anyway, I am going to have a chance to see a real American family. I go with my roommate Susan to spend Thanksgiving break with her family in Pennsylvania. When I will see her family, I will understand more.

Communication Practice

8 | LISTENING

⌒ *The Foster family is traveling in Canada. Listen to their conversation. Then listen again and mark the sentences* **T** *(true) or* **F** *(false).*

___T___ 1. Tim is still in bed.

_____ 2. The Fosters are going to the mall this morning.

_____ 3. Amy and Tim want to go to the museum.

_____ 4. Dad thinks the children can learn something at the museum.

_____ 5. The Fosters are on the tour bus now.

_____ 6. The Fosters will miss the bus if they don't hurry.

_____ 7. Tim and Amy like tours.

_____ 8. Tim thinks it's important to learn new things.

_____ 9. Amy and Tim would rather go to the museum by themselves than go on a tour.

_____10. The Fosters are going to the mall before they go on the tour.

_____11. The tour will end after 12:30.

9 | SMALL-GROUP DISCUSSION

Work in small groups. Read this quote from "This Man's Been Nearly Everywhere." Do you agree or disagree with Clouse? Why or why not? Give examples from your own experiences to support your viewpoint.

Clouse says, "I don't believe there are evil empires and evil people. Yes, there are some bad leaders in the world, but seeing people as individuals has taught me that they are all basically alike. You can be in some terrible place and someone will extend hospitality to you."

Example: **A:** I disagree with Clouse. I believe there are evil empires and evil people. Maybe there aren't many, but there are some.
B: What's an example of an empire you think is evil?

10 | WRITING

Write two or three paragraphs on one of the following topics, using present and future verbs.

- What is your response to the quote by Clouse in Exercise 9? Give examples from your own experience to support your viewpoint.

- What is your dream vacation?

Example: For most of my life, my idea of a dream vacation has been to visit China. This dream is finally going to come true. I leave next Friday for a two-week trip to China with a group from work. We're going to visit Beijing, Shanghai, and the Great Wall. We're even going to . . .

11 | ON THE INTERNET

Work in small groups. Choose a vacation spot that you might like to visit. Look it up on the Internet and find out a number of facts about it. Then describe your place to the class, describing what you'll do there, but don't say its name. The rest of the class must guess your vacation spot.

2 | Past Time

Grammar in Context

BEFORE YOU READ

1 *What do you think the term "arranged marriage" means?*

2 *Would you rather find your own person to marry or have someone else select that person for you?*

3 *Do you think an arranged marriage is likely to be a happy marriage?*

🎧 *Read this article about an unusual marriage.*

LIFESTYLES

A *Marriage* Made on the *Internet?*

How many Americans have ever considered asking friends or relatives to select their spouse for them? Not very many, apparently. Yet this is exactly what David Weinlick did.

Weinlick had apparently long been considering marriage and had known for quite some time that he was going to get married in June of 1998. When the wedding would take place and who would be invited he already knew. He just didn't know whom he would be marrying. You see, he hadn't met his bride yet.

It all started some years ago. Friends would repeatedly ask Weinlick, an anthropology student at the University of Minnesota, when he was going to tie the knot. He would say he didn't know. Eventually he got tired of these questions, so he just picked a date out of the blue: June 13, 1998. As this date was getting closer and closer, Weinlick, 28, knew he had to do something. His friend Steve Fletcher came up with the idea of a democratic selection process. Weinlick liked the idea, so he advertised for a bride on the Internet on a Bridal Nomination Committee website.

He created an application form and asked friends and relatives to interview the candidates and select the winner. They did this at a bridal candidate party before the ceremony on the day of the wedding.

Internet Marriage

Weinlick's friends and relatives took the request quite seriously. Though Weinlick wasn't sure who his bride would be, he did want to get married. He said he thinks commitment is important and that people have to work at relationships to make them successful. Weinlick's sister, Wenonah Wilms, said she thought that all of the candidates were nice but that she was looking for someone really special. Wilms added that it was important for her brother to marry someone who would fit into family celebrations like at Christmas.

So who won the election? It was Elizabeth Runze, a pharmacy student at the University of Minnesota. Runze hadn't met Weinlick before she picked up a candidate survey on the Monday before the wedding. They talked briefly on that day and again on Tuesday when Runze turned in the completed survey about her career plans and hobbies. However, neither Weinlick nor Runze knew who would ultimately be chosen by Weinlick's friends and family on Saturday, the day of the wedding. After her Saturday selection by the committee, Runze said the day was the most incredible she had ever experienced.

Weinlick was happy too. After the selection, the groom said the plan had turned out almost exactly as he had hoped.

By the time the wedding day arrived, Weinlick had prepared everything: the rings, the musicians, his tuxedo, and the reception afterwards. The two took their vows at the Mall of America in Minneapolis while about 2,000 shoppers looked on from the upper levels of the mall.

Probably few Americans would do what Weinlick and Runze did. There have been reports, however, that the newlyweds are doing well. Weinlick and Runze's union qualifies as an "arranged marriage," a phenomenon that has traditionally not been popular in America. Arranged marriages are common in many other parts of the world, though, or at least they used to be. Maybe they're not such a bad idea.

AFTER YOU READ

Read these pairs of sentences. In each pair of sentences, only one is true. Circle the letter of the true statement.

1. **a.** Weinlick didn't consider marriage for a long time before his wedding.

   b. Weinlick considered marriage for a long time before his wedding.

2. **a.** Weinlick and Runze met for the first time when Elizabeth picked up a candidate survey.

   b. They met several months before the wedding.

3. **a.** Weinlick knew who his bride would be before the day of the wedding.

   b. Weinlick didn't know who his bride would be until the day of the wedding.

Grammar Presentation

PAST TIME

PAST TIME: GENERAL OR SPECIFIC (DEFINITE)

Simple Past
Weinlick **needed** to find a bride. He **advertised** on the Internet.

Past Progressive
Was / Were + Base Form + *-ing*
He **was looking** for someone special.

PAST TIME: NOT SPECIFIC (INDEFINITE)

Present Perfect
Has / Have + Past Participle
The couple **has chosen** the date for the party. They **have** already **sent** the invitations.

PAST TIME: HABITUAL OR REPEATED

Used To + Base Form
She **used to be** a pharmacist.

Would + Base Form
Some days she **would work** 12 hours.

PAST TIME: BEFORE A TIME IN THE PAST

Past Perfect
Had + Past Participle
He **had met** her before the wedding.

Past Perfect Progressive
Had been + Base Form + *-ing*
He **had been planning** the wedding for months.

PAST TIME: AFTER A TIME IN THE PAST BUT BEFORE NOW ("FUTURE IN THE PAST")

Was / Were Going To + Base Form
He knew he **was going to marry** soon.

Would + Base Form
He knew when the wedding **would be**.

GRAMMAR NOTES

EXAMPLES

1. Use the **simple past** to express an action, event, or state completed at a general or specific time in the past.	• Runze **wanted** to get married. *(general)* • She **filled out** an application form several days before the wedding. *(specific)*
Remember that many of the most common verbs have irregular past forms and past participles.	• Weinlick and Runze **met** five days before they **got** married.

2. Use the **past progressive** to express an action that was in progress (= not finished) at a time in the past.	• Runze **was studying** pharmacy at the University when she decided to get married.

3. Use the **present perfect** to express an action, event, or state completed at an indefinite time in the past.	• How many Americans **have** ever **considered** an arranged marriage?
▶ **BE CAREFUL!** Don't use the present perfect with a past-time expression.	• Weinlick **got married a few years ago**. NOT Weinlick ~~has gotten married~~ a few years ago.
NOTE: The simple past is the definite past. The present perfect is the indefinite past.	• The two **met** on June 8, 1998. • They **have** already **met**.
Remember that the present perfect also connects the past and the present. (See Unit 1.)	• I **have attended** many weddings since then.

4. Use *used to* + base form to show a habitual action, event, or state that was true in the past but is no longer true.	• Kayoko **used to play** tennis a lot.
You can also use *would* + base form to express actions or events that occurred regularly during a period in the past.	• When we were children, we **would spend** every summer in Maine.
▶ **BE CAREFUL!** *Used to* and *would* are similar in meaning when they express past actions. However, only *used to* can show past location, state, or possession.	• I **used to live** in Chicago. • Sarah **used to be** a marriage counselor. • We **used to have** a summer home. NOT I ~~would live~~ in Chicago. Sarah ~~would be~~ a marriage counselor. We ~~would have~~ a summer home.

(continued)

5. Use the **past perfect** to show an action, event, or state that happened before a certain time in the past.

Use the past perfect with the simple past to show which of two past actions, events, or states happened first. The past perfect is often used with *by the time* and conjunctions such as *when*, *before*, *after*, and *because*.

▶ **BE CAREFUL!** In such sentences with *when*, notice the difference in meaning between the **past progressive** and the **past perfect progressive**.

- By June 13, the family **had interviewed** dozens of candidates.

- **By the time** the wedding day arrived, Weinlick **had prepared** everything.

- Weinlick and Runze **had known** each other for five days **when** they got married.

- When I left, it **was snowing**. *(It was still snowing.)*

- When I left, it **had been snowing**. *(It had stopped snowing.)*

---

6. Use the **past perfect progressive** to express an action that was in progress before another past event.

- She **had been working** when she got married.

---

7. Use *was / were going to / would* + base form to describe an action, event, or state that was planned or expected in the past (before now). Sentences with *was / were going to / would* are sometimes called **future in the past**.

- Weinlick knew that he **was going to get** married on June 13, 1998.

- He knew where the wedding **would be**.

Reference Note
For a list of **verbs with irregular past forms and past participles**, see Appendix 1 on page A-1.

Focused Practice

1 | DISCOVER THE GRAMMAR

A 1. List the simple past irregular verbs in the opening reading. Write the base form of each one next to the past form.

2. Find a sentence in the reading that shows two past actions, one happening before the other. What forms are used? Why?

B Look at these sentences based on the reading. Write the earlier-occurring action or state on the left and the later-occurring action or state on the right.

1. Weinlick had known for a long time that he was going to get married on June 13, 1998.

   Weinlick had known for a long time / he was going to get married on June 13, 1998.

2. He just didn't know whom he would be marrying.

   _____

3. Friends would repeatedly ask Weinlick when he was going to tie the knot.

   _____

4. Runze hadn't met Weinlick before she picked up a candidate survey.

   _____

5. By the time the wedding day rolled around, Weinlick had prepared everything.

   _____

C Look at these sentences containing **would**. Is the meaning of **would** future in the past (**F**) or habitual action in the past (**H**)?

  _F_ 1. He already knew when the wedding would be and who would be invited.

  ____ 2. He just didn't know who the bride would be.

  ____ 3. Friends would repeatedly ask Weinlick when he was going to tie the knot.

  ____ 4. He would say he didn't know.

  ____ 5. Weinlick's sister added that it was important for her brother to marry someone who would fit in at Christmas.

  ____ 6. Neither Weinlick nor Runze knew who would be chosen by his friends and family.

2 | DO OPPOSITES ATTRACT?

Grammar Notes 1–3, 5

Complete this story by circling the correct verb forms.

Ellen Rosetti and Mark Stevens <u>were married /</u> (<u>have been married</u>) for almost
_{1.}

a year now. Their marriage almost <u>didn't happen / wasn't happening</u>, though.
_{2.}

They <u>were meeting / met</u> on a blind date when Ellen's friend Alice <u>had / has had</u>
_{3.} _{4.}

two extra tickets for a concert.

At first, Ellen <u>thought / was thinking</u> Mark was the most opinionated man
_{5.}

she'd ever met. A couple of weeks after the concert, Mark <u>called up / was calling</u>
_{6.}

<u>up</u> and <u>had asked / asked</u> Ellen out. Ellen <u>wanted / has wanted</u> to say no, but
_{7.} _{8.}

something <u>made / was making</u> her accept. After that, one thing <u>had led / led</u> to
_{9.} _{10.}

another. Today Mark says, "Ellen is unique. I <u>'ve never met / didn't meet</u> anyone
_{11.}

even remotely like her."

Ellen says, "At first glance you might have trouble seeing how Mark and I

could be married. In certain ways, we're as different as night and day. I'm an

early bird; he's a night owl. He's conservative; I'm liberal. He <u>was always loving /</u>
_{12.}

<u>has always loved</u> sports and I <u>'ve never been able / was never able</u> to stand them.
_{13.}

I guess you might say we're a case of opposites being attracted to each other."

3 | **BEFORE AND AFTER**   *Grammar Note 4*

*Jim Garcia and Mark Stevens both got married fairly recently. Fill in the blanks in their conversation with the correct forms of **used to** or **would** and the verbs in parentheses. Use **would** if possible. If **would** occurs with a pronoun subject, use a contraction.*

MARK: So, Jim, how does it feel to be an old married man? Been about six months, hasn't it?

JIM: Yep. It feels great. It's a lot different, though.

MARK: Yeah? How so?

JIM: Well, I guess I'd say I _____*used to have*_____ a lot more freedom. Like on
                                    1. (have)

Saturdays, for example. I _____ until 11 or even noon. Then,
                                2. (sleep)

when I got up, my buddies and I _____ out for breakfast at a
                                        3. (go)

restaurant. Now Jennifer and I get up at eight at the latest. She's really an early bird.

And I either make her breakfast or she makes it for me. And then on Saturday nights I

_____ out with the guys and stay out till all hours of the night.
        4. (go)

Now it's just the two of us. Sometimes we go out on Saturday night, and sometimes we

don't.

MARK: Does that bother you?

JIM: You know, it doesn't. Life actually _____ kind of lonely. It's
                                                5. (be)

not anymore. What about you? Have things really changed?

MARK: They sure have. For one thing, the neighborhood is totally different. Remember the

apartment I _____ in, right north of downtown? Well, Ellen
                6. (live)

and I just bought a house in the suburbs. That's a trip, let me tell you.

JIM: I'll bet.

MARK: Yeah. My weekends _____ my own. I
                                7. (be)

_____ all day Saturday working on my car or going mountain
        8. (spend)

biking. Now I have to cut the grass and take care of the yard.

JIM: So would you change anything?

MARK: I sure wouldn't. You know how everyone says how great it is to be single? Well, I

_____ so too. Not now. Now I'd say "been there, done that."
        9. (think)

JIM: Me too. I wouldn't change a thing.

4 | THE REST IS HISTORY

Complete the story of how Jim Garcia and Jennifer O'Leary got married. Combine each pair of sentences into one sentence. Begin the new sentence with the connecting word or phrase in parentheses. Use the simple past and past perfect.

1. Jim Garcia and Jennifer O'Leary graduated from high school. They knew each other for three years. (when)

   When they graduated from high school, Jim Garcia and Jennifer O'Leary had known each other for

   three years.

2. Jim completed four years of military service, and Jennifer graduated from college. They both returned to their hometown about a year ago. (by the time)

   _____

   _____

3. Jennifer started teaching, and Jim took a job as a computer programmer. They saw each other again. (before)

   _____

   _____

4. Neither went out on any dates. They ran into each other in a drugstore one morning. (when)

   _____

   _____

5. Jim drove to Olson's Drugstore. He woke up with a splitting headache. (because)

   _____

   _____

6. Jennifer's younger sister fell and hurt herself and needed medicine. Jennifer also went to Olson's. (because)

   _____

   _____

7. A week passed. Jim asked Jennifer out on a date. (before)

   _____

   _____

8. Jim and Jennifer dated for three months. They got married. (when)

   _____

   _____

5 | PLANS AND EXPECTATIONS

Grammar Note 6

*Before Jim got married, he jotted down some of his plans and expectations, which are given below on the left. Some of them came true, and some didn't. On the right, complete Jim's thoughts now about those plans and expectations. Use the future-in-the-past constructions **was / were going to** + base form or **would** + base form.*

Jim's Plans and Expectations

Jim's Thoughts Now

1. I think it'll be quite a while before we have any children.

   I thought it would be quite a while

   *before we had any children*_____,

   but that's not true. Our first baby is due in four months.

2. I think I'll probably feel just a little bit trapped.

   _____

   _____,

   but I haven't felt that way at all.

3. I think we're going to live in an apartment.

   _____

   _____,

   and we do.

4. I expect that there won't be as much money to spend.

   _____

   _____,

   but that's not true. Jennifer really knows how to keep our lifestyle economical.

5. I hope that we'll be happy.

   _____

   _____,

   and we are. Tremendously.

6. I'm sure that we're going to have a lot of fun together.

   _____

   _____,

   and we do. It's a blast.

7. I don't think I'll see as much of my buddies.

   _____

   _____,

   and I don't. That's OK, though.

8. I figure that we're going to be taking a lot of trips.

   _____

   _____,

   but we haven't taken any yet.

6 | WEINLICK AND RUNZE: AN UPDATE

Grammar Notes 1–5, 7

How are David and Elizabeth Weinlick doing several years after getting married? Read this update. Then answer the questions in complete sentences.

About three years after they got married at the Mall of America in Minneapolis, David and Elizabeth Weinlick's marriage was still going strong. When telephoned in February 2001, David Weinlick was in good spirits and said their marriage was doing wonderfully. He was finishing a student teaching program in a local high school, and Elizabeth had switched to nursing school because she felt she would have more of a chance to help people as a nurse than as a pharmacist. David said they were expecting their first child in June 2001. When called a day later, Elizabeth echoed what David had said, adding that the due date for their first child was June 13, 2001—the third anniversary of their marriage. Both David and Elizabeth stressed that commitment is the thing that makes a marriage work. The feelings came later, they said. "The day we got married we had no relationship. Zero. Nothing!" Elizabeth commented. Feelings of love developed after they got to know each other. Asked how they handle conflict, Elizabeth said, "We laugh." In other words, they don't let conflict develop.

Here's an interesting postscript to their story: It turns out that David's great-grandparents went through a similar situation. His great-grandfather was scheduled to become a missionary in Alaska, but his church felt he would need a wife to stand alongside him in his work. They recommended a woman in New York State who they thought would make him a good wife. The two did in fact get married after a very short courtship. Forty-three years later, David's great-grandparents said they had never regretted the way in which they wed. An observer commented that "many young people today might have happier married lives if they got acquainted more after marriage instead of so much before."

There may well be some truth in this.

1. When David and Elizabeth were telephoned, what occupations were they pursuing?

_____

2. What did Elizabeth use to do?

_____

3. Why had she switched career plans?

_____

4. In what way is David and Elizabeth's situation similar to that of David's great-grandparents?

_____

5. Where was David's great-grandfather going to do missionary work?

_____

6. Why did the committee recommend a woman in New York State?

_____

7. What was unusual about the date June 13, 2001?

_____

7 | EDITING

Read Jennifer Garcia's journal entry. There are 11 mistakes in the use of verb constructions. The first mistake is already corrected. Find and correct 10 more.

> May 20
>
>   have been
>   I just had to write today. It's our six-month anniversary. Jim and I ~~are~~
>
> married six months as of today. So maybe this is the time for me to take
>
> stock of my situation. The obvious question is whether I'm happy I get
>
> married. The answer is "Absolutely." When I remember what my life has
>
> been like before we're getting married, I realize now how lonely I've been
>
> before. Jim is a wonderful guy. Since we both work, we took turns doing the
>
> housework. He's really good about that. When we have been dating, I wasn't
>
> sure whether or not I'll have to do all the housework. But I wasn't having
>
> any reason to worry. Today we split everything 50 / 50. The only complaint I
>
> was having is that Jim snores at night. When I tell him that, he only says,
>
> "Well, sweetie, you snore too." I don't believe it. But if this is our only
>
> problem, I guess we're pretty lucky.
>
>   Well, I would have a long and tiring day, but it's almost over. It's time to go
>
> to sleep.

Communication Practice

8 | LISTENING

🎧 *Read these questions. Listen to the news broadcast. Then listen again and answer each question in a complete sentence containing a past-time verb.*

1. What did Samantha Yang and Darrell Hammer hire Reverend Martinez to do?

   They hired him to marry them while they were

   parachute jumping from a plane.

2. To date, how many jumps have Samantha and Darrell each made?

   _____

   _____

3. How long have they been members of the jumping group?

   _____

   _____

4. How were they originally going to get married?

   _____

   _____

5. Why did they decide not to do this? (first reason)

   _____

   _____

6. Why did they decide not to do this? (second reason)

   _____

   _____

7. Had Reverend Martinez ever done this kind of wedding before?

   _____

   _____

UNUSUAL WEDDINGS

9 | INFORMATION GAP: BETTER THAN IT USED TO BE

Work with a partner to complete the text. Each of you will read a version of the same story. Each version is missing some information. Take turns asking your partner questions to get the missing information.

Student A, read the story about Jack Strait. Ask questions and fill in the missing information. Then answer Student B's questions.

Student B, turn to page 32 and follow the instructions there.

Example:
A: What kind of company did he use to work for?
B: He used to work for a large, impersonal company. How long would he stay on the road?
A: He would stay on the road for two or three weeks at a time.

Jack Strait's life is quite different now from the way it used to be. He used to work for

_____ company. His job required him to do a lot of

traveling. He would stay on the road for two or three weeks at a time. It was always the same:

As soon as he pulled into a town, he would look for _____.

The next morning he'd leave his business card at a lot of different establishments, hoping that

someone would agree to see him. If he'd been lucky enough to arrange an appointment in

advance, he'd show them _____. Occasionally they would

buy something; most often they wouldn't.

Jack's marriage began to suffer. He missed his wife a lot, but there wasn't much he could

do about the situation. And when he was on the road, he hardly ever saw his children. He

would try to call them _____ if he had a spare moment, but

usually it was so late that they had already gone to bed. They were growing up without him.

Finally, his wife laid down the law, saying, "Why should we even be married if we're never

going to see each other?" Jack decided she was right. He took a risk. He quit his job and

started his own business. Things were difficult at first, but at least the family was together.

That was five years ago. Things have changed a lot since then. Jack and his family used to

live in a small apartment. Now they own a house. Life is good.

Compare your story with your partner's. Are they the same? Now discuss these questions: What did Jack's occupation use to be? Is it important to take risks in life as Jack did? Can you think of an example of a risk you have taken in your life?

10 | PICTURE DISCUSSION

*With a partner, discuss the picture. Describe the situation. What is happening?
Approximately how long do you think these people have been married? Do you think their
relationship is less interesting or satisfactory than it used to be, or is it just different?
Present your opinions to the class.*

11 | WRITING

Choose one of the following topics and write two or three paragraphs about it.

1. Describe a situation that has turned out differently from what you expected—for example, a marriage or other relationship, or college plans. First talk about what you thought would happen; then talk about what actually happened.

2. Did marriages use to be arranged in your culture or a culture you are familiar with? How would young people meet their mates when your parents or grandparents were young? Ask an older person you know about the situation.

> **Example:**   I've been happily married for some time now, but when I was introduced to the man who is now my husband, it never occurred to me that we would end up husband and wife. In fact, when I met Dave, I thought he was the most arrogant man I had ever met. Here's how it happened . . .

12 | ON THE INTERNET

Use the Internet to find five interesting statistics about marriage. Share your information with the class.

> **Examples:**
> - the country with the highest percentage of married adults
> - the country with the lowest percentage of married adults
> - the longest marriage on record

INFORMATION GAP FOR STUDENT B

Student B, read the story about Jack Strait. Answer Student A's questions. Then ask your own questions and fill in the missing information.

Example: **A:** What kind of company did he use to work for?
B: He used to work for a large, impersonal company.
How long would he stay on the road?
A: He would stay on the road for two or three weeks at a time.

Jack Strait's life is quite different now from the way it used to be. He used to work for a large, impersonal company. His job required him to do a lot of traveling. He would stay on the road for _____. It was always the same: As soon as he pulled into a town, he would look for a cheap motel to stay in. The next morning he'd leave _____ at a lot of different establishments, hoping that someone would agree to see him. If he'd been lucky enough to arrange an appointment in advance, he'd show them his samples. _____ they would buy something; most often they wouldn't.

Jack's marriage began to suffer. He missed his wife a lot, but there wasn't much he could do about the situation. And when he was on the road, he hardly ever saw his children. He would try to call them _____ if he had a spare moment, but usually it was so late that they had already gone to bed. They were growing up without him. Finally, his wife laid down the law, saying, "Why should we even be married if we're never going to see each other?" Jack decided she was right. He took a risk. He quit his job and started his own business. Things were difficult at first, but at least the family was together.

That was five years ago. Things have changed a lot since then. Jack and his family used to live _____. Now they own a house. Life is good.

Compare your story with your partner's. Are they the same? Now discuss these questions: What did Jack's occupation use to be? Is it important to take risks in life as Jack did? Can you think of an example of a risk you have taken in your life?

Simple and Progressive: Action and Non-Action Verbs

Grammar in Context

BEFORE YOU READ

1 *What are some benefits that technology provides us? Write down several.*

2 *What are some problems caused by technology?*

Read this article about the effects of technology on our lives.

TRENDS MAGAZINE

What Is Technology Doing to Us?

Technology is such a major part of our lives today that it's difficult to think of life without its products. Where would we be without such things as cell phones, CD players, automobiles, and computers? There's no doubt that technology serves us and enriches our lives. The trouble is, technology has a downside also. Are there ways to gain the benefits of technology without being at the mercy of it? Let's look at the pros and cons of three technological products.

The telephone

Pros: Since its invention in 1876, the telephone has become more important to people's lives with each passing year. It's hard to imagine life without it, as we learn when we move and don't have phone service for a day or two. The telephone is just about everywhere these days. If we want to go to a popular movie but are afraid it will be sold out when we get to the theater, all we have to do is call in advance and order tickets. Telephones save lives;

if there's an emergency, we call 911. The telephone allows us to stay in touch with people who live on the other side of the street, the country, or the world.

Cons: Consider the cell phone; it's a wonderful technological product. We carry a cell phone with us in case our car breaks down. We use it to talk with our friends at our convenience and to take care of business matters when we can't get to a regular phone. But the downside is that cell phones can be troublesome and even dangerous. Increasingly these days, teachers are having problems with students who

(continued)

What Is Technology Doing to Us?

bring cell phones to class and insist on using them. Teachers try to prohibit cell phone use in class, but students feel strongly about their right to use their cell phones, and school districts are often reluctant to forbid them. Much more significantly, many serious and even fatal accidents are caused by people talking on their cell phones while driving. A few cities and states have passed laws against using hand-held devices in cars, but they are few and far between.

The automobile

Pros: As with the telephone, there are countless benefits of cars. Let's assume you just bought a new one, and today you're driving it for the first time. Everyone says it looks good, and you're discovering that it performs beautifully. It takes you places speedily. It gives you freedom and mobility. Together with the telephone, it can save a life if someone is in an accident or is sick and has to get to a hospital quickly. It allows you to go places at speeds undreamed of in the past. This week you're working at a job that is far from your home, but your car will get you there fast. And the manufacture of cars provides millions of jobs worldwide.

Cons: The automobile is a victim of its own success because almost everyone wants one. It does its job so well that cars are everywhere—and that's the problem. We have built freeways to handle the steadily increasing traffic generated by the car's popularity. As soon as a new freeway is built or lanes are added to an existing freeway, however, traffic simply increases to the point that it often takes longer to get somewhere by freeway than on city streets. There are other negatives: Cars are the major cause of air pollution, and each year in the United States over 40,000 people are killed in auto accidents—more than from diseases such as kidney failure.

The computer

Pros: We live in the Information Age, and the computer is the key element of it. Let's say you have a new computer, and you love it. The music you listen to on it sounds wonderful. Your computer gives you access to the world: you e-mail your friends, do research on the Internet, create documents and edit them easily, check up on sports scores, and read news articles without even having to subscribe to a daily paper. What a marvelous invention technology has provided us. How could we do without it?

Cons: Yesterday your computer was working fine, but today it's being difficult. You don't know much about fixing computer problems, so you call for technical support. The technician determines that you have two computer viruses. You download and install anti-virus protection, and everything is fine for a while. It's a good thing, because you're working at home today. But you've also agreed to take a friend to a doctor's appointment, and you're printing a document to take along and work on. You have just enough time to print the document and jump into the car, but the printer chooses this moment to stop functioning. By the time you've figured out how to fix the printer and you pick up your friend, you're late. You feel bad about this, but what can you do?

Technology is so important that our world would have difficulty surviving without its constant advances. If a technological product is there, people will use it. Our problem is over-dependence on it. We need to learn how to use technology moderately, and we'll explore ways of doing that in next month's issue.

AFTER YOU READ

What does each sentence mean? Circle the correct answer.

1. Your car performs beautifully.
   a. It does a good job.
   b. It looks beautiful.

2. You feel bad about getting your friend to the appointment late.
   a. You're unhappy about this.
   b. You're ill because of this.

3. Your computer is being difficult today.
   a. It is difficult for you to understand how to use it.
   b. Your computer is not doing what you want it to do.

Grammar Presentation

ACTION AND NON-ACTION VERBS

Action Verbs	
Simple Form	**Progressive Form**
They normally **drive** to work.	Today they**'re taking** the bus.

Most Non-Action Verbs
Simple Form
People **know** he is a good employee.   They **want** to understand his problem.   This building **belongs** to the company.

Some Non-Action Verbs	
Simple Form (Stative Use)	**Progressive Form (Active Use)**
I **have** a new cell phone. She **appears** very happy about the job. They **think** they need a new car.	I'm **having** problems with it. She is **appearing** in a new play. Please don't bother me; I'm **thinking**.

Action Verbs
+ Adverb
He **works constantly**.   The computer **is working well** today.

(continued)

Some Non-Action Verbs	
+ Adjective (Stative Use)	+ Adverb (Active Use)
Your car **looks good**.	He **looked thoughtfully** at the message.
The soup **tastes delicious**.	You should **taste** that **carefully**—it's hot!
She **feels bad** about what she said.	The doctor **felt** the bruise **gently**.

THERE + BE

Simple Form
There were many requests for a new version.
There are some problems with the invention.
There won't be an alternative technology.
There appears to be a need for a simple device.

GRAMMAR NOTES

EXAMPLES

1. Action verbs describe actions. Use **simple** verb forms (without *-ing*) to describe all of an action—the action in general. Use **progressive** verb forms (with *-ing*) to describe part of an action—in progress at a specific time.	• Computers **perform** tasks quickly. • Martha **works** for a high-tech company. • The mechanic **is fixing** my car.

2. Non-action verbs describe states, such as appearance *(seem)*, emotions *(love)*, mental states *(know)*, perceptions *(hear)*, possession *(own)*, and wants *(need)*. They are often called **stative** verbs. These verbs are generally used in the simple form and not in the progressive. Some stative verbs can be used to describe either states or actions. When they are used to describe actions, they usually have different meanings.	• The boss **seems** angry. • I **know** my co-workers very well. • Sam **owns** three cell phones. • We **need** a new car. NOT We ~~are needing~~ a new car. • People **are** basically equal, or should **be**. *(a state)* • The children **are being** difficult today. *(an action—behaving)* • I **see** what you mean. *(a state—understand)* • Two of my co-workers **are seeing** each other. *(an action—dating)*

3. We normally use adverbs with **action verbs**. Remember that many adverbs end in **-ly**. There are a few irregular adverbs such as *well*, *hard*, and *fast*.

- Bill always **drives carefully**.
- The children **speak** Chinese **well**.
- Sarah **works hard**.

4. We normally use the verbs *look*, *sound*, *feel*, *smell*, and *taste* to show states, in which case they are used with adjectives, not adverbs.

▶ **BE CAREFUL!** These verbs are sometimes used to show actions, in which case they are used with adverbs. When they are used to describe actions, these verbs usually have different meanings.

- Sarah **doesn't look good** today. Is she depressed?
- Your idea **sounds good** to me.
- I don't **smell well** when I have a cold. *(an action—using one's nose)*.
- The fire alarm **sounded** a warning **loudly**. *(an action—making a noise)*.

5. To show the existence of something, we often use *there* + *be*. The verb can be past, present, or future.

NOTE: *There* is used with simple, not progressive, verb forms. Verbs like *seem* and *appear* can also be used with *there*.

▶ **BE CAREFUL!** The verb in a *there* construction agrees in number with the noun following it.

- **There was** no other option.
- **There won't be** anywhere to park.
- **There seems** to be a problem with the TV.

- **There have been** several accidents here.
- NOT ~~There's been~~ several accidents here.

Reference Notes
For a list of **non-action verbs**, see Appendix 2 on page A-2.
For a list of **non-action verbs sometimes used in the progressive**, see Appendix 3 on page A-3.

Focused Practice

1 | DISCOVER THE GRAMMAR

A *Look again at the opening reading. Read the "Pros" paragraphs on the three technological products. Make a list of all the non-action verbs.*

B *Look at these sentences. Do the underlined verbs describe actions or states? Write **A** or **S**.*

___S___ 1. Too many people <u>don't know</u> their neighbors anymore.

_____ 2. Miranda <u>feels</u> things deeply.

_____ 3. Your computer <u>is being</u> difficult today.

_____ 4. I've been sick, so I don't <u>feel</u> strong yet.

_____ 5. I don't <u>feel</u> strongly about the proposal, one way or another.

_____ 6. Everyone <u>needs</u> food, shelter, and love.

_____ 7. The majority of people today <u>own</u> an automobile.

_____ 8. I haven't met Bill, but he <u>sounds</u> nice over the telephone.

_____ 9. He<u>'s having</u> trouble getting his printer to work.

_____ 10. <u>Are</u> you <u>thinking</u> about buying a new car?

_____ 11. Marty <u>has</u> three computers at home.

_____ 12. Anne <u>hears</u> quite well now that she has a hearing aid.

_____ 13. I <u>don't think</u> technology is harmful.

_____ 14. The food <u>tastes</u> awful.

_____ 15. I <u>felt</u> bad about getting here late.

C *Look again at the reading. Underline the six sentences that use* there *to show existence.*

2 | STATEMENTS WITH ACTION AND NON-ACTION VERBS

Grammar Notes 2–3

Complete these statements with a non-action verb in the simple present or an action verb in the present progressive. Use the verbs in the box.

be	have	hear	see	smell	taste	think

1. Some consider the computer to be a machine that _____*thinks*_____.

2. People who are dating are said to be _____ each other.

3. One _____ with one's nose.

4. One _____ with one's eyes.

5. The bald eagle is a large North American bird that _____ a white head and neck.

6. One _____ with one's ears.

7. A person who _____ is using his or her brain.

8. One _____ primarily with one's tongue.

9. That child _____ normally well-behaved.

10. But at the moment, he _____ difficult and causing lots of trouble.

11. Your day has gone badly so far; you _____ a bad day.

3 | EFFECTS OF TECHNOLOGY

Grammar Note 3

Complete these sentences about the effects of technology. Use adverbs with action verbs and adjectives with non-action verbs. Circle the correct word.

1. Freeways throughout the world look (similar) / similarly.

2. Democracy gives us the opportunity to use technology <u>free / freely</u>.

3. In theory, technology helps us to perform tasks <u>simple / simply</u>.

4. Technology allows food to be prepared and distributed <u>rapid / rapidly</u>.

5. An attraction of fast food is that it smells and tastes <u>good / well</u>.

6. Technology has many benefits. Eyeglasses help people see <u>clear / clearly</u>.

7. Hearing aids help people hear <u>good / well</u>.

8. Computers help people communicate <u>quick / quickly</u>.

9. Freeways are designed to help drivers get places <u>easy / easily</u>.

10. Unfortunately, they also cause people to feel <u>angry / angrily</u> when they're stuck in traffic.

4 | **THE WORLD: PAST, PRESENT, AND FUTURE**   *Grammar Note 4*

*Look at the chart. Write a sentence using **there** (meaning existence) plus the time word to describe each phenomenon. Make the sentences negative if it is logical to do so. Use the correct form.*

Phenomenon	Time
1. taxes	always
2. complete peace in the world	never
3. between 200 and 300 million people on the Earth	in 1 A.D.
4. automobiles	after 1910
5. television	before 1920
6. humans on other planets	now
7. deaths from smallpox	before the 20th century
8. personal computers	before 1950
9. DVD players	since the 1990s
10. just under 8 billion people on the Earth	by 2025

1. _There have always been taxes._

2. _____

3. _____

4. _____

5. _____

6. _____

7. _____

8. _____

9. _____

10. _____

5 | A PERSONAL INVENTORY

Complete each sentence according to your own experience. Use adjectives or adverbs, depending on the type of verb.

1. do / bad / on written tests

   I do badly on written tests.

2. play / a sport / good

   _____

3. a food / taste / good

   _____

4. feel / bad / when

   _____

5. do / good / in / a school subject

   _____

6. feel / strong / about

   _____

7. look / good in / a color

   _____

8. a vacation / sound / interesting

   _____

9. something / smell / awful

   _____

10. a place / look / beautiful

    _____

6 | EDITING

Read this student essay. There are 13 mistakes in the use of verbs, adjectives, and adverbs.
The first mistake is already corrected. Find and correct 12 more.

No Cell Phone Restrictions!

It seems
~~It's seeming~~ that I constantly hear the same thing: "Cell phones are dangerous.

We're needing to severely restrict them. People are dying because of cell phones."

Well, I'm thinking cell phones themselves aren't the problem. I'm completely

opposed to restrictions on them, and here's why.

First, people say cell phones are dangerous to health, so they should be limited.

Supporters of this idea say there are being studies showing that cell phones produce

radiation that is harmful to users. I think this is nonsense. There hasn't been any real

proof. It's sounding like just another study that ultimately isn't meaning anything.

Second, a lot of teachers are proposing that we not allow cell phones in classes

because they're a distraction. I feel pretty angrily about this. Here's a good example.

Two weeks ago in my history class, one of the students was having her cell phone on

because her mother was really sick and might need a ride to the hospital. The

student's mother couldn't contact anyone else. In fact, the student's mother did call,

and the student found someone to help her mother. What if her cell phone hadn't been

on? The teacher would have felt pretty badly.

Third, people argue that using a cell phone while driving is dangerous. I disagree.

It's no more dangerously than turning on the car radio or eating a sandwich. People

do those things when they drive. The law says you must have one hand on the steering

wheel. It's possible to use a cell phone correct with one hand. I use my cell phone

careful; I always keep one hand on the wheel. Maybe there should be training in ways

to use a cell phone good, but we shouldn't prohibit using cell phones in cars.

This has always been a free country. I hope it stays that way.

Communication Practice

7 | LISTENING

🎧 *Read these questions. Listen to the conversation. Then listen again and answer the questions in complete sentences.*

1. How are things going for Mary?

Things aren't going well for her.

2. What kind of problem is Mary having?

_____

3. What is wrong?

_____

4. What is this a good example of?

_____

5. How much money is involved?

_____

6. How did this probably happen?

_____

7. When are people supposed to report problems like this?

_____

8. When did Mary report the problem?

_____

9. Why?

_____

10. According to Jim, what is the downside of the Internet?

_____

8 | SMALL-GROUP DISCUSSION

Look at the chart. Fill it out for yourself, adding two other inventions not mentioned. Then discuss your answers in a small group. Talk about which inventions are important for your life and which are not. Share your conclusions with the class.

Example:
A: I have a good bicycle, but it's not really important in my life.
B: Why not?
A: Well, it works well, and it's a great way to exercise, but I seldom ride it.
C: Why don't you ride it more often?
A: It's too dangerous because there aren't any bike trails in my neighborhood.

Invention	Have one	Don't want one	Works well	Often use it	Seldom use it	Pros	Cons
bicycle	✓		✓		✓	*great way to exercise*	*too dangerous*
car							
TV set							
dishwasher							
cell phone							
computer							
other							
other							

9 | WRITING

What do you consider the most important invention of the last 200 years? Write two or three paragraphs about it, explaining your choice. Talk about the invention's benefits and disadvantages. Use one of these topics or develop your own.

| the airplane | the automobile | the computer | photography | television |

Example: In my opinion, the most important invention in the last 200 years is the automobile. It's obvious that cars have changed the way people live. They have created jobs. They've given us mobility and freedom. They've changed the way towns and cities are built. . . .

10 | ON THE INTERNET

 Look at the following list of inventions. When were they invented? By whom? Use the Internet to find the answers. Compare your answers with those of the rest of the class.

| the bicycle | the microscope | the telescope | the VCR | the X-ray machine |

From **Grammar** to **Writing**
The Sentence

In formal English a sentence must have a subject and a verb that shows person, number, and time. Only one type of sentence has no subject: an imperative sentence. In imperative sentences, the subject *you* is understood.

Word groups that contain a subject or a verb but are not sentences are called **fragments**.

Look at the sentences. The complete subjects are underlined once and the complete verbs twice.

Examples: Sherry and her friends are students.

They are spending a year studying in Spain in an exchange program.

All of the students in the program arrived a month ago.

Most of them will stay for the entire year.

Sherry's sister Martha has received three letters from her.

The letters were written over a period of three months.

Write soon.

Are exchange programs good learning experiences?

These word groups are fragments:

Sherry sitting and writing a letter. (no verb)

Were taking the train to Barcelona. (no subject)

Such an exciting year. (no subject or verb)

1 *On the line below each of the word groups, write **sentence** if the group is a sentence. If the word group is not a sentence, write **fragment** and explain why by writing **no subject**, **no verb**, or **no subject and no verb**.*

1. Sherry at the library doing research.

fragment—no verb

2. All afternoon.

_____

3. Akiko and Lisa were at home.

_____

4. Has been an exciting year.

_____

5. A worthwhile experience meeting students from many nations.

_____

6. They would do it again.

_____

7. Akiko waiting at the bottom of the stairs.

_____

8. Think about this question.

_____

2

Read the description of a trip to Barcelona. There are eight sentences and eight groups of words that are not sentences. Underline the eight sentences.

In late December. Sherry, Akiko, and Lisa took a one-day trip to Barcelona. Not knowing anyone there. They stayed in a youth hostel for a very reasonable price. On their one day in the city. They visited the Sagrada Familia, Gaudí's famous church. All three girls were impressed by the church's beauty. And decided to climb to the top instead of taking the elevator. Nearing the top, Akiko began to feel dizzy and had to start down again. Sherry and Lisa continued climbing. However, even Sherry, who had done a great deal of mountain climbing in Canada. Felt nervous and unprotected at the summit. Both she and Lisa agreed that the view was magnificent. And the climb well worth it. The three decided to return to Barcelona. As soon as they could.

Now rewrite the paragraph, eliminating all the word groups that are not sentences by combining them as necessary.

_____

The first word of a sentence begins with a capital letter. A sentence ends with some punctuation, most commonly a period. Question marks are used at the end of direct questions. Exclamation points are placed at the end of sentences that express very strong feelings. Commas are used within sentences to show short pauses or to separate single things in a list or parts of a sentence.

capital (upper-case) letter	**T**	question mark	**?**
small (lower-case) letter	**t**	exclamation point	**!**
period	**.**	comma	**,**

Examples: They met in Spain.

Who knows the answer?

Leave me alone or I'll call the police!

She visited Singapore, Malaysia, and Thailand.

In late August, he got a new job.

French food is very delicious, and it is known all over the world.

3 | *Read this description of an experience in Morocco. It contains 16 sentences. Find the sentences and insert initial capitalization and end punctuation in the appropriate places. Do not add or eliminate any commas.*

last summer when my wife and I were traveling in Morocco, we had one of the most interesting bargaining experiences ever. we were in an open-air market in Rabat, and I really wanted to buy a Moroccan *jellaba*, a long, heavy, ankle-length garment there were several different shops where jellabas were sold, but Heather and I were drawn to one shop in particular I tried one jellaba on it fit perfectly, and I knew it was the one I wanted, so I asked the merchant how much it was he said it was $200 now I've always been uncomfortable about bargaining, so I was ready to pay his price Heather took me aside, however, and said that was too much and that he expected me to bargain when I said I couldn't bargain, she told me that bargaining was part of the game and that I should offer him less I sighed, tried to swallow the lump in my throat, and suggested $100 he smiled and asked for $150, whereupon I offered $110 he looked offended and shook his head Heather grabbed my hand and we started walking away I thought that was going to be the end of the experience, but then the merchant came running after me, saying he'd accept $125 I ended up buying the jellaba for that amount, and I still have it since then I've never been afraid to bargain

4 | *Write two paragraphs about an experience you have had while traveling. Be careful to avoid sentence fragments. Then work with a partner. Your partner will check your paragraph, and you will check your partner's. Try to discover and correct any fragments.*

Review Test

I Read the conversation between Sherry, Akiko, Lisa, and Jaime, who are spending the school year in an international exchange program in Spain. Complete the conversation, using the cues in parentheses. Use **would** or **will** and correct forms of **be going to** (was / were going to or is / are going to). Use **will** or **would** if **be going to** is not specified. Use contractions with pronoun subjects.

SHERRY: I wonder where Jaime and Demetrios are. Demetrios said _____*they'd be*_____
1. (they / be)

here by 12:30. It's already 12:45.

AKIKO: Well, when I talked to Jaime this morning, he told me he _____
2. (be going to)

stop at the post office to mail a package. That's the only thing I can think of.

LISA: These men! They can never be anywhere on time. We _____ miss
3. (be going to)

the train if they don't come soon.

SHERRY: What about lunch? Did Jaime say _____ bring sandwiches?
4. (he / be going to)

AKIKO: No. He said _____ at a restaurant near the castle . . . Oh,
5. (we / eat)

here they come . . . At last! Where have you guys been? _____
6. (you / not / be going to / turn over)

a new leaf and not be late anymore? That's what you said.

JAIME: Well, we promised that _____ not to be late all the time! We're
7. (we / try)

working on it. Oh, by the way, Igor is coming after all. He says

_____ a later train and meet us at three o'clock. OK, time's
8. (he / take)

a-wasting. Let's get on the train!

II *Read the conversations. Fill in the blanks with the correct forms of the words in parentheses. Use **would** if possible; otherwise, use **used to**. Use contractions with pronoun subjects.*

1. A: You _____*used to smoke*_____, didn't you?
      a. (smoke)

    B: Yeah, sometimes I _____ after meals, but I quit six months ago.
      b. (smoke)

    A: Good. I _____ too. It was terrible. When I was a serious smoker, I
      c. (smoke)

    _____ two packs a day. I'm glad I stopped.
      d. (smoke)

2. A: When I was a child, my family spent every summer at a lake in the mountains. We kids

    _____ a hike every morning. In the afternoon, we
      e. (take)

    _____ swimming.
      f. (go)

    B: Yeah, our summers were like that too. My parents _____ a cottage
      g. (own)

    on the beach. They sold it after we grew up, but when I was a kid, we

    _____ every July there. Ah, those were the good old days! Life
      h. (spend)

    _____ carefree. Now it's just hectic.
      i. (be)

3. A: Did you play many sports when you were growing up?

    B: Well, I _____ an avid softball player when I was in elementary
      j. (be)

    school. There was a park near where we _____, and the kids from
      k. (live)

    my neighborhood _____ there almost every weekend from May to
      l. (go)

    October.

    A: How about high school?

    B: I was on the football team. I remember how tough the practices were.

    A: How so?

    B: We _____ daily practices in the summer before the fall season, and
      m. (have)

    it _____ really hot. Not only that, but practices
      n. (be)

    _____ at 6:30 in the morning, so we _____
      o. (start)   **p. (feel)**

    really tired when we began and even worse when we finished.

    A: Well, I never had to worry about the heat; my sport was ice hockey!

III *Read the itinerary for the Mendozas' Italian tour. Today is the morning of July 20. Fill in the blanks with the correct forms of the verbs in parentheses. Use negative forms where necessary.*

Fred and Alice Mendoza	**Itinerary**	**Italy Trip, July 15–23**
Date	**Destination**	
July 15	Arrive at Rome airport; check in at hotel in Rome	
July 16	Tour Vatican City, including Sistine Chapel	
July 17	Day trip to Pompeii; return to Rome to spend night	
July 18	Visit other attractions in Rome: Colosseum, Forum, Trevi Fountain; stay in Rome that night	
July 19	Take train to Venice; arrive in Venice late afternoon	
July 20	Take walking tour of Venice, morning; go on gondola ride, afternoon; tour St. Mark's Cathedral; take evening train to Florence; arrive early morning	
July 21	Tour Florence	
July 22	Another day touring Florence; late afternoon: take train to Pisa; spend night there	
July 23	Tour Pisa; return to Rome late afternoon; take 11:00 P.M. flight home	

1. The Mendozas _____*have been*_____ in Italy since the night of July 15.
   (be)

2. They _____ the first four nights in Rome.
   (stay)

3. On their first full day in Rome, they _____ Vatican City.
   (tour)

4. Since touring the Vatican, they _____ Pompeii, the Colosseum, the Forum, the
   (see)
   Trevi Fountain, and some of Venice.

5. Right now it's 11:00 A.M. They _____ around Venice since 9:00 this morning.
   (walk)

6. They _____ on a gondola ride yet.
   (go)

7. Tonight they _____ the train to Florence.
   (take)

8. They _____ in Florence early tomorrow morning.
   (arrive)

9. They _____ two days in Florence and one night in Pisa.
   (spend)

10. By the evening of July 23, they _____ to Rome.
    (return)

11. They _____ home at 11:00 P.M. on the 23rd.
    (fly)

IV *Look at the pictures. Complete each pair of sentences. Use a simple verb form in one sentence and a progressive verb form in the other. Use the verbs* **develop**, **taste**, **be**, **have**, *and* **write**.

1. Mr. Schoenberg's students _____ usually well
<small>a.</small>
behaved. Today, for some reason, they _____
<small>b.</small>
difficult.

2. Amy Tanaka is a novelist. She _____ five
<small>a.</small>
novels already. She _____ a sixth novel since
<small>b.</small>
last October and expects to complete it in July.

3. The employees of Excelsior Computer _____
<small>a.</small>
their annual holiday party this evening. They always

_____ it sometime in December.
<small>b.</small>

4. Excelsior Computer _____ an amazing new
<small>a.</small>
software program since last summer and expects to release it

in four months. In the past ten years, the company

_____ 15 major software programs.
<small>b.</small>

V Circle the letter of the one underlined word or phrase in each sentence that is not correct.

1. Just before the telephone <u>rang</u>, I <u>was hoping</u> someone <u>called</u>

A   B   C
   and <u>suggest</u> going somewhere.

    D
                                           A   B Ⓒ D

2. Igor <u>doesn't go</u> with us to Toledo today; <u>he's</u> <u>staying</u> home because

       A   B   C
   he <u>has to</u> finish a term paper.

   D
                                             A   B C D

3. <u>I'll</u> <u>have returned</u> to Barcelona by the time <u>you'll</u> <u>get</u> to Manila.

 A   B   C   D
                                             A   B C D

4. I <u>promised</u> <u>to be</u> ready, but when he <u>arrived</u>, I <u>took</u> a shower.

  A   B   C   D
                                             A   B C D

5. I <u>hope</u> dinner <u>is going to</u> <u>be</u> ready soon. <u>It's smelling</u> delicious.

  A   B   C   D
                                             A   B C D

6. I <u>didn't</u> even <u>think</u> there would be a party. Akiko and Jaime <u>have done</u>

   A   B   C
   a great job, and last night's get-together <u>was</u> great.

                                     D
                                             A   B C D

7. Sherry <u>felt</u> <u>terribly</u> when she <u>forgot</u> Lisa's birthday and <u>had</u> no present.

       A   B   C   D
                                             A   B C D

8. The plane <u>has</u> just <u>taken off</u> when I <u>realized</u> I <u>had given</u> my parents the

          A   B   C   D
   wrong arrival date.
                                             A   B C D

9. <u>There</u> <u>didn't used to</u> <u>be</u> a factory on this corner, <u>did</u> there?

  A   B   C   D
                                             A   B C D

10. We <u>haven't</u> <u>been visiting</u> Venice since 2001. <u>Wouldn't</u> it be

     A   B   C
    fun <u>to go</u> there again?

   D
                                              A   B C D

VI Go back to your answers to Exercise V. Write the correct form for each item that you believe is incorrect.

1. _____ *would call* _____   6. _____

2. _____   7. _____

3. _____   8. _____

4. _____   9. _____

5. _____   10. _____

▶ *To check your answers, go to the Answer Key on page RT-1.*

PART II

Modals
and Other Auxiliaries

4 *Be* and Auxiliaries in Additions, Tags, and Short Answers

Grammar in Context

BEFORE YOU READ

1 *In your view, can people change their character, or is it basically determined at birth?*

2 *Do you think the order in which children are born determines their character? Explain your answer.*

⌒ *Read this article about birth order.*

Psychology Monthly

DOES IT MATTER *WHEN* YOU WERE BORN?

Dear Reader,

Let's see if you can answer the following question: There are two men, one named Sam and the other named Jerry. They're pretty similar: Sam is a perfectionist; so is Jerry. Jerry, always a high achiever, was president of his high school class. So was Sam. Neither man went to college. Both did become successful businessmen, though. Jerry has been a leader in most of his enterprises. So has Sam. Sam always tries to obey rules. Jerry does too. Jerry has never liked liberal ideas. Neither has Sam. The question is, why are they so similar?

"Wait!" you say, "I know what the explanation is: They're identical twins. That's why they're so similar." Well, dear reader, I'm sorry to disappoint you, but that isn't it. They're not twins, or even related to each other. But they are both firstborns. Sam and Jerry are examples of what researchers are calling the birth-order theory. According to this theory, the order in which children are born plays a significant role in the formation of their personalities and in the way they ultimately turn out. Does this sound like some crazy new theory? It isn't. It's been around for a while.

Psychology Monthly

The main idea behind the birth-order theory is quite simple: Firstborn children enjoy a special relationship with their parents simply because they were there before any other children were. When other children come along, firstborns understand that these new arrivals represent a challenge to their special relationship. For this reason, firstborns tend to be conservative, rule-oriented, and opposed to change. They want to keep things as they are. Later borns have a different challenge. They must somehow find a place in their parents' affections. They sense that they have to become different from the oldest child, so they do.

One of the main supporters of the birth-order theory is Frank Sulloway, a researcher who did a 26-year study about 7,000 famous people in history. The results of the computer analysis led Sulloway to develop his theory that first, second, and later borns often have very different characteristics. According to Sulloway, firstborns are usually self-confident, assertive, conscientious, and conservative. They can also be jealous, moralistic, and inflexible. Winston Churchill, John Wayne, Oprah Winfrey, and Joseph Stalin were all firstborns. Based on this idea, we might expect powerful political figures, such as U.S. presidents, to be firstborns. They generally are, says Sulloway.

Last borns, Sulloway observes, are usually more social, more agreeable, and more open to new and even revolutionary ideas. This is because, sensing the power of the already established relationship between the oldest sibling and the parents, they have to turn outward to establish their place in the world. Famous last borns are Joan of Arc, Thomas Jefferson, and Leon Trotsky.

What about families in which there are more than two children, or only one? If there are three children in a family, the middle child is usually more flexible than the other two and often has a talent for compromise. And a family in which there's only one child is the least predictable configuration, Sulloway says. Only children aren't as inflexible as firstborns. Like firstborns, they do identify with their parents, however.

Perhaps you're saying to yourself, "But this is all just too much of a generalization, isn't it?" Yes, maybe it is. Sulloway is the first to acknowledge that there are many exceptions to the birth-order theory. A child's temperament has a great deal to do with how he or she turns out. Shy children, for example, may not become leaders even if they are firstborns. And, as Sulloway notes, there have been a lot of famous firstborns who became revolutionaries, as well as later borns who became conservatives. Still, the theory of birth order does appear to be generally valid.

Assuming that there is some validity to the birth-order theory, what can parents do to achieve the best possible relationships with their children? In Sulloway's view, they should give each child unique time and attention. If they do, they probably won't significantly change the influences of birth order, but they will maximize the quality of those relationships.

AFTER YOU READ

1 *Look at these two sentences. Based on them, which is true, **a** or **b**? Circle the letter of the answer.*

Sam always tries to obey rules. Jerry does too.

a. Jerry normally obeys rules.

b. Jerry normally doesn't obey rules.

2 *Look at these two sentences. Based on them, which is true, **a** or **b**? Circle the letter of the answer.*

Jerry has never liked liberal ideas. Neither has Sam.

a. Sam is a liberal.

b. Sam is not a liberal.

3 *Look at these two sentences. What does* do *at the end of the second sentence stand for? Circle the letter of the answer.*

They must somehow find a place in their parents' affections. They sense that they have to become different from the oldest child, so they do.

a. become different from the oldest child

b. find a place in their parents' affections

Grammar Presentation

BE AND AUXILIARIES IN ADDITIONS, TAGS, AND SHORT ANSWERS

ADDITIONS REFERRING TO PRECEDING INFORMATION

Statement	Addition
You might think this **is** crazy.	It **is**.
It sounds like it**'s** a ridiculous idea.	It **isn't**.
You wonder if he might **be** wrong.	He **is**.
Some people **believe** in you.	I'm not sure I **do**.
See if you **can solve** it.	Michael thinks you **can**.
He **is working** on this problem right now.	At least he says he **is**.
Many of us **have worked** on this.	All my friends **have**.

ADDITIONS OF SIMILARITY WITH *SO, TOO, NEITHER, NOT EITHER*

Statement	Addition
Michael **is** a good leader.	**So is** Dennis.
	Dennis **is too**.
Carolyn **isn't** jealous of her siblings.	**Neither is** Alice.
	Alice **isn't either**.
Annie **doesn't play** sports.	Karen **doesn't either**.
George **can't ski**.	**Neither can** Martin.
George **is studying** engineering.	**So is** Martin.
Annie **has visited** Japan several times.	Karen **has too**.

ADDITIONS OF CONTRAST AND EMPHASIS

Statement	Addition
They**'re not** rich,	**but** they **ARE*** successful.
They**'re** rich;	**however**, they **AREN'T** powerful.
She**'s never studied** Italian,	**but** she **CAN speak** it fairly well.
He**'s had** many years of German;	he **CAN'T speak** it, **though**.
I **don't have** a computer at home,	**but** I **DO use** one at work.
We **have** a lot of money;	**still**, we **DON'T manage** to be happy.
My mother **is never** home;	she **DOES keep** in touch, **however**.
They **didn't go** to college;	they **DID become** successful, **though**.

*Capital letters are used here to show which words are stressed for emphasis.

TAG QUESTIONS

Statement	Tag
That**'s** a good idea,	**isn't** it?
You**'re working** with Sam,	**aren't** you?
Jeff **has worked** hard for this,	**hasn't** he?
We **can visit** your office,	**can't** we?
Annie **works** at the lab,	**doesn't** she?
That**'s not** a good idea,	**is** it?
I**'m not doing** well,	**am** I?
Jason **hasn't called**,	**has** he?
They **can't come** now,	**can** they?
Megan **didn't study**,	**did** she?

Short Answers	
	it **is**.
	I **am**.
Yes,	he **has**.
	you **can**.
	she **does**.
	it**'s not**.
	you**'re not**.
No,	he **hasn't**.
	they **can't**.
	she **didn't**.

GRAMMAR NOTES	EXAMPLES
1. Auxiliaries are helping verbs (HV) that are used with main verbs (MV) to make negative statements, questions, progressive forms, and perfect forms, and to express meanings such as possibility and advice.	• It **doesn't** make sense to me. (HV MV) • **Does** this sound like a crazy theory? (HV MV) • He **might** be a last born. (HV MV)

2. Auxiliaries can be used:
  a. without a main verb in additions to statements
  b. in the tags of tag questions
  c. in short answers
 	
The main verb *be* is also used in additions, tags, and short answers.
	• Let's see if you can understand this. I think you **can**. *(addition)*
	  A: She went to college, **didn't** she? *(tag)*
	  B: Yes, she **did**. *(short answer)*
	• You might assume presidents are firstborns. They usually **are**.
	  A: Sulloway is a last born, **isn't** he?
	  B: Yes, he **is**.

3. In **additions** that refer to previous information, we use *be* if it is present or implied in the previous statement. If *be* is not present in the previous statement, **other auxiliaries** are used to refer to previous information.	• We might think firstborns are conservative. They often **are**. • Frank seems like a good parent. In fact, he **is**. • Jerry owns a company. Or at least he says he **does**. • Alice says we've solved the problem. I'm not sure we **have**.

4. To make an affirmative addition to an affirmative statement, use *so* or *too*.
 	
To make a negative addition to a negative statement, use *neither* or *not either*.
 	
▶ **BE CAREFUL!** When you make additions with *so* and *neither*, place these words at the beginning of the sentence, and invert the subject and the auxiliary.
	• Sam is a perfectionist. **So is** Jerry.
	       OR
	 Jerry **is too**.
	• Jerry has never liked liberal ideas. **Neither has** Sam.
	       OR
	 Sam **hasn't either**.
	• Martha got married last year. **So did Helen**.
	 NOT So ~~Helen did~~.
	• Sam didn't go to college. **Neither did Jerry**.
	 NOT Neither ~~Jerry did~~.

5. Use auxiliaries to make a contrast with a preceding statement. Use a negative addition to make a contrast to an affirmative statement. Use an affirmative addition to make a contrast to a negative statement.

NOTE: In additions of contrast, there is sometimes a contrast word such as *but*, *though*, *however*, or *still*.

To place special emphasis on a word, pronounce it with stress. To emphasize a verb in the simple present or simple past, use *do*, *does*, and *did* in affirmative sentences.

To emphasize a verb with *be* and other auxiliaries, use full forms, not contracted forms.

- Some think all leaders are firstborns. They **aren't**, **though**.
- They're not twins, **but** they **are** both firstborns.

- I don't have any children of my own. **Still**, I **do** love children.

- Neither of them got a college education. They **did** have successful careers.

- He's not a conservative. He **is** a Republican.
- I've never read Sulloway's book. I **have** read two of his articles.

---

6. In **tag questions**, use a negative tag after an affirmative statement. Use an affirmative tag after a negative statement.

Use tag questions to check information or to comment on a situation. You expect the listener to agree with you, and your voice falls on the tag.

Use tag questions to get information. You expect an answer, and your voice rises on the tag.

- The birth-order theory **makes** sense, **doesn't it**?
- Young children **shouldn't** be left alone, **should they**?

A: You're an only child, **aren't you**?
B: Uh-huh. So was my dad.
A: That's an interesting idea, **isn't it**?
B: Yeah. It's fascinating.

A: You have a sister, **don't you**?
B: No. Actually, I have a brother.

(continued)

7. Use **auxiliaries without main verbs** in short answers.

- Sulloway is a writer, isn't he? Yes, he **is**.
- Have you read his book? No, I **haven't**.
- Is she an only child? Yes, she **is**. NOT Yes, ~~she's.~~

▶ **BE CAREFUL!** Use full forms, not contractions, in affirmative short answers. You can use contracted forms or full forms in negative short answers.

    A: Had you heard about the birth-order theory previously?

    B: No, I hadn't.

               OR

    No, I **had not**.

Focused Practice

1 | DISCOVER THE GRAMMAR

A *Look at these sentences. The verbs that are circled refer to a preceding word or phrase. Find and underline the preceding word or phrase referred to by the circled verbs. Draw an arrow between the two.*

1. Let's see if you can <u>answer the following question</u>. No doubt you (can).

2. Sam is a perfectionist; so (is) Jerry.

3. Jerry, always a high achiever, was president of his high school class. So (was) Sam.

4. Jerry has been a leader in most of his enterprises. So (has) Sam.

5. Sam always tries to obey rules. Jerry (does) too.

6. Jerry has never liked liberal ideas. Neither (has) Sam.

7. Does this sound like some crazy new theory? It (isn't).

8. They were there before any other children (were).

9. They sense that they have to become different from the oldest child, so they (do).

10. Based on this idea, we might expect powerful political figures, such as U.S. presidents, to be firstborns. They usually (are), says Sulloway.

11. But this is perhaps too much of a generalization. Yes, maybe it (is).

B *Look again at the reading. Read the first two and the last three paragraphs. Find six sentences in which auxiliaries are used to show contrast or emphasis. Write the main parts of those sentences here and underline the auxiliary.*

1. *Both did become successful businessmen, though.* _____

2. _____

3. _____

4. _____

5. _____

6. _____

2 | ADDITIONS   *Grammar Notes 2–5*

Match the statements on the left with the correct additions on the right.

___f___ 1. Jefferson was a last born,   **a.** Neither had my wife.

_____ 2. My favorite cousin is an only child,   **b.** Everyone in my family has.

_____ 3. Does her idea sound silly?   **c.** He won't be, though.

_____ 4. Everyone expected the plan to fail.   **d.** but she does read it well.

_____ 5. Most people support that plan.   **e.** It isn't.

_____ 6. Tim hasn't done the work.   **f.** and so was Joan of Arc.

_____ 7. Sarah can't speak Japanese,   **g.** I'm not sure I do.

_____ 8. Dan thinks he'll be successful.   **h.** and I am too.

_____ 9. I've graduated from college.   **i.** It didn't, however.

_____ 10. I'd never heard of birth order.   **j.** He says he hasn't, anyway.

3 | **FAMILY DYNAMICS** *Grammar Notes 3–5*

Read a dinner table conversation in the Grant family. Complete the conversation with verbs or verb phrases to show contrast and emphasis or to refer to what was said before.

MRS. GRANT: Kids, come on, now. You need to eat your asparagus.

SAMANTHA: Do I have to, Mom? I don't like asparagus.

MOLLY: Neither _____*do I*_____, Mom.
1.

MRS. GRANT: Yes, you _____ have to eat it. It's good for you.
2.

MOLLY: Mom, if I eat it, it'll make me sick. I know it _____.
3.

MRS. GRANT: No, _____. Don't be silly.
4.

MR. GRANT: Steve, what about your homework? You promised me you were going to do it

before dinner.

STEVE: I _____ it, Dad.
5.

MR. GRANT: You _____? When? While you were watching TV?
6.

STEVE: From 5:00 to 5:30. It only took me a half hour.

MR. GRANT: What about you, girls? Have you finished your homework? We need to be leaving

for the concert pretty soon.

SAMANTHA: I _____, Dad.
7.

MOLLY: So _____.
8.

MRS. GRANT: What was that you said about a concert, John?

MR. GRANT: You know, the big Shania Twain concert—the one we've had tickets to for a month.

MRS. GRANT: It's not tonight, is it?

MR. GRANT: Yes, _____, Helen. You forgot, didn't you?
9.

MRS. GRANT: Oh, no! I'm not ready. Come on, now. Everyone needs to help. Who'll clear the table?

STEVE: I _____, Mom.
10.

MR. GRANT: What about loading the dishwasher?

SAMANTHA: Can't we just leave the dishes in the sink if we're in such a hurry?

MR. GRANT: No, _____. Now, who'll do it?
11.

STEVE: Sam _____, Dad.
12.

SAMANTHA: Thanks a lot, pal!

MR. GRANT: Come on, kids. Let's get going.

4 | **SENTENCES ABOUT FAMILIES**   *Grammar Notes 4–5*

Read these sentences. Use the words in parentheses to write additions of similarity or contrast.

1. The kids don't like to eat vegetables. (my husband / similarity)

   My husband doesn't either. OR *Neither does my husband.*

2. My cousin is an only child. (I / contrast)

   _____

3. I don't work in the field of pediatrics. (my brother and sister / contrast)

   _____

4. I'd never read anything about family dynamics. (anyone else in my family / similarity)

   _____

5. Some parents favor one child over another. (should / contrast)

   _____

6. Our family has taken a vacation every year for 10 years. (my brother's family / contrast)

   _____

7. My daughter doesn't read or write Spanish. (speak / contrast)

   _____

8. Our son hasn't been accepted at the university. (daughter / similarity)

   _____

9. Bob has always been an excellent student. (Katie / similarity)

   _____

10. Steve doesn't want to leave home. (Theresa / contrast)

    _____

5 | LET'S TALK IT OVER

🎧 *Listen to Brent Washburn's conversation with his thirteen-year-old son, Jeremy, about Jeremy's recent behavior. As you listen, read the tapescript and pay special attention to the use of stress for contrast and emphasis. There are ten auxiliary verbs that show emphasis or make a contrast with a preceding statement. The first one is circled. Find and circle the other nine.*

BRENT: Jeremy, come on into the living room. There are some things we need to talk about.

JEREMY: Dad, if it's about the broken window in the bathroom, I can explain. I guess I (did) break it, but I didn't mean to. It was an accident, really.

BRENT: It wasn't the window I wanted to talk about. I was wondering how it got broken, though.

JEREMY: It's not the window? What do you want to talk about, then?

BRENT: Well, for one thing, I got a letter from your teacher, Ms. Hammond. She says you haven't been studying and you might fail. You do want to pass the seventh grade, don't you?

JEREMY: Of course, Dad. And I have been studying. I just keep forgetting to turn in my homework.

BRENT: She says you don't pay attention in class, either, and you're always staring out the window.

JEREMY: Dad, she just doesn't like me. I do pay attention. Just because I'm not looking at Ms. Hammond doesn't mean I'm not paying attention to what she's saying . . . She's boring, too.

BRENT: Jeremy, I've known Ms. Hammond for a long time. Her classes may not always be fun, but she does know how to teach. From now on, I want you to study every evening from 7:00 until 9:00, and I'm going to call Ms. Hammond every week to see if you're turning in your homework. And I will call every week. Don't think I won't.

JEREMY: Do I still get to watch TV and play video games?

BRENT: Not during the week until your grades improve. You can't have any of your friends over during the week either. Of course, you can read a book if you've finished your homework. OK. Now, let's talk about the window. What did happen to the window?

6 | EDITING

Read this letter from Jeremy Washburn's seventh-grade teacher to Jeremy's parents, reporting on his progress at school. There are ten mistakes in the making of additions and the use of auxiliaries. The first mistake is already corrected. Find and correct nine more.

MADISON JUNIOR HIGH SCHOOL

February 12

Dear Mr. and Mrs. Washburn,

I'm writing to give you a progress report on Jeremy. In general,
I'd say he's doing better than before, though he ~~is~~ *isn't* doing as well as
he could. He still has a tendency to daydream a little too much, but
he doesn't seem to be paying better attention in class. One of his
weak subjects is science; neither is math. He scored high in math on
the national achievement tests a month ago, though, so he is have a
chance of passing his math class. However, he is passing at the
moment. Either is he passing science. He is doing very well in
English, though, and he's doing reasonably well in history and art
either. The main problem I'm having is getting Jeremy to turn in his
work; still, he didn't submit three assignments last week. I
appreciate your efforts to monitor his study time in the evenings.
Children today have so many distractions, do they? Your son is lucky
to have parents who care about education; many don't. Jeremy is
doing better; he isn't out of trouble yet. Please keep up the
supervised work at home, and call me if you have any concerns.

Sincerely,

Priscilla Hammond

Priscilla Hammond

Communication Practice

7 | LISTENING

🎧 *Listen to a segment of the radio talk show* Do the Right Thing. *Then listen again. Read the statements and check* **True** *or* **False.**

	True	False
1. Sally says she never really loved Bob.	☐	☑
2. Sally thinks a lot of Bob as a person.	☐	☐
3. A few weeks ago Sally tried to tell Bob her feelings.	☐	☐
4. Bob accepted what Sally told him.	☐	☐
5. Sally says she's unsure of her feelings.	☐	☐
6. Mary Mobley says Sally doesn't have to tell Bob the truth.	☐	☐
7. Jerry is rich.	☐	☐
8. Jerry has put money away for his children.	☐	☐
9. Jerry and his children live in the same vicinity.	☐	☐
10. Jerry's son can afford to make the payments on a house.	☐	☐
11. Mary Mobley thinks Jerry's children don't really sound selfish.	☐	☐
12. Mary Mobley thinks not giving the children their inheritance now might be a good thing to do.	☐	☐

8 | GROUP DISCUSSION

A *Read this article about raising children. As you read, think about points you agree or disagree with.*

Example: American parents have lost their way. (disagree)

PARENTING *Monthly*

ASIAN PARENTS DIFFER ON CHILD REARING

by John Rosemond

A man called the other day from Milwaukee with an interesting story that illustrates how much American parents have lost their way.

He and his wife took their three children, ages 6, 4, and 3, to the zoo for what was supposed to be a pleasant afternoon. Instead, it was a disaster. The children ran in three directions at once, requiring that the two parents run even faster. The children's activity levels were matched by their continuous yelling. They demanded everything they saw. The parents saying no resulted in dramatic displays of anger. So, they said yes more often than not. The children then began complaining that their toys and souvenirs were too heavy, so the parents wound up carrying armloads of worthless junk.

"Needless to say, John," he went on, "we didn't have a good time. In fact, my wife and I took the kids home early because we were getting angry at one another."

To many, this story will sound very familiar. Some might even say, "Well, what did they expect, taking three young children to the zoo?"

But that's not where this father's story ends. In the course of all this noise and confusion, he and his wife noticed an Asian woman with three equally young children. But her children were well behaved, calm, quiet, and followed their mother like ducklings. She spoke with her children, but only rarely. It was apparent that this woman was not giving her children many instructions. They seemed to know what she expected of them. Neither the mother nor the kids were carrying any junk, yet everyone seemed to be having a good time.

"What's her secret?" asked my man from Milwaukee.

It just so happens I've had several conversations lately with Asian parents; all of them have arrived here recently. They tell me they are shocked by the behavior of American children, and fear their bad influence. In the course of these conversations, I've discovered that these parents have assumptions about child rearing as different from those of average American parents as China is from the United States.

The first assumption is that children should pay more attention to parents than parents pay to children. These parents understand that you cannot discipline a child who is not paying attention to you. They also understand that the more attention parents pay to children, the less children will pay to parents.

Second, no attempt should be made to persuade children to cooperate. In fact, since cooperation implies a state of equality, these parents don't even seek cooperation. Instead, they expect obedience.

Third, they don't explain themselves to their children. Therefore, their children's questions are about what the world is made of and how it works, rather than

(continued)

ASIAN PARENTS DIFFER ON CHILD REARING

about the "why?" and "why not?" of their parents' rules and expectations. In fact, these parents are amazed at the amount of time American parents waste dealing with such things.

Lastly, these parents do not tolerate misbehavior. Therefore, they do not bribe their children, nor do they threaten them.

The truly sad thing is that most of America's children used to be as well-behaved as those Asian kids. The good news is, it's not too late, however, to save ourselves.

B *Now read the article again. Form small groups and discuss Rosemond's article. In two columns, list points you agree with and disagree with. Say why you agree or disagree in each case. Discuss your points with the class.*

Example: **A:** American parents have lost their way.
B: I basically disagree. Some American parents have lost their way, but not all of them have.

9 | PICTURE DISCUSSION

With a partner, discuss the picture. Compare the American family and the Asian family. What differences do you see? Which family is behaving more like a family in your culture?

Example: **A:** Which family looks more similar to a family in your culture?
B: The Asian family does. They're . . .

10 | WRITING

Is child rearing better when children pay more attention to parents than parents pay to children, or when the opposite is true? Write three or four paragraphs explaining your viewpoint. Give examples to support your ideas.

Example: In my opinion, children should pay more attention to their parents than parents pay to their children. I don't believe that parents should ignore or neglect their children. I do think, however, that many parents these days are too worried that their children won't like them and are not willing to use their parental authority. Let me explain my viewpoint . . .

11 | ON THE INTERNET: FAMOUS PEOPLE AND BIRTH ORDER

Use the Internet to find out information about a famous person you are interested in. Is the person an only child? If the person has siblings, where does he or she come in birth order? Does what you know about this person fit the birth-order theory? Report your findings to the class.

Example: I researched President George W. Bush. He is the oldest of five children in the Bush family. I think he fits the birth-order theory because his conservative values are similar to those of his father, President George H.W. Bush.

5 Modals to Express Degrees of Necessity

Grammar in Context

BEFORE YOU READ

1 *Look at the picture on page 73. What are the people doing? Is this a practice in your culture?*

2 *What are some things that should and shouldn't be done in your culture? Make a short list.*

Read this article about cultural differences.

What We Should and Shouldn't Have Done

Recently my wife and I had a cross-cultural experience that taught us about some things we should have done differently. Six months ago my company sent me to work at our branch office in Japan. My Japanese co-workers have been friendly and gracious, and last week one of them invited my wife and me to his house for dinner. We were honored to be invited, and the food was delicious. But even though Masayuki and Yukiko, his wife, were most polite and friendly and never gave an indication that anything was wrong, we felt a bit uncomfortable about the evening. I decided to ask my friend Junichi about it. He's lived in both Japan and the United States, so he knows the differences be-

tween the two cultures. He gave me a lot of pointers. Now we know what we should and shouldn't have done.

The first tip was about taking off our shoes. We knew that you're supposed to take off your shoes when you enter a Japanese home, so we did. We didn't know we were supposed to arrange them so they'd be pointing toward the door when we left so that we'd be able to put them on without having to turn around. But this wasn't a big mistake, Junichi said.

The second pointer was about gifts. Helen and I knew you're supposed to take a gift to a Japanese home. Masayuki and Yukiko seemed a little shocked, though, when we pulled the present out of a plastic bag and said, "We thought

What We Should and Shouldn't Have Done

you'd like this CD. It's rock and roll." Junichi chuckled and said, "Well, you should have wrapped the CD. It's OK to bring it in a plastic bag, but the gift itself has to be wrapped. And you mustn't say anything about the gift. Just give it to your hosts. The main problem, though, was the gift itself."

"You mean we should have taken something different?"

"Yes. A rock and roll CD isn't really an appropriate gift."

"Well, what should we have taken?"

"Maybe a box of chocolates. Or you could have taken some flowers."

After that I told Junichi about what happened before dinner. Masayuki and Yukiko had invited us to sit down for some tea and snacks. The tea was delicious, but we had trouble eating the raw sushi. I was able to finish mine, but Helen couldn't finish hers. Masayuki and Yukiko seemed a little puzzled. Junichi chuckled again and said, "Well, in Japan it's considered impolite to leave half-eaten food on a plate."

"You mean you've got to eat everything that's offered to you?" I asked.

"You don't have to. But if you take something, you must finish it."

After we ate, Helen asked Yukiko if she could help her in the kitchen. This is the way we do things back in the United States, but Junichi says you are not to do this in Japan. According to the rules of Japanese culture, visitors aren't allowed to go into the kitchen.

The other thing you probably shouldn't do, he says, is praise pictures or ornaments in the house. If you do, your Japanese

(*continued*)

What We Should and Shouldn't Have Done

hosts might feel they have to give the object to you. Fortunately, we didn't do that.

At the end of the evening, Masayuki asked us if we'd like to have another drink. We thought it wouldn't be polite to say no, so we accepted and stayed for another half hour. Finally we felt that we absolutely had to leave, so when Masayuki invited us to have an additional drink, I said, "We'd really like to, but it's late. We'd better get going, or we won't be able to get up in the morning." Masayuki and Yukiko seemed relieved. Junichi said, "That's what you should have done in the first place. When a Japanese host invites you to have a drink at the end of the evening, you should refuse gently. Otherwise, you could be there all night. Leaving earlier would have been fine."

I asked what he thought we might do to rectify the situation. "Shall we invite them over?" I asked. He said, "Yes, you ought to do that. Just remember all the things I've told you. But don't invite them to an informal, Western-style party with a lot of loud music. Just make it a simple dinner for the four of you."

Good advice, I thought. What really struck me is how much we all have to learn about other cultures.

AFTER YOU READ

Complete these sentences. Circle the correct answer. Discuss your answers.

1. The author and his wife _____.
   a. followed exactly the Japanese custom of taking your shoes off
   b. should have left their shoes pointing toward the door, but didn't

2. In Japan, it's a good idea to _____.
   a. bring something like a rock and roll CD as a house gift
   b. wrap a gift instead of just bringing it in the original bag

3. In Japan, it's wrong to _____.
   a. talk about a gift when you give it to your host
   b. bring a gift in a plastic bag

4. According to their Japanese friend, the author and his wife should _____.
   a. ask Masayuki and Yukiko to join them for a quiet dinner party
   b. ask Masayuki and Yukiko to a typical Western-style party

Grammar Presentation

MODALS TO EXPRESS DEGREES OF NECESSITY (RANGING FROM OBLIGATION TO NO OBLIGATION)

Obligation (Necessity)								
You	**must** **have to** **have got to**	**call**	them.	You	**must not** **can't** **are not allowed to**	**call**	them.
You	**had to**	**call**	them.	You	**couldn't** **weren't allowed to**	**call**	them.

Advice								
You	**had better** **should** **ought to**	**leave**	early.	You	**had better not** **shouldn't**	**leave**	early.
You	**should have** **ought to have**	**left**	early.	You	**shouldn't have**	**left**	early.

Expectation								
You	**are supposed to** **are to**	**take**	a gift.	You	**are not supposed to** **are not to**	**do**	this.
You	**were supposed to** **were to**	**take**	a gift.	You	**were not supposed to** **were not to**	**do**	this.

Suggestion		
You	**could** **might**	**give**	roses.
You	**could have** **might have**	**given**	roses.

No Obligation (No Necessity)		
You	**don't have to**	**call**	them.
You	**didn't have to**	**call**	them.

Necessity
100%

0%

GRAMMAR NOTES   **EXAMPLES**

1. **Modals** are auxiliary verbs. The modals are *can*, *could*, *had better*, *may*, *might*, *must*, *ought to*, *shall*, *should*, *will*, and *would*. Each modal has only one form for all persons.

- I / You / He / She / We / They **could take** some flowers.

Use **simple modals** (modal + base form) for the present and the future.

- We **should invite** Jim to the party tonight.

Use **perfect modals** (modal + *have* + past participle) to show degrees of necessity in the past.

- We **should have invited** Jim to last week's party too.

When referring to degrees of necessity, modals show speakers' attitudes toward the actions they are describing. Modals are used to talk about obligations, advice, expectations, and suggestions.

- You **could invite** them over.
- You **should leave** early.

---

2. Some **modal-like expressions** have meanings similar to modals:

must	*have to*
should	*be supposed to*

- You **must finish** everything on your plate. / You **have to finish** everything on your plate.
- You **should take** a gift. / You**'re supposed to take** a gift.

---

3. Use *must*, *have to*, and *have got to* to show strong necessity. They are similar in meaning.

- You **must / have to / have got to arrive** on time.

USAGE NOTES

Use *must* formally to show very strong obligation that can't be escaped.

Use *have to* in all forms and situations, formal and informal.

A: You mean you **must eat** everything they offer you?

B: No, you **don't have to**.

Use *have got to* informally in conversation. It is rarely used in the negative. Use *don't have to* instead.

Use *will have to* to show future necessity.

- We**'ll have to invite** them over to our house.

Use *had to* to show past necessity.

- We felt we **had to take** a gift.

▶ **BE CAREFUL!** Don't use *must have* + past participle to show past necessity.

- We **had to leave**.
  NOT We ~~must have left~~.

4. Use *must not* to say that it is necessary not to do something (that it is prohibited).	• You **must not smoke** here.
▶ **BE CAREFUL!** Although *must* and *have to* have similar meanings, *must not* and *don't have to* have very different meanings. For *don't have to*, see note 9.	• We **must not miss** the flight. NOT We ~~don't have to~~ miss the flight.

5. Use *had better* to give a warning that something bad or negative will happen if advice isn't followed.	• We**'d better get going**, or we'll be late. • You**'d better not discuss** politics during dinner.

6. Use *should* or *ought to* to offer advice. They mean "it would be a good idea if . . ." and are basically the same in most situations. Use *should*, not *ought to*, in questions and negatives.	• You **should / ought to refuse** gently.
	  A: Should I invite a guest?
	  B: No, you **shouldn't.**

Use *should have / ought to have* to express advice about past situations. *Should have* and *ought to have* suggest that the action did not happen. *Shouldn't have* and *ought not to have* suggest that it did.	• You **should / ought to have done** that the first time. • You **shouldn't / ought not to have mentioned** your gift.
NOTE: We sometimes use *shall* in questions to ask for advice. In this meaning, *shall* is used only with *I* or *we*. When it is used with *we*, it is often followed by a sentence with *let's*. In this meaning, *shall* is somewhat similar to *should*.	**A: Shall** we **get** them some flowers? **B:** Yes, **let's do** that.

7. Use *be supposed to* to show an expectation. It is used only in the present and the past. In the past, the affirmative suggests that the action didn't happen. The negative suggests that the action did happen.	• You**'re supposed to take off** your shoes when you enter a Japanese home. • We **were supposed to take** flowers. • We **weren't supposed to mention** the gift we'd brought.
You can use *be to* + base form formally to express a strong expectation.	• All employees **are to attend** the company office party. • You**'re not to ask** any personal questions.

(continued)

<table>
<tr>
<td>

8. Use *could* or *might* to make polite, not-too-strong suggestions about the present or future.

Use *could have / might have* + past participle to make polite suggestions about a past opportunity. In this meaning, *might have* and *could have* mean that the action didn't happen.

</td>
<td>

- You **could / might take** them some chocolates.

- You **could have / might have taken** some flowers.

</td>
</tr>
</table>

<table>
<tr>
<td>

9. To say that something is not necessary, use *don't / doesn't have to*.

In the past, use *didn't have to* + base form to show that something was not necessary.

</td>
<td>

- You **don't have to eat** everything offered to you.

- You **didn't have to bring** a gift.

</td>
</tr>
</table>

Focused Practice

1 | DISCOVER THE GRAMMAR

Look at these sentences. Each sentence can be said in another, similar way. Circle the letter of the choice that is closer in meaning to the sentence given.

1. We knew that you're supposed to take off your shoes when you enter a Japanese home, so we did.
   a. Japanese people expect guests to remove their shoes.
   b. It doesn't matter whether or not you wear your shoes in a Japanese home.

2. Well, you should have wrapped the CD.
   a. You wrapped the CD, and that was the right thing to do.
   b. You didn't wrap the CD, and that was a cultural mistake in Japan.

3. And you mustn't say anything about the gift.
   a. It's sometimes acceptable to say something about the gift.
   b. It's definitely wrong to say anything about the gift.

4. Or you could have taken some flowers.
   a. Flowers are an acceptable gift in Japan, but the author and his wife didn't take any.
   b. The author and his wife made a cultural mistake by not taking flowers.

5. According to the rules of Japanese culture, visitors aren't allowed to go into the kitchen.
   a. The Japanese expect visitors to stay out of the kitchen.
   b. It's OK for visitors to go into a Japanese kitchen.

6. If you do, your Japanese hosts might feel they have to give the object to you.

    a. Japanese hosts might feel a strong obligation to give the object to you.

    b. Japanese hosts might feel they can choose not to give the object to you.

7. When a Japanese host invites you to have a drink at the end of the evening, you should refuse gently.

    a. The hosts don't expect you to refuse gently.

    b. It's a good idea to refuse gently.

8. Yes, you ought to do that.

    a. It doesn't matter whether you do that.

    b. It would be a good idea to do that.

9. Junichi says you are not to do this in Japan.

    a. People won't care if you do this in Japan.

    b. It's a cultural mistake to do this in Japan.

2 | SHOULD WE LEAVE A TIP?   *Grammar Notes 3, 6–9*

Read this conversation between Fumiko, a visiting exchange student, and her American friend Jane. Complete the conversation with items from the box. Use each item once.

~~are you supposed to leave~~	could have left	don't have to leave	had to worry
ought to have given	should we have left	should you leave	should you tip
supposed to do	were supposed to leave	you're supposed to do	

    JANE: Hi, Fumiko. How are things going?

FUMIKO: Really well. But there's something I wanted to ask you about.

    JANE: OK. What?

FUMIKO: Tipping. I just don't understand it. _____*Are you supposed to leave*_____ a tip
                                   1.

everywhere you eat? This is really bothering me. I've never

_____ about this before. We don't tip in Japan.
           2.

    JANE: You don't?

FUMIKO: No. You're not really _____ that. It's all included in
                                   3.

the service charge.

    JANE: Tell me more. Have you had a problem with this?

(continued)

FUMIKO: Yeah. Last week a Chinese friend of mine and I had dinner at a restaurant. We knew

we _____ a tip, but we didn't know how much.
4.

JANE: How much did you leave?

FUMIKO: About 25 percent. _____ more?
5.

JANE: Wow! Twenty-five percent. That's a lot. The service must have been really good.

FUMIKO: Actually, it wasn't. The waiter was pretty rude . . . and slow.

JANE: Well, if you're not really satisfied with the service, you

_____ anything.
6.

FUMIKO: So how much _____ the waiter if you're satisfied?
7.

JANE: Between 15 and 20 percent. Fifteen is the usual.

FUMIKO: Hmmm. OK. Now here's another question. I'm confused about what

_____ if you're sitting at a lunch counter instead of
8.

at a table. _____ anything for the person behind the
9.

counter?

JANE: It's a nice gesture. Why do you ask?

FUMIKO: Yesterday I had lunch at a cafeteria counter. The waitress was really nice and polite. I

felt like I _____ her something.
10.

JANE: Did you?

FUMIKO: No.

JANE: Well, you _____ something. Maybe 5 to 10 percent.
11.

FUMIKO: Oh. OK. Next time I will.

3 | GIFT GIVING IN TWO OTHER CULTURES

A *Read this short essay about gift giving.*

A Chinese woman had lived in Australia for a few years. On her birthday, she was invited to the home of an Australian friend to celebrate. When she was presented with a gift, she thanked her friend and put the gift away. Her friend asked, "Aren't you going to open it?" The Chinese lady said, "Oh no! I don't want to open it now."

In Chinese culture, one is not expected to open a gift immediately after receiving it. In Australian culture, however, the opposite is true. There are other rules about gift giving in Chinese culture. It is important, for example, to avoid giving umbrellas, knives, scissors, and clocks.

Iranian culture has its rules too. Amanda, a young North American woman, went to the home of her fiancé's sister. She saw a small statue, and when she said she liked it, the sister insisted on giving it to her. Why? Many Middle Easterners feel obligated to give something to someone who admires it. Amanda didn't want to accept the statue, but Fariba, the sister, kept insisting. Amanda should have kept on refusing. Iranians may keep on insisting, but you are under no obligation to accept.

B *Now complete these sentences, using modals or modal-like expressions. Make some sentences negative if necessary.*

1. According to the rules of Australian culture, the Chinese lady _____ opened the gift at the party.

2. In Chinese culture, one _____ open a gift immediately after receiving it.

3. In Chinese culture, one _____ avoid giving umbrellas, knives, scissors, and clocks.

4. Iranians feel one _____ give something to someone if that person admires it.

5. Amanda _____ refused to accept the statue.

6. Even if an Iranian keeps on insisting, you _____ acccpt.

4 | SHOULDS AND COULDS

Grammar Notes 6, 8

Look again at the opening reading. Write six sentences about what the American couple should have done and shouldn't have done. Then write four sentences about what they could or might have done.

1. *They should have wrapped the CD.* _____

2. _____

3. _____

4. _____

5. _____

6. _____

7. _____

8. _____

9. _____

10. _____

5 | EDITING

Read this letter from Tong-Li, an international exchange student in Australia, to her friend Masako in Singapore. There are 11 mistakes in the use of modals or modal-like expressions. The first mistake is already corrected. Find and correct 10 more.

Dear Masako,

                                      should

    Sorry it's taken me so long to write. I ~~shouldn't~~ have gotten to this

weeks ago, but I've been so busy. I'm really looking forward to the holidays

and seeing all you guys again.

    School is going well. It's tough but really interesting, and I'm sure I should to be studying even

more than I have been. Part of the problem is that I'm taking too many classes. You're only suppose

to take five a term, but I'm taking six.

Anyway, I've gotten to know a lot of new people, including several Australians. I have this one really good friend, a girl named Jane. She invited me to her house last week for a party. Actually, it was my birthday, but I didn't know she knew that. I thought it was a party like any other. I figured I better take some kind of gift, but I couldn't decide what it must be. Finally I came up with the idea of a bouquet of flowers. As soon as I got to the party, I gave it to Jane, and she was really happy to get it. But then the funniest thing happened. I guess I should expect something was up from the mysterious way Jane was acting, but I didn't. This was a surprise party—for me! As soon as I took off my coat and sat down, a lot of people jumped up from behind sofas and other places where they'd been hiding and shouted "Surprise! Happy birthday!" I was embarrassed, but I might not have been, because everyone was really friendly, and pretty soon I forgot about my embarrassment. Then they gave me presents. I was about to put them away, but Jane said, "Aren't you going to open them?" I didn't know what to do. In China you shouldn't have opened gifts right when you get them, but apparently you are supposed to in Australia. So I opened them. The nicest gift was a new blouse from Jane. She told me I must have gone and try it on immediately, so I did. It's beautiful. Anyway, what a party! I thought I knew all about Australian culture, but I guess I'm not as familiar with it as I thought. The custom of opening up presents in front of the gift giver is a strange one to me.

The weather is kind of chilly. How is it back in Singapore? Nice and warm? Must I bring you something special from Australia when I come?

Well, Masako, I'm running out of space, so I got to sign off. Write soon.

Best,

Tong-Li

Communication Practice

6 | LISTENING

🎧 *Listen to the telephone conversation. Read the questions. Then listen again. Complete the answers, using modals or modal-like expressions.*

1. Why do Dad and Ray need to get home as soon as possible?

   Mom's surprise party is supposed to start in 15 minutes.

2. What's Bev's opinion about delaying Mom's present, and why?

3. What does Dad say when Bev reminds him about not putting things off till the last minute?

4. What's Dad's opinion about Bev's camera suggestion?

5. What's Bev's opinion about a dress?

6. What's Bev's blouse suggestion?

7. What's Bev's scarf suggestion?

8. What does Bev say about getting home as soon as possible, and why?

7 | INFORMATION GAP: WHY WON'T THEY WAIT ON US?

Work with a partner to complete this story. Each of you will read a version of the same story. Each version is missing some information. Take turns asking your partner questions to get the missing information.

Student A, read the story. Ask questions and fill in the missing information. Then answer Student B's questions.

Student B, turn to page 88 and follow the instructions there.

Example: **A:** Where were they supposed to stay?
B: They were supposed to stay at the Grand State Hotel. What should they have gotten?
A: They should have gotten a confirmation number.

A married couple was traveling in Europe and had just entered a new country. They had been having a wonderful time, but now everything was going wrong. The first problem was finding accommodations. They were supposed to stay at _____, but when they got to the hotel there was no record of their reservation. The wife said they should have gotten a confirmation number. They hadn't, unfortunately, so they had to spend the night _____. The next day they finally found a room at a hotel far from the center of town. There were two rooms available: a large one and a tiny one. Since they were on a tight budget, they decided they had better take the tiny one. The second problem was communication. They were starving after spending hours looking for accommodations, so they went into a restaurant. A waiter brought them a menu, but they couldn't understand it. The husband said they should have _____. They hadn't done that, though, so they didn't know what to order.

Time passed. Other people were being served but they weren't. Frustrated, they decided they had to do something. But what? They noticed that a boy about 11 years old seemed to be listening to their conversation. Soon the boy came over to their table. "Excuse me," he said. "You have to _____. Then they'll take your order." The husband and wife were both astonished but grateful. The wife said, "You speak our language very well. Did you study it somewhere?" The boy said, "I lived in Australia for three years. I learned English there." He asked, "Shall I help you order? I can translate the menu."

When they got back home, their friends asked them what they had liked best about the trip. The wife said, "Well, the best part was visiting that country where everything went wrong. At some point, everybody should _____. You don't have to be miserable, but you need a challenge. That's when you learn things. Maybe that's what people mean when they say travel is broadening."

8 | SMALL-GROUP DISCUSSION: IS IT OK IN YOUR CULTURE?

Work in small groups. Decide individually whether each of the behaviors is required, advised, allowed, or unimportant in your culture or another culture you are familiar with. Check the appropriate boxes. Then discuss the results with the others in your group.

Example: A: When you're invited to dinner in your culture, are you supposed to take a gift?

B: Absolutely. You must take a gift. And it has to be wrapped. What about in your culture?

A: It's pretty much optional. You should take a gift if it's a birthday party, but . . .

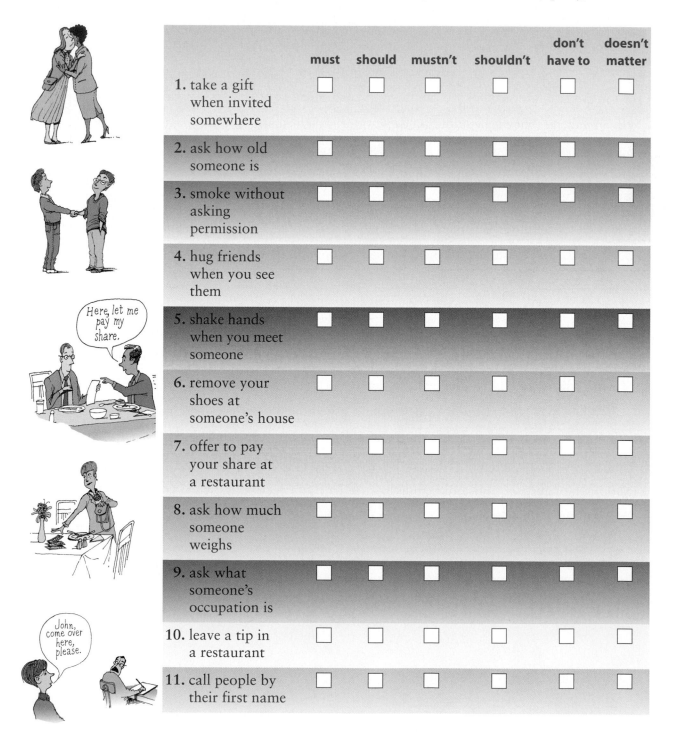

	must	should	mustn't	shouldn't	don't have to	doesn't matter
1. take a gift when invited somewhere	☐	☐	☐	☐	☐	☐
2. ask how old someone is	☐	☐	☐	☐	☐	☐
3. smoke without asking permission	☐	☐	☐	☐	☐	☐
4. hug friends when you see them	☐	☐	☐	☐	☐	☐
5. shake hands when you meet someone	☐	☐	☐	☐	☐	☐
6. remove your shoes at someone's house	☐	☐	☐	☐	☐	☐
7. offer to pay your share at a restaurant	☐	☐	☐	☐	☐	☐
8. ask how much someone weighs	☐	☐	☐	☐	☐	☐
9. ask what someone's occupation is	☐	☐	☐	☐	☐	☐
10. leave a tip in a restaurant	☐	☐	☐	☐	☐	☐
11. call people by their first name	☐	☐	☐	☐	☐	☐

9 | WRITING

Write two or three paragraphs about a past situation that you feel you should have handled differently. Tell what you should or could have done (past) and what you should, could, or might do in a similar future situation.

Example: Two years ago my husband and I were traveling on a train in Europe. It was the middle of the night, and we were the only travelers in a sleeping car. We were both deeply asleep when suddenly our compartment door was loudly opened and several young people came in and began looking for their beds. They were talking very loudly and did not settle down and go to sleep. For a while we tolerated this and tried to go back to sleep but couldn't. Finally, my husband got very angry and started to yell at them. He shouldn't have done this, because the young people just laughed at him. Instead of this, he should have . . .

10 | ON THE INTERNET

Use the Internet to find answers to questions you have about what you should and shouldn't do in another culture. Share your questions and answers with the class.

Examples: In Japanese culture, should you shake hands with someone you meet?

In Lebanese culture, are you supposed to tip in a restaurant?

INFORMATION GAP FOR STUDENT B

Student B, read the story. Answer Student A's questions. Then ask your own questions and fill in the missing information.

Example: A: Where were they supposed to stay?
B: They were supposed to stay at the Grand State Hotel. What should they have gotten?
A: They should have gotten a confirmation number.

A married couple was traveling in Europe and had just entered a new country. They had been having a wonderful time, but now everything was going wrong. The first problem was finding accommodations. They were supposed to stay at the Grand State Hotel, but when they got to the hotel there was no record of their reservation. The wife said they should have gotten _____. They hadn't, unfortunately, so they had to spend the night at the train station. The next day they finally found a room at a hotel far from the center of town. There were two rooms available: a large one and a tiny one. Since they were on a tight budget, they decided they had better _____. The second problem was communication. They were starving after spending hours looking for accommodations, so they went into a restaurant. A waiter brought them a menu, but they couldn't understand it. The husband said they should have brought along a phrase book. They hadn't done that, though, so they didn't know what to order.

Time passed. Other people were being served but they weren't. Frustrated, they decided they _____. But what? They noticed that a boy about 11 years old seemed to be listening to their conversation. Soon the boy came over to their table. "Excuse me," he said. "You have to pay for your meal first. Then they'll take your order." The husband and wife were both astonished but grateful. The wife said, "You speak our language very well. Did you study it somewhere?" The boy said, "I lived in Australia for three years. I learned English there." He asked, "_____? I can translate the menu."

When they got back home, their friends asked them what they had liked best about the trip. The wife said, "Well, the best part was visiting that country where everything went wrong. At some point, everybody should experience difficulty. You don't have to _____, but you need a challenge. That's when you learn things. Maybe that's what people mean when they say travel is broadening."

Modals to Express Degrees of Certainty

Grammar in Context

BEFORE YOU READ

1 When people say, "Columbus discovered the New World," what do they mean?

2 What theories have you heard of as to who besides Columbus might have "discovered" the New World?

🎧 Read this article about the discovery of America.

Who *Really* Discovered America?

A well-known school rhyme goes like this: "In fourteen hundred and ninety-two, Columbus sailed the ocean blue." However, Columbus may not have been the first to visit the Western Hemisphere. So many other groups have been nominated for the honor that the question might almost be rephrased as follows: "Who *didn't* discover America?" But what does the evidence show? Who *really* discovered the New World? Those suggested include the Vikings, the Japanese, the Chinese, the Egyptians, the Hebrews, the Portuguese, and some Irish monks.

The Vikings are perhaps the best-known candidates. Some assume there were several Viking trips to the New World, but the most famous is the voyage of Leif Erickson. Evidence suggests that Erickson and some companions visited the New World in about the year 1000, almost 500 years before Columbus. Viking records and artifacts found in the New World indicate that they arrived at a place they named "Vinland the Good"—the land of grapes. Scholars originally assumed that Vinland must have been present-day Newfoundland. Today, though, the assumption is that Vinland couldn't have been Newfoundland, since that island is too far north for grapes to grow. Could the climate have been warmer in Erickson's day? Perhaps. However, the current theory is that Vinland may have been what is now Rhode Island, Cape Cod, the Boston area, or Nova Scotia.

The Japanese are more recent candidates. In 1956 on the Pacific coast of Ecuador, an amateur archaeologist discovered pottery fragments dating back about 5,000 years. Where did

Christopher Columbus

(continued)

Who *Really* Discovered America?

they come from? Intrigued by the mystery, Betty Meggers of the Smithsonian Institute concluded that individuals may have sailed from Japan across the Pacific to Ecuador about 5,000 years ago. Meggers based her conclusion on the similarity of the pottery found in Ecuador to Japanese pottery of the same era. Besides this, said Meggers, it has been established that there was no pottery in Ecuador in 3000 B.C., so the Japanese may have introduced it. If this theory is true, how could the voyage have happened? Some think Japanese fishermen might have been swept out to sea and carried across the Pacific for 10,000 miles. The theory may sound unlikely and may be disproved eventually, but the pottery evidence must mean something.

One interesting theory is the story of St. Brendan, an Irish monk born in A.D. 484, who made many voyages in northwestern Europe to establish monasteries. Maps of the time of Columbus showed an island far out in the Atlantic called "St. Brendan's Isle." Brendan's journey is mentioned in a document called "Voyage of St. Brendan the Abbot." The journey supposedly took place in the sixth century, and reports of it may have influenced Columbus to believe that there really was a New World. The text says that when Brendan and his fellow monks took this tremendous journey, they saw "sea monsters" and "crystals that rose up into the sky" and described "a rain of bad-smelling rocks." In 1976, British navigation scholar Tim Severin decided to test the theory to see if Brendan and his companions could really have accomplished this voyage. Using the specifications described in the St. Brendan text, they built a curragh, an Irish boat made out of leather, and attempted the journey. On the way, they passed Greenland and wintered in Iceland, where they saw whales, a volcano, and icebergs. They theorized that Brendan's sea monsters could have been large, friendly whales, that the crystals rising to the sky might have been icebergs, and that volcanoes in Iceland might have produced the rain of bad-smelling rocks. Severin's group did eventually get to Newfoundland, proving that a curragh could have made the journey to North America. Religious artifacts and stone carvings showing vocabulary and grammatical constructions from Old Irish have been found in Virginia in the United States. This suggests that other missionaries could have gone to the New World after Brendan's return. So the story may be true.

However, we come back to the original question: Who really "discovered" America? Continued future research should get us closer to an answer. Whatever the results of such future investigations, Columbus did <u>not</u>, of course, really discover America. The Native Americans who migrated across the Bering Strait 10,000 or more years ago were, of course, the real discoverers, and they deserve most of the credit. The statement that Columbus "discovered" the New World really means that he started two-way communication between the Old World and the New. In that sense, therefore, Columbus's reputation is still safe.

Could this boat have made it across the Atlantic?

AFTER YOU READ

What does each sentence mean? Circle the correct answer.

1. Leif Erickson and some companions must have visited the New World around the year 1000.
   a. It's almost certain that they visited it then.
   b. It's absolutely certain that they visited it then.
   c. It's possible that they visited it then.

2. The story of St. Brendan may have influenced Columbus to believe there was a New World.
   a. It's almost certain that it influenced him.
   b. It's possible that it influenced him.
   c. It's absolutely certain that it influenced him.

3. Future research should get us closer to an answer.
   a. It's possible that it will get us closer.
   b. It's absolutely certain that it will get us closer.
   c. It's almost certain that it will get us closer.

Grammar Presentation

MODALS TO EXPRESS DEGREES OF CERTAINTY

	Speculations about the Present						
It	must has (got) to	be	true.	It	can't / couldn't must not	be	true.
It	may / might could	be	true.	It	may not might not	be	true.

	Speculations about the Past						
It	must have had to have	been	true.	It	can't have couldn't have must not have	been	true.
It	may have might have could have	been	true.	It	may not have might not have	been	true.

Speculations about the Future							
We	should ought to	**solve**	it soon.				
We	**may** **might** **could**	**solve**	it soon.	We	**may not** **might not**	**solve**	it soon.

GRAMMAR NOTES

EXAMPLES

1. We use **modals** and **modal-like expressions** to express different degrees of certainty. With these modals we speculate, or make guesses, about things based on logic and facts as we understand them.

- The story **must** be true. *(approximately 90% certain)*
- The story **might** be true. *(approximately 50% certain)*

Remember that we use modals in progressive as well as in simple forms.

- He **may** be planning another trip.

When we want to state a fact we are absolutely—100 percent—sure of, we don't use modals.

- That story is true.
- He was planning another trip.

2. Use *must / have to / have got to* + base form when you are speculating about the present and are almost certain.

- The evidence **has to / has got to** mean something.

To make a negative speculation, use *can't / couldn't* + base form.

- That theory **can't** be / **couldn't** be right.

Use *must not* + base form when you are slightly less certain.

- It **must not** be right.

NOTE: We usually don't contract *must not* in this meaning of *must*.

- The explorer **must not** be famous.
  NOT The explorer ~~mustn't~~ be famous.

In questions, use **could / couldn't** + base form.

- **Could** that be the case?
- **Couldn't** that be the explanation?

3. Use ***may / might / could*** + base form when you are speculating about the present and are less certain.

Use *may not / might not* + base form in the negative.

▶ **BE CAREFUL!** We usually do not contract *might not*, and we never contract *may not*.

In questions, use *could / might* + base form.

- We **may / might / could** know the answer.

- They **may not / might not** have any evidence.
  NOT They ~~mayn't~~ have any evidence.

- **Could / Might** that be correct?

---

4. Use ***must have / had to have*** + past participle when you are speculating about the past and are almost certain.

In the negative, use ***can't have / couldn't have*** + past participle.

Use ***must not have*** + past participle when you are slightly less certain.

In questions, use ***can have / could have*** + past participle.

- They **must have / had to have** visited America.

- That **can't have / couldn't have** happened.

- He **must not have** made the trip.

- **Can / Could** that **have** been the reason?

---

5. When you are speculating about the past and are less certain (50%), use ***may have / might have / could have*** + past participle.

▶ **BE CAREFUL!** *Could have* + past participle has two meanings.

In the negative, use ***may not have / might not have*** + past participle.

In questions, use ***might have / could have*** + past participle.

- They **may / might / could have** reached the New World.

- He **could have** gone. (*It's a possibility—a degree of certainty*)
- He **could have** gone. (*He didn't—a missed opportunity*)

- They **may / might not have** found what they were looking for.

- **Might / Could** they **have** had trouble?

---

6. Use ***should / ought to*** + base form when you are almost certain about a future action or event.

- Continued research **should / ought to** get us closer to an answer.

---

7. Use ***may / might / could*** + base form when you are less certain about a future action or event.

In the negative, use ***may / might + not / never*** + base form.

- We **may / might / could** know the answer soon.

- However, we **may / might never** know the answer.

Focused Practice

1 | DISCOVER THE GRAMMAR

A *Look again at the opening reading. Read the first three paragraphs. Underline all the modals and modal-like expressions that show a degree of certainty.*

B *Look at these sentences based on the reading. For each sentence, circle the letter of the statement that is closer in meaning.*

1. Columbus may not have been the first to visit the Western Hemisphere.
   (a.) He might not have been the first.
   b. He could not have been the first.

2. It must have been about the year 1000 when Erickson visited the New World.
   a. I'm almost certain it was about the year 1000.
   b. I think maybe it was about the year 1000.

3. The assumption is that Vinland couldn't have been Newfoundland.
   a. It must not have been Newfoundland.
   b. It can't have been Newfoundland.

4. How could the voyage have happened?
   a. I'd like an explanation of how the voyage was impossible.
   b. I'd like an explanation of how the voyage was possible.

5. Individuals may have sailed from Japan to Ecuador.
   a. It's possible they did it.
   b. It's certain they did it.

6. The pottery evidence must mean something.
   a. I'm almost sure it means something.
   b. I strongly doubt it means something.

7. Other missionaries could have gone to the New World after Brendan's return.
   a. It's possible that they went.
   b. They had the opportunity to go but didn't.

8. Continued research should get us closer to an answer.
   a. It's possible that it will.
   b. It's almost certain that it will.

2 | WHERE'S HARRY?

Read this conversation. Complete it with modal constructions from the box.

could be working	~~could have gotten~~	may have had to	might be
might be meeting	must have	must have been visiting	should be

BLAKE: I wonder what's keeping Harry. He's usually on time for office parties. I suppose he

_____*could have gotten*_____ stuck in traffic.
　　　　　　1.

SAMANTHA: Yeah, that's a possibility. Or he _____ work late. I've never
　　　　　　　　　　　　　　　　　　　　2.

known him to be late for a party.

BLAKE: You know, I've always felt there's something a little puzzling—or even mysterious—

about Harry.

SAMANTHA: What makes you say that?

BLAKE: Well, he never says much about his past. He's really an interesting guy, but I don't

know much about him. For all I know, he _____ an
　　　　　　　　　　　　　　　　　　　　　　　　　3.

international spy.

SAMANTHA: I think I know what you mean. Or he _____ as a government
　　　　　　　　　　　　　　　　　　　　　　　　4.

agent.

BLAKE: Something tells me this is a case of *cherchez la femme.*

SAMANTHA: What does that mean?

BLAKE: It means "look for the woman." I figure he _____ a girlfriend
　　　　　　　　　　　　　　　　　　　　　　　　　5.

that he doesn't want us to know about.

SAMANTHA: Yeah, maybe so. You know, now that I think of it, he always leaves work early on

Friday afternoons. I see him go to the parking garage about 4:00, and it always seems

like he's trying not to be seen. He _____ his secret love.
　　　　　　　　　　　　　　　　　　　　　6.

[The doorbell rings.]

BLAKE: Oh, wait a minute. There's the doorbell. Everyone else is here. That

_____ him.
　　　7.

(continued)

HARRY: Hi, folks. Sorry I'm late. Had some business to take care of.

SAMANTHA: Business, huh. You mean romantic business?

HARRY: Romantic business? What are you talking about?

BLAKE: We figure you _____ your lady love. After all, we see you
8.
leave early every Friday afternoon.

HARRY: Pretty funny. Well, there is a lady, and I love her. But it's not what you think.

SAMANTHA: What is it, then?

HARRY: My mother. She's 88 years old, and she lives in a retirement home. I go to see her
every Friday.

3 | MYTH, LEGEND, OR REALITY?   *Grammar Notes 3–5*

Read this article about past cultures. Complete the sentences, using the words in
parentheses. Be careful to put the verbs in the past or present form.

🌐 World Review

Where do we draw the line between myth or legend and reality? How much is true

and how much invented? What happens to groups or cultures when they disappear?

We at *World Review* decided to explore some of these questions.

Let's first consider the saga of the ancient Pueblo people of the U.S. Southwest.

Scholars think that these people, called the Anasazi or "ancient ones" by the Navajo,

_____*may have settled*_____ about A.D. 100 in the Four Corners area, where today
1. (may / settle)

the corners of the states of Arizona, Utah, Colorado, and New Mexico come together.

The Anasazi are known to have developed agriculture and to have built impressive

cities and spectacular cliff dwellings. About the year 1300, however, something

happened to the Anasazi. They abandoned their dwellings and migrated to other

locales, such as the Rio Grande Valley in New Mexico and the White Mountains in

Arizona. What _____ this?
2. (could / cause)

Today many anthropologists assume that the present-day Pueblo peoples in

the Southwest _____ the descendents of the Anasazi.
                     3. (must / be)

However, for other scholars, questions remain: What _____
                                               4. (might / bring)

an end to their flourishing culture? Drought? Attacks by unfriendly tribes? Are

certain present-day Native Americans really the descendants of the Anasazi? Or

_____ they actually _____?
                  5. (could / disappear)

Next, let's turn our attention to the story of Atlantis, the famed "lost continent"

which is said to have existed in the Atlantic Ocean thousands of years ago.

Atlantis was supposedly located west of the Strait of Gibraltar. Is Atlantis a myth, or

_____ it _____? Plato wrote about Atlantis in two of his
                6. (could / exist)

dialogues, describing it as a fabulous island, larger than Libya and Turkey. He believed

that Atlantis _____ about 9,000 years before his time. The
                7. (had to / exist)

Atlanteans were reputed to have conquered many lands around the Mediterranean

and, he thought, _____ evil and greedy in the process. Their
                8. (must / become)

island or continent was supposed to have sunk into the sea after being hit by

earthquakes. _____ an Atlantis? Certain writers think the
            9. (Could / there really / be)

present-day Basques _____ the descendants of survivors of the
                10. (might / be)

catastrophe, if there was one. Is the Atlantis story just an entertaining legend invented

by Plato? Or, if Atlantis was real, is the problem simply that it existed so long ago that

traces of its memory are all that remain? Many scholars think that reports of a disaster

on the island of Thíra _____ the Atlantis legend. Thíra, in the
                11. (may / influence)

Mediterranean Sea north of Crete, was destroyed about 1500 B.C. by volcanic eruptions

and accompanying earthquakes, which also devastated civilization on nearby Crete.

Perhaps the Thíra disaster was the basis for the Atlantis legend, or the descendants of

Atlanteans _____ still _____ among us. At this point, we
                12. (might / be)

simply don't know.

4 | PREDICT YOUR FUTURE

Grammar Notes 6–7

Think for a few minutes about things you might accomplish or are likely to accomplish in the next 10 years. Write 10 sentences describing these potential accomplishments. Use **should**, **ought to**, **may**, **might**, *and* **could**. *Then compare your sentences with a partner's.*

Examples: I **might get married** within three years.

I **should finish** my college education by 2010.

5 | EDITING

Read this student essay. There are nine mistakes in the use of modals. The first mistake is already corrected. Find and correct eight more.

WHY WE ITCH

One ~~must~~ *might* think that with all the scientific progress that has been made in the last century, researchers would be able by now to answer this very simple question: Why do we itch? Unfortunately, scientists can't answer this question with any certainty. They simply don't know.

There are some clear cases involving itching. If a patient goes to her doctor and complains of terrible itching and the doctor finds hives or some other kind of rash, the doctor will probably say that she must eat something she was allergic to—or that she must not have been stung or bitten by some insect. This kind of case can be easily explained. Most itching, however, does not have an obvious cause.

Here's what scientists do know: Right under the surface of the skin there are sensory receptors that register physical stimuli and carry messages to the brain. These receptors detect pain and let the brain know about it. If there is a high level of physical stimulation to the body, the sensory receptors might carried a message of pain to the brain. If the level of physical stimulation is low, the sensors might be report it as itchiness.

There has been a lot of speculation about the function of itching. Some researchers think it's possible that the function of itching has to be to warn the body that it is about to have a painful experience. Others theorize that early humans might developed itching as a way of knowing that they needed to take insects out of their hair. Still others believe that itching could have been a symptom of serious diseases such as diabetes and Hodgkin's disease.

One of the most interesting aspects of itching is that it may have be less tolerable than pain. Research has shown, in fact, that most of us tolerate pain better than itching. Many people will allow their skin to be painfully broken just so they can get rid of an itch.

Communication Practice

6 | LISTENING

🎧 *Listen to a discussion in a biology class. Then listen to certain statements made during the discussion. For each statement, choose the sentence, **a** or **b**, that gives the same information.*

1. **a.** It's almost impossible that it was me on the tape.
   b. It's possible that it was me on the tape.

2. **a.** There's probably a mistake.
   b. There's possibly a mistake.

3. **a.** It's possible that all of you have had this experience before.
   b. It's almost certain that all of you have had this experience before.

4. **a.** You have probably figured out the answer.
   b. You will probably be able to figure out the answer.

5. **a.** It's probably because we hear the sound in a different way.
   b. It's possibly because we hear the sound in a different way.

(continued)

6. **a.** It's possibly because the sound travels through different substances.

   b. It's almost certainly because the sound travels through different substances.

7. **a.** It's certain that it's a combination of the two things.

   b. It's possible that it's a combination of the two things.

8. **a.** It's almost certain that the sound others hear is the real sound.

   b. It's unlikely that the sound others hear is the real sound.

9. **a.** The sound we heard was probably the real sound.

   b. The sound we hear is probably the real sound.

10. **a.** It's certain that internal hearing is more accurate than external hearing.

    b. It's almost certain that internal hearing is more accurate than external hearing.

7 | SOLVE THE PUZZLE

Work with a partner to solve these puzzles. Using past modals, suggest several possible solutions to each puzzle and write them down—from most likely to least likely—and label them accordingly.

1. On November 22, 1978, an 18-year-old thief broke into a lady's house and demanded all her money. She gave him all she had: $11.50. The thief was so angry that he demanded she write him a check for $50. Two hours later, the police caught the thief. How?

   Example: **A:** The thief might have given the lady his real name for the check.
   B: It could be that the lady just recognized him.
   A: Or there may have been a security camera in the building.

2. A dog owner put some food in a pan for her cat. Then, because she didn't want her dog to eat the cat's food, she tied a six-foot rope around his neck. Then she left. When she came back, she discovered that the dog had eaten the cat's food. What happened?

3. A young girl named Michelle decided to ride her bicycle from her own town to a town 10 kilometers away. After a while she reached a crossroads where she had to change direction. She discovered that the signpost with arrows pointing to different towns in the area had blown down. She didn't know which road was the right one. Nevertheless, she was able to figure out which road to take. What do you think she did?

4. Roy Sullivan, a forest ranger in Virginia, had several experiences in his life in which he was struck by a powerful force. Two times his hair was set on fire. He had burns on his eyebrows, shoulder, stomach, chest, and ankle. Once he was driving when he was hit and was knocked 10 feet out of his car. What do you think happened to him?

8 | SMALL-GROUP DISCUSSION

Form small groups. Look again at the story of Atlantis in Exercise 3. Which explanation do you think is the most likely? Which do you like best? Discuss your opinions with your partners. Report your opinions to the class.

Example: A: Which explanation do you like best about Atlantis?
B: Well, the one I like best is that the Basques are descendants of the Atlanteans. But I don't think it's the most likely explanation.
A: What is it, then?
B: I think it must have been . . .

9 | PICTURE DISCUSSION

Look at the photograph of Stonehenge, located on the Plain of Salisbury in southern England. With a partner, discuss the photograph. Who do you think built it? What do you think it was used for? Use modals in your discussion.

Example: It might have been used for religious ceremonies.

10 | WRITING

Write about an important world mystery you have heard of. Using present and past modals of certainty, speculate on the causes and possible explanations. Use one of the following topics or choose your own.

- How were the great pyramids in Egypt built?
- Who or what is making the crop circles in Britain?
- Does the Loch Ness monster really exist?
- How did the great statues get to Easter Island?

Example: Does the Loch Ness monster really exist? I've always wanted to believe it does, and for years I did believe that. Recently, however, I've come to a different conclusion. Reports of seeing the monster might be from people's imaginations. Or they could just be tricks. But the legend can't be true. Here's why I think this . . .

11 | ON THE INTERNET

Use the Internet to find information about a mystery that intrigues you. You may choose a topic mentioned in this unit or create your own topic. Share your information with the class.

From **Grammar** to **Writing**
Topic Sentences

A common way of organizing a composition or other piece of writing in English is to begin with a **topic sentence**. A topic sentence is a general sentence that covers the content of the entire paragraph. All the supporting examples and details of the paragraph must fit under this sentence. It is usually the first sentence in the paragraph. Look at this paragraph from an essay.

> For me, a dog is a better pet than a cat. When I come home from work, for example, my dog comes to meet me at the door. He is always glad to see me. My cat, on the other hand, couldn't care less whether I'm at home or not, as long as I keep filling her food dish. Another good thing about a dog is that you can teach him tricks. Cats, however, can't be bothered to learn anything new. The best thing about a dog, though, is that he's a great companion. I can take my dog on hikes and walks. He goes everywhere with me. As we all know, you can't take a cat for a walk.

The topic sentence for this paragraph is "For me, a dog is a better pet than a cat." This sentence tells the reader what to expect in the paragraph: some reasons why the writer considers a dog a superior pet.

1 | *This paragraph contains many supporting details but no topic sentence. Read the paragraph. Then circle the letter of the best topic sentence for the paragraph.*

> For one thing, you should always remove your shoes when you enter a Japanese home, and you should leave them pointing toward the door. Another suggestion is to make sure that you bring a gift for your Japanese hosts, and to be sure to wrap it. A third recommendation is to be appreciative of things in a Japanese house, but not too appreciative. Finally, remember that when you sit down to eat, you do not have to accept every kind of food that you are offered, but you are expected to finish whatever you do put on your plate.

Choices

a. Visiting a Japanese home is very enjoyable.

b. Taking a gift is very important when you visit a Japanese home.

c. There are a number of things to keep in mind when you visit a Japanese home.

d. When you visit a Japanese home, be sure not to eat too much.

Remember that an English sentence must contain a subject and a verb in at least one independent clause. The following groups of words are potential topic sentences, but they are fragments (they are not independent clauses, or they lack a subject or verb):

Reasons why the birth order theory makes sense. (not an independent clause)

Correction: There are several reasons why the birth order theory makes sense.

Relaxing and doing nothing. (no verb)

Correction: Relaxing and doing nothing can be beneficial sometimes.

2 | *Each of the following word groups is a fragment but is also a potential topic sentence. Make necessary additions to each.*

1. A city where exciting and mysterious things happen.

   _____

2. Reasons why college isn't for everybody.

   _____

3. Wild animals not making good pets.

   _____

4. Regular exercise and its benefits.

   _____

3 | *Read this paragraph. Then look at the four possible topic sentences. With a partner, discuss which one is the best. Why? What is wrong with each of the other choices?*

One reason is that when commercial flights began, all pilots were male. Men were hired because they had flight experience obtained in combat. Women, not having been in combat, had no flight experience. A second reason is simply prejudice: The powers in the airline industry presumably believed the stereotype that there are certain jobs that women cannot do as well as men. A third reason is inertia and the status quo—flying has mostly been a male-dominated profession since it began, and it takes time to change things. Eventually we will see more and more female commercial airline pilots, but for the present, old ideas die hard.

Choices

a. Why there are so few women commercial pilots today.

b. There are three principal reasons why there are so few women commercial pilots today.

c. Women pilots in aviation.

d. Men are still prejudiced about women's capabilities.

4 | *Look at the following sets of supporting details. For each set, write an appropriate topic sentence.*

1. _____

    a. For one thing, there's almost always a traffic jam I get stuck in, and I'm often late to work.

    b. Also, there's not always a parking place when I do get to work.

    c. Worst of all, I'm spending more money on gas and car maintenance than I would if I took public transportation.

2. _____

    a. One is that I often fall asleep when watching the TV screen, no matter how interesting the video is.

    b. Another is that watching movies is basically a social experience, and I'm usually alone when I watch videos.

    c. The main reason is that the TV screen, no matter how large it is, diminishes the impact that you get when watching a movie on the big screen.

3. _____

    a. Nothing spontaneous usually happens on a guided tour, but I've had lots of spontaneous experiences when I planned my own vacation.

    b. Tour guides present you with what *they* think is interesting, but when you are in charge of your own vacation, you do what *you* think is interesting.

    c. Individually planned vacations can often be less expensive than guided tours.

4. _____

    a. Cats don't bark and wake up the neighbors or bite the letter carrier.

    b. Dogs have to be walked at least two times a day, but cats handle their own exercise.

    c. Cats eat a lot less than dogs.

5 | *Write a paragraph of several sentences about one of the following topics, a similar topic that interests you, or a topic suggested by your teacher. Make sure that your paragraph has a topic sentence. Then share your work with three or four other students. Read each other's paragraphs. Identify topic sentences. Make sure that each one is not a fragment and that it is appropriate for the paragraph.*

Topics

- An annoying habit
- The best part of the day
- Night owls versus early birds
- The ideal vacation
- A problem in society
- Expectation versus reality

Review Test

I *Read the conversations between a job interviewer and various applicants. Fill in the blanks using the cues in parentheses. Use full forms for auxiliaries used to emphasize or show stress; use contracted forms for all other auxiliaries.*

1. A: What languages are you familiar with, Ms. Suzuki? Do you speak Mandarin?

   B: No, I _____*don't speak*_____ Mandarin. I _____*do speak*_____ Japanese

                a. (not / speak)   **b. (speak)**
   and Spanish, though.

   A: Are you fluent in those languages?

   B: I _____ fluent in Japanese. I _____ fluent

            c. (be)   **d. (not / be)**
   in Spanish, but I _____ conversant in it.

                       e. (be)

2. A: Mr. Quinn, your résumé says that you attended college. Did you earn a bachelor's degree?

   B: No, I _____ a B.A. I _____ an associate

             a. (not / earn)   **b. (earn)**
   degree, though.

3. A: Ms. Liu, this job requires overseas experience. Have you lived abroad?

   B: I _____ abroad, but I _____ extensively in

             a. (not / live)   **b. (travel)**
   Europe and Eastern Asia.

4. A: Mr. Travolta, this _____ a full-time position. It

                   a. (not / be)
   _____ a three-quarter-time job, however, and it

             b. (be)
   _____ an extensive benefits package. Are you interested?

             c. (have)

   B: The job sounds interesting. I _____ some time to think it over,

                                       d. (would like)
   though. Could I let you know by next Monday?

II *Complete the conversations using* **so**, **neither**, **too**, *or* **not either** *plus the appropriate auxiliary to make additions. Use contractions whenever possible.*

1. A: Avocados have a disgusting texture, I think. I can't stand them.

 B: _____*Neither can*_____ I. They're at the bottom of my list.

2. A: What did you think of *The Lord of the Rings*? I thought it was pretty neat.

 B: _____ I. I really liked Viggo Mortenson and Elijah Wood.

3. A: Janice has never been to Mexico City.

 B: Joe _____. He wants to go this summer, though.

4. A: Helena won't be able to come to the party Wednesday afternoon.

 B: _____ Josh. He has a doctor's appointment.

5. A: How do you feel about hunting whales? I'm against it.

 B: I _____. I can understand both sides of the issue, but it still seems cruel to the whales.

6. A: Did you hear that Bill spent $2,000 on a new bicycle? I wouldn't spend that much.

 B: _____ I. There are better things to do with your money.

7. A: Can you believe it? Mandy had never heard of Peter Jackson.

 B: Well, I _____ before *The Lord of the Rings* came out. You just can't know everything.

8. A: I can't believe it! My mother says she believes in UFOs.

 B: Really? _____ my mother. She says she saw one once.

III *Complete this letter to a columnist and the columnist's response. Circle the correct modals and modal-like expressions.*

Dear Pamela:

My wife, Jeannine, and I invited a Japanese colleague to dinner last week. We'd invited her once before, but she'd (had to)/ must decline because of other commitments. This time, she was able to
   1.
come. Things were going well at first. Yoko, my co-worker, seemed a little nervous, but that was understandable. I thought she was probably trying to remember how you 'd better / 're supposed to
   2.
act when you visit an American home. She brought a beautifully wrapped present, which my wife opened right away. Yoko seemed to think Jeannine shouldn't have / must not have done that,
   3.

(continued)

because she looked upset. I thought maybe in Japan you <u>don't have to / aren't supposed to</u> tear the
4.
paper. Maybe you <u>could / 're supposed to</u> take it off gently and fold it, or something. Anyway, my
5.
wife tore it off and pulled out a box of excellent chocolates. She <u>should have / might have</u> waited
6.
until after dinner, but she insisted on passing them around and having everyone eat some of them.

Before dinner! Yoko was embarrassed. She said she thought she <u>should bring / should have brought</u>
7.
something else for a gift. Pamela, what went wrong? It think it was all Jeannine's fault.

Puzzled in Pittsburgh

Dear Puzzled:

You <u>aren't allowed to / don't have to</u> blame anybody for this problem. It's a clear case of cultural
8.
misunderstanding. What you <u>must / are to</u> understand is that in Japan when someone takes a gift to a
9.
friend's house, the friend <u>shouldn't / doesn't have to</u> open it in front of the visitor. It is more polite to
10.
wait until later to open it, so it was probably something of a shock to your Japanese friend to see your

wife make such a big scene. That's not what one <u>might have done / is supposed to do</u> in Japan.
11.

Don't be too concerned about it. I'm sure your friend will understand when you explain to her
and apologize.

Pamela

IV *Read the story. Fill in the blanks with modals or modal-like expressions.*

One of the most puzzling experiences I've ever had happened last winter. It was one of those

typical dark and stormy nights that you read about in mystery novels. Sitting on the sofa in the

living room, I could hear thunder and see an occasional flash of lightning. It _____*must have*_____
1.
been at least 1:00 A.M. I was reading an exciting mystery novel. Suddenly the phone rang, startling

me out of my wits. I picked up the receiver, muttering to myself something like, "Who

_____ that be at this hour of the night? Someone _____ died." But
2.   **3.**
no. There were a few seconds of silence; then a low, scary voice said, "Help me. Help me." "Who

are you?" I asked. "Who is this?" No answer. The phone went dead.

The next morning it all seemed like a bad dream. I was troubled enough by the experience to

tell my friend Josh about it. "It _____ been a crank call," he said. "Or it

4.

_____ been one of your friends playing a joke on you."

5.

"What do you think I _____ do?"

6.

"Do? Why do anything? It won't happen again."

It did happen again, though, the following night. At precisely 1:12 A.M. (I looked at my watch

this time) the phone rang, waking me out of a sound sleep. The same deep, scary voice was on the

other end of the line. I responded in the same way, but the voice just said, "Help me, help me."

Then there was silence, and the line went dead as before.

The next day I told Josh about it again. "I still say it _____ to be some friend of

7.

yours playing a joke. Don't you recognize the voice?"

"Not at all," I said. "It _____ be anyone I know."

8.

"Well, call the phone company. They _____ have an idea about what to do."

9.

I never did call the phone company, for some reason. This experience went on for the next five

nights. At precisely 1:12 A.M., the phone would ring, and I would pick it up, only to hear the same

thing: "Help me, help me." After that, it stopped. Since then I haven't stopped wondering if I

_____ called the police.

10.

I wonder if it _____ been someone who needed help. Or was it just a joke? I

11.

_____ never find out.

12.

V *Look at the pictures. Write a sentence using the modal or modal-like expression in parentheses to describe each situation, making sure to use the correct form.*

1.

(should)

They should all be

wearing their seat belts.

2.

(must)

_____

_____

3.

(had better)

_____

_____

4.

(be supposed to)

_____

_____

5.

(might)

_____

_____

6.

(could)

_____

_____

7.

(may)

_____

_____

8.

(should)

_____

_____

VI *Circle the letter of the one underlined word or phrase in each sentence that is not correct.*

1. I think we <u>ought</u> <u>look into</u> a nice guided tour—that is, if we
   _A   _B
   <u>can find</u> one that <u>won't bankrupt</u> us.
   _C   _D
       (A) **B** **C** **D**

2. Fortunately, I <u>was able to get</u> a scholarship to attend college, and my
   _A
   sister was <u>either</u>; otherwise, we never <u>could have</u> <u>afforded</u> it.
   _B   _C   _D
       A **B** **C** **D**

3. You <u>had better</u> <u>to set</u> your alarm, or you <u>might not</u> <u>wake up</u> on time.
   _A   _B   _C   _D
       A **B** **C** **D**

4. The only idea I <u>have</u> as to why Joe <u>isn't</u> here is that he might <u>have been</u>
   _A   _B   _C
   <u>working</u> late.
   _D
       A **B** **C** **D**

5. All employees <u>were to</u> <u>attend</u> the company party on Saturday, and
   _A   _B
   everyone <u>should</u> <u>bring</u> a present for the gift exchange.
   _C   _D
       A **B** **C** **D**

6. Frank <u>has</u> always <u>been</u> against capital punishment, and <u>so</u> <u>had</u> I.
   _A   _B   _C _D
       A **B** **C** **D**

7. We <u>ought to</u> <u>take</u> some extra cash along on the trip, but we
   _A   _B
   absolutely <u>don't have to</u> <u>forget</u> our passports.
   _C   _D
       A **B** **C** **D**

8. Joe called to say that he won't <u>be able to</u> <u>get here</u> by seven o'clock,
   _A   _B
   but he <u>shouldn't</u> <u>manage to be</u> here by eight.
   _C   _D
       A **B** **C** **D**

(continued)

9. If <u>you want</u> flowers from your rose bushes, you'll <u>have to</u> <u>water</u>
A   B   C
them, <u>haven't</u> you?
D

A   B   C   D

10. I suppose they <u>could be</u> <u>working</u> late at the office, but Amy didn't
A   B
mention it, and <u>either</u> <u>did</u> Mary.
C   D

A   B   C   D

VII *Go back to your answers to Exercise VI. Write the correct form for each item that you believe is incorrect.*

1. _____ *ought to* _____   6. _____

2. _____   7. _____

3. _____   8. _____

4. _____   9. _____

5. _____   10. _____

▶ *To check your answers, go to the Answer Key on page RT-1.*

PART III

Nouns

Count and Non-Count Nouns

Grammar in Context

BEFORE YOU READ

1 *Do you think food today is basically safe and nutritious, or do you have concerns about it?*

2 *What do you think the most important food issues are today?*

3 *Do you believe diets are effective?*

🎧 *Read this transcript of part of a TV presentation by a food and nutrition expert.*

Concerned about Food?
ASK THE EXPERT

Mel Brand:	Good afternoon, everyone, and welcome to *Ask the Expert*. I'm Mel Brand. The other day I glanced at a depressing headline in the local paper, which said "Is Anything Safe to Eat These Days?" With reports of mad cow disease, bird flu, contaminated water, and other food scares, it's not a bad question. Food and diet are things people are highly interested in these days, and our guest today is Dr. Miranda Olsen from the International Nutrition Institute. We'll be taking your questions in a moment. Dr. Olsen, welcome. What's the biggest issue in food today?
Dr. Olsen:	Thanks for inviting me, Mel. I can answer your question in one word: convenience. The most obvious recent change is that we're living fast lives, with less time at our disposal. Everything revolves around speed and convenience, so there's a push for convenience eating and convenience food. More of us are eating out. If we don't eat out, we often go to supermarkets to pick up already-prepared food. Supermarkets have changed greatly from what they were in the past. They now sell full meals to take out. They also offer new products like packaged salad.

Mel Brand:	All right, Dr. Olsen. Thanks for that overview. Now let's have some questions from our audience. Please give your name and tell us where you're from. Yes, the gentleman in the back.
Bob:	I'm Bob Gonzales from Tampa, Florida. My question is about school lunches. My three children are all in high school, and they take lunches from home, which is OK. What I'm really concerned about, though, are the vending machines in the schools. They sell soda, candy, and snacks. I'm worried that the kids are filling up on sodas and chips and not eating what they should. Is there any nutrition in that kind of stuff? Am I worrying for nothing?
Dr. Olsen:	No, you're not, Bob. You have reason to be concerned. There's very little nutrition in soda and snacks. Soda is loaded with sugar, and most snacks are just empty calories. School vending machines have become a big problem in many places. What usually happens is that big companies pay school districts to have vending machines there. The districts find it difficult to turn down the money. There's more and more opposition to having these machines in schools, though, and you <u>can</u> get rid of them.
Mel Brand:	OK. Another question? Yes, ma'am—in the third row.
Maria:	Yes, good morning, Dr. Olsen. I'm Maria Spring from Toronto, Ontario. My question is about diets. In my family we're really concerned about losing weight, so we've started using low-fat or fat-free food. The trouble is, we all hate it because it tastes so bland. Can you give me any advice?
Dr. Olsen:	Well, there's evidence that a nonfat or low-fat diet can actually lead to weight gain. My advice is to stay away from such diets. You can eat regular food in moderate quantities. Avoid sodas. Drink plenty of water and juice, and minimize your intake of salt and sugar. Make sure you eat five to eight servings a day of fruits and vegetables. And exercise at least three times a week. Play a couple of games of tennis. Take brisk walks. That should help your family to lose weight.
Mel Brand:	All right. Next question? Yes, the man in the back …

AFTER YOU READ

What does the underlined word refer to? Circle the correct answer.

1. People are highly interested in <u>food</u>.
   - **a.** food in general
   - **b.** a specific type of food

2. There's very little nutrition in <u>soda</u>.
   - **a.** an individual serving of soda
   - **b.** soda in general

3. My question is about <u>diets</u>.
   - **a.** diets in general
   - **b.** particular diets

Grammar Presentation

NOUNS

Proper Nouns
Professor Lee heads the **Nutrition Institute**.

Common Nouns
The **professor** teaches **nutrition**.

COUNT AND NON-COUNT NOUNS

Count Nouns			
Article or Number	Noun	Verb	
A One	**snack**	is	refreshing.
The Two	**snacks**	are	

Non-Count Nouns		
Noun	Verb	
Rice	is	nourishing.
Nutrition		important.

NOUNS WITH COUNT AND NON-COUNT MEANINGS

Count Meaning
There's **a hair** in my soup!
A chicken escaped from the henhouse.
My favorite **works** of art are from China.

Non-Count Meaning
Sandra has black **hair**.
We had **chicken** for dinner.
It takes **work** to prepare a meal.

NON-COUNT NOUNS IN COUNTABLE FORM

Non-Count Noun
I'll have **tea**.
You need **advice**.
Let's play **tennis**.
The stew needs more **spice**.
Fruit is nutritious.

Countable Form
I'll have **a cup of tea**.
Let me give you **a piece of advice**.
Let's play **a game of tennis**.
There are several **spices** in this stew.
Many different **fruits** are grown in California.

USES OF NON-COUNT NOUNS

Non-Count Nouns in Uncountable Use
I'd like some **coffee**.
Cheese is produced in France.
The sun provides **light**.

Non-Count Nouns in Countable Use
Please bring us **two coffees**.
Brie is **a soft cheese**.
I see **a light** in the window.

GRAMMAR NOTES

EXAMPLES

1. **Nouns** represent persons, places, and things. There are two types of nouns: proper nouns and common nouns.

    Proper nouns name particular persons, places, or things. They are usually unique and are capitalized in writing.

- Dr. Olsen, Ichiro Suzuki, São Paulo, China, the Empire State Building, Harrod's

    Common nouns refer to people, places, or things but are not the names of particular individuals.

- scientist, athlete, city, country, building, department store

2. There are two types of **common nouns**: count nouns and non-count nouns.

    Count nouns refer to things that you can count separately. They can be singular or plural. You can use *a* or *an* before count nouns.

- one **woman**, nine **planets**
- This **sandwich** is delicious.
- Some **vegetables** are tasty.
- That's **an** interesting **question**.

    Non-count nouns refer to things that you cannot count separately. They usually have no plural form. We usually do not use *a* or *an* with non-count nouns, though they are often preceded by *some* or *the*.

- I bought **rice**.
  NOT I bought ~~a rice.~~
- Let me give you **some advice**.
  NOT Let me give you ~~an advice.~~

▶ **BE CAREFUL!** Many nouns have both count and non-count meanings. Check your dictionary to avoid mistakes.

- She heard **a noise** in the attic.
- **Noise** can be harmful to health.
  NOT ~~A noise~~ can be harmful to health.

    We normally use a **singular verb** with a non-count noun. We use a **singular pronoun** to refer to the noun.

- **Rice feeds** millions.
  NOT Rice ~~feed~~ millions.
- **It** feeds millions.

(continued)

3. Notice the following categories and examples of **non-count nouns**.

Abstractions	• chance, energy, honesty, love
Activities	• basketball, dancing, tennis
Diseases	• AIDS, cancer, influenza, malaria
Foods	• beef, bread, fish, fruit, meat
Gases	• air, carbon dioxide, oxygen, smoke
Liquids	• coffee, gasoline, milk, tea, water
Natural phenomena	• electricity, heat, rain, thunder
Occupations	• dentistry, nursing, teaching
Particles	• dust, pepper, salt, sand, sugar
Solid elements	• gold, iron, plutonium, silver
Subjects	• Chinese, English, physics, science
Others	• equipment, furniture, money, news

4. We frequently **make non-count nouns countable** by adding a phrase that gives them a form, a limit, or a container.

NON-COUNT NOUN	COUNTABLE FORM
furniture	a piece of furniture
lightning	a bolt / flash of lightning
meat	a piece of meat
rice	a grain of rice
tennis	a game of tennis
thunder	a clap of thunder
water	a cup of water

5. We use many **non-count nouns** in a **countable sense** without the addition of a phrase (such as "a piece of"). We can use these nouns with *a / an* or in the plural to mean *kind / type / variety of*.

• Do you like **pasta**?
• In Italy, I tasted **a** new **pasta**.

• I drink **tea** every morning.
• That shop has many different **teas**.

A / an and plurals can also be used to indicate discrete amounts.

• I drank **a soda**.
• Please bring us two **orange juices**.

| 6. When **non-count nouns** are preceded by *some* or occur alone, they refer to things that don't have any particular boundaries. | • I drank **some soda**.
• **Orange juice** is produced in Florida. |

| 7. Some nouns are irregular.

   a. A few **non-count nouns** end in *-s*.

   b. A few **count nouns** have **irregular plurals**. |

• news, mathematics, economics, physics

• criterion, phenomenon, nucleus
(singular count nouns)

• criteria, phenomena, nuclei
(their irregular plural forms) |

| 8. **BE CAREFUL!** In its normal usage, the word *people* is **plural** and means "more than one person." In this meaning, it does not have a singular form, and it takes a plural verb.

The word *people* meaning "a particular group (or particular groups) of human beings" can have a singular and a plural form. | • Hawaiian **people use** food in unusual ways.
NOT Hawaiian people ~~uses~~ food in unusual ways.

• The Hmong are **a people** of southern China and nearby areas.
• Many different **peoples** have settled in Hawaii. |

Reference Notes
For a list of **non-count nouns**, see Appendix 5 on page A-4.
For a list of phrases for **counting non-count nouns**, see Appendix 6 on page A-5.
For a list of **irregular plurals**, see Appendix 4 on page A-3.

Focused Practice

1 | DISCOVER THE GRAMMAR

Read the sentences based on the opening reading. Underline the count nouns. Circle the non-count nouns.

1. With <u>reports</u> of (mad cow disease,) bird (flu,) contaminated (water,) and food <u>scares</u>, it's not a bad <u>question</u>.

2. Food and diet are things people are interested in these days.

3. What's the biggest issue in food today?

4. We're living fast lives with less free time, so we seek convenience.

5. I'm concerned about the vending machines that sell soda, candy, and snacks.

6. Is there any nutrition in that kind of stuff?

7. My family is concerned about losing weight, so we've started using low-fat or fat-free food.

8. There's evidence that a nonfat or low-fat diet can actually lead to weight gain.

2 | NON-COUNT NOUNS IN COUNTABLE FORM

Grammar Note 4

Complete each sentence with the correct phrase to give the non-countable noun a countable form. Refer to Appendix 6 on page A-5 for help in completing this exercise if necessary.

1. When we moved to the new office, we lost _____*a piece of*_____ equipment.
   (a piece of / a pound of)

2. Let me give you _____ advice: don't buy that item.
   (a speck of / a piece of)

3. The floor was so clean that there wasn't _____ dust anywhere.
   (a speck of / a piece of)

4. Please get _____ sugar when you're at the store.
   (a pound of / a piece of)

5. Our office bought several new _____ furniture.
   (pieces of / matters of)

6. There hasn't been _____ rain here for over a month.
   (a drop of / a grain of)

7. We heard an interesting _____ news on the radio last night.
   (amount of / piece of)

8. In our family it's customary to have _____ tea late in the afternoon.
   (a kilo of / a cup of)

9. What you order at a restaurant is _____ choice.
   (a piece of / a matter of)

10. You've had a reasonable _____ time to finish the job.
    (branch of / period of)

3 | **BLENDING** *Grammar Notes 3, 5*

Read the article about fusion cooking and complete it with words from the box.

century	chefs	~~cooking~~	cuisines	flavoring	foods
fusion	menu	rolls	rules	spices	ways

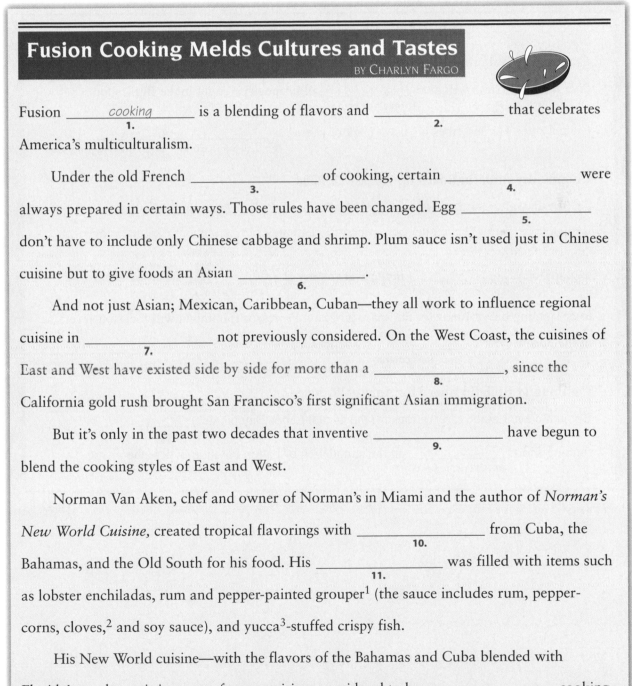

Fusion Cooking Melds Cultures and Tastes
BY CHARLYN FARGO

Fusion _____*cooking*_____ is a blending of flavors and _____ that celebrates
      1.   **2.**

America's multiculturalism.

Under the old French _____ of cooking, certain _____ were
                               3.   **4.**

always prepared in certain ways. Those rules have been changed. Egg _____
                                                          5.

don't have to include only Chinese cabbage and shrimp. Plum sauce isn't used just in Chinese

cuisine but to give foods an Asian _____.
                                        6.

And not just Asian; Mexican, Caribbean, Cuban—they all work to influence regional

cuisine in _____ not previously considered. On the West Coast, the cuisines of
                7.

East and West have existed side by side for more than a _____, since the
                                                               8.

California gold rush brought San Francisco's first significant Asian immigration.

But it's only in the past two decades that inventive _____ have begun to
                                                              9.

blend the cooking styles of East and West.

Norman Van Aken, chef and owner of Norman's in Miami and the author of *Norman's*

New World Cuisine, created tropical flavorings with _____ from Cuba, the
                                                      10.

Bahamas, and the Old South for his food. His _____ was filled with items such
                                              11.

as lobster enchiladas, rum and pepper-painted grouper[1] (the sauce includes rum, pepper-

corns, cloves,[2] and soy sauce), and yucca[3]-stuffed crispy fish.

His New World cuisine—with the flavors of the Bahamas and Cuba blended with

Florida's produce—is just one of many cuisines considered to be _____ cooking.
                                                                        12.

[1]*grouper:* a large fish   [2]*cloves:* a tropical spice
[3]*yucca:* a desert plant of Mexico and the southwestern United States

4 | COMMUNITY BULLETIN BOARD

Grammar Notes 5–8

Interactive websites on the Internet give people information about entertainment, cultural events, and the weather. Fill in the blanks in the bulletin board messages, choosing the correct count or non-count form in parentheses. Refer to Appendices 4 and 6 on pages A-3 and A-5 for help in completing this exercise if necessary.

COMMUNITY BULLETIN BOARD

[Follow Ups] [Post a Reply] [Message Board Index]

Community Bulletin Board for August 26, 2006

Poet Jefferson Saito will give ___*a reading*___ of his poetry tonight in the Burlington
                     1. (reading / a reading)

Civic Center. He describes his latest book of poems as _____ in _____.
                               2. (work / a work)   **3. (progress / a progress)**

Community Bulletin Board for August 27, 2006

On Tuesday afternoon at 4 PM at City Hall, Professor Helen Hammond, who has

written _____ of the space program, will give _____ on the
      4. (history / a history)   **5. (talk / a talk)**

exploration of _____ in the 21st century at _____ when we seem
       6. (space / a space)   **7. (time / a time)**

to be running out of funds for the space program. Professor Hammond will focus on several

of the government's _____ for suggesting budget cuts.
          8. (criterion / criteria)

Community Bulletin Board for August 28, 2006

If you have not made reservations for the annual Labor Day picnic, _____ is
                                      9. (time / a time)

running short. _____ on the remodeling of Patton Pavilion, where the picnic
     10. (Work / A work)

```
┌─────────────────────────────────────────────────────────────────────┐
│ □ ▐▐▐▐▐▐▐▐▐▐▐═══ COMMUNITY BULLETIN BOARD ═══▐▐▐▐▐▐▐▐▐         回 ▤ │
├─────────────────────────────────────────────────────────────────┬───┤
```

will be held, is complete. All residents of Burlington are invited, but you must have a ticket,

which will cover the price of dinner. The menu will include _____, meat, and
                                                      11. (fish / a fish)

pasta as main courses. _____ and _____ are free.
                        12. (Soda / A soda)   **13. (milk / a milk)**

Community Bulletin Board for August 29, 2006

On Friday evening at 8:00 P.M. in the Civic Auditorium, Professor Mary Alice Waters will

present a program on the Hmong, _____ of China and Laos. Professor Waters
                                14. (peoples / a people)

will show _____ about marriage customs of the Hmong and other   ,
          15. (film / a film)

_____ of Eastern Asia.
16. (people / peoples)

---

5 | A PIECE OF ADVICE   *Grammar Notes 3–6, 8*

Write your own sentence for each of the nouns and noun phrases in the box. Then share
your sentences with a partner. Discuss and correct them if necessary.

a people	a piece of advice	a soda	a TV	fruits
furniture	peoples	pieces of furniture	spices	time

    Example: My boss gave me a great piece of advice: Check your e-mail just three times a day.

1. _____

2. _____

3. _____

4. _____

5. _____

6. _____

7. _____

8. _____

9. _____

10. _____

6 | EDITING

Read this letter. There are 12 mistakes in the use of count and non-count nouns. The first mistake is already corrected. Find and correct 11 more.

Miramar Ipanema Hotel

Dear kids,

Your mom and I are having a wonderful time in Brazil. We landed in Rio de Janeiro on Tuesday as scheduled and made it to our hotel without any problems. On Wednesday we walked and sunbathed on Copacabana and Ipanema beaches. The only problem was that I dropped my camera and got ~~sands~~ *sand* in it, and now it's not working. Actually, there's one other problem: We don't have enough furnitures in our hotel room. There's no places to put anything. But everything else has been great. We went to a samba show, and even though it was intended for tourist, it was a lot of fun.

The Brazilian people is very friendly and helpful. On Friday we had a flight to São Paulo scheduled for 9:00 A.M., and we missed the bus and couldn't get a taxi. But we were saved by one of the hotel employee, who gave us a ride to the airport. We got there just in time. Now we're in São Paulo. It's an exciting place, but I can't get over the traffics. It took two hour to get from our hotel to the downtown area. Yesterday we had lunch at a famous restaurant where they serve feijoada, which is typical Brazilian foods. It had so much spice in it that our mouths were on fire, but it was delicious. Tonight we're going to have dinner at another restaurant where they serve all kinds of meat. They raise a lot of cattle in Brazil, and meats are very popular. This restaurant is one of the most famous ones.

The other thing about Brazil that's really interesting is the amount of coffee the Brazilians drink. They have little cups of coffees several times a day—called caffezinho. We tried it; it's very strong and sweet.

That's all for now. Your mom hasn't had a time to go shopping yet, which is good. You know how much I hate shopping.

Love,

Dad

Communication Practice

7 | LISTENING

🎧 **A** *Read the sentences. Then listen to the cooking show.*

1. Pelmeni is ____*a (traditional) Russian*____ dish.
   (national origin)

2. The principal ingredient of pelmeni is _____.
   (type of meat)

3. Other meats that can be used to make pelmeni are _____.
   (types of meat)

4. You need _____ meat to make pelmeni.
   (amount)

5. You need _____ egg _____ to make pelmeni.
   (number) **(item)**

6. You need _____ water for the meat mixture.
   (amount)

7. You need _____ salt for the meat mixture.
   (amount)

8. To make the dough, you need _____ flour.
   (amount)

9. Each dough circle should be approximately _____ in diameter.
   (size)

10. One person can easily eat _____ pelmeni at a meal.
    (number)

🎧 **B** *Now listen again. Complete the sentences. Refer to the clues in parentheses.*

8 | INFORMATION GAP: A GRAIN OF SAND

Student B, turn to page 127 and follow the instructions there. Student A, read statements 1–5 aloud. Student B will read the best completion for each statement, including a phrase from the box below in each statement. Then reverse the process for statements 6–10. Refer to Appendix 6 on page A-5 for help in completing this exercise if necessary.

a branch of	a clap of	a flash of	a game of
a grain of	a piece of	a speck of	an article of

Student A's statements

1. A particle of a cereal grown in Asia is called . . .

2. A small piece of powdery material is called . . .

3. An athletic competition played on a field and using a ball is called . . .

4. A part of the science that studies planets and stars is called . . .

5. A loud sound that usually comes with a sudden light from the sky is called . . .

(continued)

Student A's completions

f. jewelry

g. sand

h. lightning

i. furniture

j. advice

9 | WRITING

Write two or three paragraphs about the best or worst meal experience you have ever had. Your essay can be serious or funny. Describe the kind of meal it was and what was good, bad, interesting, or funny about it.

Example: The worst meal experience I've ever had happened about a year ago. I'd been studying French for three years, and I guess I wanted to show my parents how much I'd learned about French culture and language. It was my mother's birthday, so I made reservations at a very nice French restaurant in town. The trouble started right after we got there . . .

10 | ON THE INTERNET

Use the Internet to research one of the following.

- the preparation of an exotic dish

- a particular diet you are interested in

Then report your findings to the class. If you learn about the preparation of a dish, tell the class how the dish is made. If you learn about a particular diet, explain what the diet is and discuss its advantages and disadvantages.

Examples: **A:** I learned how to make Mexican *mole*. It's a traditional dish with 20 ingredients: turkey or some other kind of meat, chili peppers, peanuts, chocolate, and . . .

  B: I learned about the Atkins diet. It's a high-protein, low-carbohydrate diet. The advantages of it are that you can lose weight on it and eat foods like beef, chicken, fish . . .

INFORMATION GAP FOR STUDENT B

Listen as Student A reads statements 1–5. Read aloud the best completion for each statement, including a phrase from the box below. Then read statements 6–10. Student A will read the best completion for each statement. Refer to Appendix 6 on page A-5 for help in completing this exercise if necessary.

a branch of	a clap of	a flash of	a game of
a grain of	a piece of	a speck of	an article of

Student B's completions

a. soccer

b. astronomy

c. rice

d. thunder

e. dust

Student B's statements

6. A statement of recommended behavior is . . .

7. A particle of a material found on beaches is called . . .

8. A sudden light from the sky is called . . .

9. An object on which one sits or sleeps is called . . .

10. A decorative object worn on the body or the clothes is called . . .

8 Definite and Indefinite Articles

Grammar in Context

BEFORE YOU READ

1 *What is an example of an environmental problem that you consider serious?*

2 *Do you think people exaggerate the seriousness of hazards to the environment? What would be an example?*

3 *How can serious environmental problems be remedied?*

🎧 *Read this article about an environmental disaster.*

The Real Mystery of EASTER ISLAND

This area was once a subtropical forest

Most of us have seen pictures of the gigantic statues of Easter Island, and a big mystery has been this: Who built the statues, and how were they moved? Recently, however, we've become aware of an even greater mystery: What happened to Easter Island? What changed it so drastically?

Easter Island lies in the South Pacific about 2,300 miles west of Chile, the country to which it belongs. According to current estimates, it was settled about the year 900 by Polynesians. If you go to Easter Island today and visit Rano Raruku, the quarry where the statues were carved, you'll see almost 400 statues in various stages of disrepair. On roads leading out from Rano Raruku, a volcanic crater about 600 yards across, there are about 100 more statues. Many if not most of these statues are toppled over and damaged. Elsewhere on the island you'll see more than 100 gigantic platforms on which the statues stood.

Easter Island was discovered by Dutch explorer Jacob Roggeveen on April 5, 1722—Easter day. When Roggeveen landed, he saw the island much as it is today: a rather desolate place covered mostly by grassland, with no trees taller than 10 feet. It is clear today, however, that Easter Island was once much different: Most of it was a subtropical forest. At one time, the island was home

The Real Mystery of EASTER ISLAND

to as many as 15,000 people, while today there are only about 200. What occurred to cause such drastic changes?

Explorer Thor Heyerdahl theorized that the building and moving of the statues was somehow linked with the activities of the Incas and with the Egyptians and their Pyramids. Author Erich Von Däniken proposed that extraterrestrials made and moved the statues. However, it is believed today that the Easter Islanders did all the work themselves. But how could they have done this? They didn't have cranes, metal tools, large animals, or wheels. (The wheel had been invented long before, but the Easter Islanders didn't have access to it.) One very convincing explanation is that they invented their own devices, called canoe rails, which are ladders with parallel wooden logs connected by crosspieces. The islanders used the rails to drag the statues. But large trees would have been required to build the rails, along with other kinds of trees to provide bark to make rope to pull the statues. Had such trees ever existed there?

Botanist John Flenly and anthropologist Paul Bahn have concluded that these trees did exist. Studies have established that the island was once covered with forests. One of the principal trees was the Chilean wine palm, which grows as high as 65 feet and as wide as 3 feet. The assumption is that the trunks of the wine palm were used to lift and move the statues and that the bark of other trees was used to make rope for hauling. But what happened to the trees?

Today some consider the deforestation of Easter Island one of the greatest environmental disasters of all time. The disaster was almost certainly caused by humans. No one knows for sure how or why it happened, of course, but it seems likely that a few hundred years after it was settled, the island began to experience a decline. It came to be ruled by 11 chiefs, who apparently constructed the statues as competitive demonstrations of their power. As the population increased, competition among the chiefs became fiercer. More and more land was cleared to grow crops to feed the people, and more and more trees were cut down to provide firewood and wood for use in moving and raising the statues. This deforestation led to the drying of the land, the loss of nutrients in the soil, and eventually less and less rainfall. In effect, the climate was changed.

Why did the Easter Islanders allow the disaster to happen? Did they simply fail to recognize an eventual problem? Was the problem too far advanced to do anything about it when they figured out what was happening? Perhaps more significantly for us, are there parallels today? Are we acting as the Easter Islanders did, but on a global scale? For example, does the push to cut down trees (such as in the Amazon rain forest) in the name of jobs and economic development make environmental sense? Are we over-fishing the ocean in our current belief that the supply of seafood is limitless? Are future catastrophes in the works? We mustn't shy away from these questions.

AFTER YOU READ

What does the underlined phrase refer to? Circle the correct answer.

1. Most of it was covered with <u>a subtropical forest</u>.

   a. subtropical forest in general   **b.** one particular subtropical forest

2. <u>The wheel</u> had been invented millennia before.

   a. one particular wheel   **b.** wheels in general

3. Tree bark provided <u>the rope</u> used to raise the statue.

   a. one particular rope   **b.** rope in general

Grammar Presentation

INDEFINITE AND DEFINITE ARTICLES

A/AN: INDEFINITE ARTICLE

	Non-Specific	**Generic**
SINGULAR COUNT NOUNS	He saw **a statue** at **an exhibition**.	**A statue** is **a** three-dimensional **figure**.

ZERO ARTICLE (NO ARTICLE)

	Non-Specific	**Generic**
PLURAL COUNT NOUNS	Easter Island has impressive **statues**.	**Statues** are made in all shapes and sizes.
NON-COUNT NOUNS	The statues are made of **stone**.	**Stone** is an important building material.
PROPER NOUNS	**Ms. Johnson** spent a year on **Easter Island**. She worked in **Egypt** and **Hawaii**. She now lives in **New York City**.	

THE: DEFINITE ARTICLE

	Specific	**Generic**
SINGULAR COUNT NOUNS	He finally got a computer. **The computer** he got is good. It's **the best computer** in **the world**.	**The computer** is a great invention.
PLURAL COUNT NOUNS	**The rain forests** in South America are being cut down.	**The rain forests** are in danger everywhere.
NON-COUNT NOUNS	**The stone** from that quarry is very soft.	
PROPER NOUNS	She crossed **the Sahara**, visited **the Pyramids**, and sailed down **the Nile**.	

GRAMMAR NOTES	EXAMPLES
1. When speakers do not have a particular person, place, or thing in mind, the nouns they use are **non-specific**. Use the indefinite article, *a / an*, with non-specific singular count nouns.	• He wants to buy **a statue**. • She wants to be **an anthropologist**.
2. A noun is often **indefinite** the first time a speaker mentions it. It is usually **definite** after the first mention.	• I heard of **an** interesting **mystery**. • **The mystery** is about Easter Island.
3. Use **zero article** (no article) with non-specific plural count nouns, non-specific non-count nouns, names of people, names of most countries, and habitual locations.	• The island used to have tall **trees**. • **Platinum** and **gold** are valuable minerals. • **Mr. Flenly** is a botanist. • Many statues have been found in **Egypt**. • People spend most of their time at **work**, at **school**, or at **home**.
4. A noun is **generic** when it represents all members of a class or category of persons, places, or things. In other words, generic nouns talk about things in general. Three common ways to use nouns generically are: **a.** zero article + plural count noun **b.** indefinite article + count noun **c.** zero article + non-count noun ▶ **BE CAREFUL!** Don't use *the* before a non-count noun used generically. **NOTE:** You can also make a generic statement with the definite article + adjective. A head noun such as *people* or *individuals* is implied. The adjective is plural in meaning and takes a plural verb.	• **Computers** are **machines** that do calculations and process information. • **A computer** is **a machine** that does calculations and processes information. • **Water** is essential for survival. • **Rainfall** is essential for crops. NOT ~~The rainfall~~ is essential for crops. • **The rich are** fortunate. **They need** to help **the poor**, who **are** not so fortunate. (= the rich people, the poor people)

(continued)

5. A noun is **definite** when the speaker and listener both know which particular person, place, or thing is being talked about. Use the definite article, **the**, with non-count nouns and singular and plural nouns that are definite for you and your listener.

NOTE: A noun or noun phrase is normally definite if you can ask a *which* question about it. Nouns of this type are often followed by a phrase with *of*.

- **The food** we had for lunch was terrible.
- **The island** used to be covered by forests.
- **The statues** were made by tribal chiefs.
- **The population** of the island has declined a great deal.

6. Use the **definite article** with nouns that describe something unique.

An adjective can often make a noun represent something unique. Examples of such adjectives are *first*, *last*, *only*, *right*, *wrong*, and the comparative and superlative form of adjectives.

- **The sun** gives us light and heat.
- It's one of **the worst disasters** in the world.

7. You can use the **definite article** generically in two ways:

a. in the singular: We often use this construction with inventions and musical instruments.

b. in the plural: We often use this construction with the names of peoples and of animal species.

- **The wheel** was invented thousands of years ago.
- She plays **the harp**.

- **The Hawaiians** are a resourceful people.
- There are many attempts today to save **the whales**.

8. Note these other uses of the **definite article** with nouns and noun phrases:

a. with public places

b. with the names of many geographical regions or features

c. with the names of a few countries

d. with the names of ships

- the bank, the post office, the library, the movies
- the Middle East, the Grand Canyon, the Colorado River, the Pacific Ocean
- the Netherlands, the United States, the Dominican Republic
- the *Titanic*, the *Queen Mary*

Reference Note
For more complete lists of **nouns used with the definite article**, see Appendices 7–9 on pages A-5–A-6.

Focused Practice

1 | DISCOVER THE GRAMMAR

A *Read the sentences based on the opening reading. For each sentence, classify the underlined word or phrase as indefinite (**I**), definite (**D**), or generic (**G**).*

___I___ 1. We've become aware of <u>an even greater mystery</u>.

_____ 2. Chile is <u>the country</u> to which Easter Island belongs.

_____ 3. There are gigantic <u>platforms</u> all over the island.

_____ 4. The building and moving of the statues was somehow linked with the activities of <u>the Incas</u> and the <u>Egyptians</u>.

_____ 5. Von Däniken thought the statues had been made by <u>extraterrestrials</u>.

_____ 6. <u>The wheel</u> had been invented long before.

_____ 7. <u>Canoe rails</u> are <u>ladders</u> with parallel wooden logs connected by crosspieces.

_____ 8. <u>The Chilean wine palm</u> grows as high as 65 feet.

_____ 9. Did they simply fail to recognize <u>an eventual problem</u>?

_____10. Is <u>the supply</u> of seafood limitless?

B *Read the sentences based on the reading. Circle the letter of the statement that correctly explains the meaning of each sentence.*

1. Who built the statues there, and how were they moved?
   a. Who built some of the statues there?
   b. Who built all of the statues there?

2. The island was settled by Polynesians.
   a. Some of the Polynesians settled the island.
   b. All of the Polynesians settled the island.

3. One of the principal trees in the forest was the Chilean wine palm.
   a. There was one Chilean palm tree in the forest.
   b. There were many Chilean palm trees in the forest.

4. But what happened to the trees on the island?
   a. What happened to all of the trees on the island?
   b. What happened to some of the trees on the island?

5. Trees were cut down to provide firewood.
   a. All of the trees were cut down.
   b. Some of the trees were cut down.

2 | DISASTERS

Read the descriptions of two notable environmental disasters that have occurred in recent decades. Fill in the blanks with the correct article in parentheses (— means no article is needed).

CHERNOBYL DAMAGE WIDER THAN PREVIOUSLY REPORTED

DETAILS ARE FINALLY EMERGING. On April 26, 1986, _____ fires and explosions following
1.(— / The)

_____ unauthorized experiment caused _____ worst accident in _____ history of
2.(an / the)   3.(a / the)   4.(— / the)

nuclear power at the nuclear power plant in Chernobyl, Ukraine. At least 31 people were

killed in _____ disaster itself, and _____ radioactive material was released into
5.(— / the)   6.(—, the)

_____ atmosphere. Approximately 135,000 people were evacuated from _____
7.(an / the)   8.(a / the)

vicinity. _____ scientists warned of _____ possible future cancer deaths and birth
9.(— / The)   10.(— / the)

defects.

MASSIVE OIL SPILL IN ALASKA

MARCH 24, 1989. _____ oil tanker *Exxon Valdez* struck Bligh Reef in Prince William
1.(An / The)

Sound, Alaska, tonight, causing _____ worst oil spill in _____ U.S. history. More
2.(a / the)   3.(— / the)

than 10 million gallons of _____ oil were spilled, causing the deaths of _____ many
4.(an / —)   5.(— / the)

animals and resulting in _____ great environmental catastrophe. The captain of
6.(— / a)

_____ *Valdez* was not present in _____ wheelhouse at _____ time of _____
7.(— / the)   8.(a / the)   9.(— / the)   10.(an / the)

accident; _____ ship was being piloted by _____ first mate, who was inexperienced.
11.(a / the)   12.(— / the)

It was determined that _____ captain, rather than _____ first mate, should have been
13.(a / the)   14.(— / the)

piloting _____ vessel. _____ Exxon agreed to pay for _____ cost of cleaning up
15.(a / the)   16.(— / The)   17.(— / the)

_____ spill.
18.(— / the)

3 | EARTHWEEK: A DIARY OF THE PLANET
Grammar Notes 2, 4–6, 9

Read the two excerpts from the article "Earthweek: A Diary of the Planet." Fill in the blanks with the articles needed. Leave a blank if no article is necessary.

Permafrost Warning

____The____ melting of permafrost in Sweden's sub-Arctic region due to global warming is
  1.

believed to be releasing vast quantities of the greenhouse gas methane into _____
                                                    2.

atmosphere. _____ research team, led by _____ GeoBiosphere Science Center at
             3.   4.

Lund University, said their research shows _____ part of _____ soil that thaws
                                 5.   6.

during summer has become deeper since 1970, and the permafrost has disappeared entirely

in some locations. "This has led to significant changes in the vegetation and to a subsequent

increase in emission of the greenhouse gas methane," _____ team announced. They
                                             7.

added that methane is 25 times more damaging to _____ atmosphere than _____
                                      8.   9.

carbon dioxide and often is overlooked in _____ discussion of greenhouse gases.
                                     10.

Plastic Pollution

_____ German magazine *Geo* published _____ report that said _____ plastic
  1.   2.   3.

trash has created _____ environmental hazard that stretches across _____ Pacific
                  4.   5.

from California to Hawaii, resulting in more plastic than plankton on _____ water's
                                              6.

surface. _____ March issue quotes biologist Charles Moore of the Algalita Marine
          7.

Research Foundation as saying: "Most plastic floats near _____ sea surface where some
                                           8.

is mistaken for _____ food by birds and fishes." The masses of plastic find their way
                   9.

into _____ Pacific from _____ western United States and _____ Canada after
      10.   11.   12.

storms flush the debris downstream and ultimately into _____ ocean. Maritime
                                         13.

observers have witnessed areas of floating plastic that stretch as far as the eye can see in

_____ central Pacific.
  14.

4 | INVENTIONS AND INSTRUMENTS

Grammar Notes 4, 8

Write two sentences about each invention or instrument. In the first sentence, write about the item's characteristics. In the second sentence, use the definite article to say when the item was invented.

Example: computer / electronic device / process information and perform high-speed calculations / 1944

A computer is an electronic device that processes information and performs high-speed calculations. / Computers are electronic devices that process information and perform high-speed calculations.

The computer was invented in 1944.

1. television set / electronic device / receive electromagnetic waves, convert waves into images, display them on a screen / 1920s by Farnsworth and Zorinsky

   _____

   _____

2. wheel / circular device / turn around central point / 5,000 to 6,000 years ago

   _____

   _____

3. clarinet / woodwind instrument / use a reed / around 1700

   _____

   _____

4. guitars / stringed instruments / typically have six strings / in the 1400s in Spain

   _____

   _____

5. automobiles / self-powered traveling vehicles / 1874 by Siegfried Marcus in Vienna

   _____

   _____

6. telephones / communication devices / convert sound signals into waves and reconvert them into sounds / 1878 by Alexander Graham Bell

   _____

   _____

5 | EDITING

Read this composition about genetic engineering and the environment. There are 15 mistakes in the use of articles. The first mistake is already corrected. Find and correct 14 more.

Genetic Engineering

People say we are now able to perform ~~a~~ genetic engineering. I am against this for several reasons. First, it is dangerous to tamper with the nature because we don't know what will happen. We could upset balance of nature. For example, people are against a mosquito because it carries malaria. Suppose we change the DNA of the mosquito so that it will die off. That will stop a malaria, but it will upset ecological balance because certain other species depend on mosquito. If we destroy it, these other species won't be able to survive. This will have serious effect on environment.

Second, genetic engineering will take away people's control over their own lives. Suppose scientists develop the capability to isolate gene for violent behavior and they eliminate this gene from future generations. This may eliminate a violence, but I believe that behavior is matter of choice, and this type of genetic engineering will eliminate choice. It will make people behave as others have determined, not as they have determined, and it will take away an individual responsibility.

Third, genetic engineering will remove chance from our lives. Part of what makes the life interesting is unpredictability. We never know exactly how someone, or something, is going to turn out. It's interesting to see what happens. As far as I am concerned, we should leave genetic engineering to Creator.

Communication Practice

6 | LISTENING

⌒ *Read the statements. Then listen to the conversation between a husband and a wife. Listen again and circle the answer that correctly completes each sentence.*

1. According to the husband, the newspaper is on the side of _____.
   a. the Indians   (b.) the environmentalists

2. Whose point of view does he think is ignored?
   a. the Indians'   b. the environmentalists'

3. The husband supports the point of view of _____.
   a. the Indians   b. the environmentalists

4. The wife supports the point of view of _____.
   a. the Indians   b. the environmentalists

5. The issue is whether _____ can hunt whales.
   a. one particular group of Indians   b. all Indians

6. The husband is in favor of allowing hunting because _____.
   a. it will reduce the surplus of whales   b. it will allow the Indians to support themselves

7. The wife thinks it's cruel to hunt _____.
   a. some whales   b. all whales

8. She says _____ animals are raised for food.
   a. all   b. some

9. The wife thinks it's acceptable to use _____ animals for food.
   a. all   b. some

10. The wife thinks _____ are intelligent.
    a. some whales   b. all whales

7 | PICTURE DISCUSSION

Form small groups and discuss this picture. Identify the items you see. Then discuss the situation. How can we dispose of items we no longer need or want? Are there solutions to this problem?

Example: A: I see an electric skillet and two axes.
　　　　　　 B: How do you think we should dispose of things like those?
　　　　　　 C: Well, I think each city should send trucks to pick up things people don't want.
　　　　　　 D: They could sell the items at special centers.

Yard sale

8 | WRITING

Work in small groups. Choose an environmental issue from the list below or develop your own idea. Write about the topic you select. Say why you think the issue is important and what should be done about it. Exchange papers with another group and correct any mistakes in the use of articles.

Possible Issues

- saving endangered animals
- improving air quality
- getting rid of nuclear weapons
- disposing of garbage
- ensuring the supply of clean water

> **Example:** Laws against air pollution have been in effect for decades now, but we haven't seen much progress in reducing air pollution. Actually, air pollution has gotten worse in many areas. If we want to make real progress, we need stricter laws, and we need to enforce them. There are three areas where we can improve: automobiles, factories, and the burning of forests. Let's look at each of these separately.
>
> The automobile . . .

9 | ON THE INTERNET

Form teams of four or five. Each team creates five questions about the environment, inventions, or musical instruments. Use the Internet to find answers to your questions. Then play a game in class. Teams take turns asking their questions. A team responding with the correct answer receives one point. The team with the most points at the end of the game is the winner.

Quantifiers

Grammar in Context

BEFORE YOU READ

1 *Do you pay for most things with cash, with credit cards, or by some other means?*

2 *What would be the advantages and disadvantages of living in a cashless society?*

🎧 *Read this article about money.*

AUGUST 6, 2006   BUSINESS TODAY

What's Happening to CA$H?

How did money originate, and where? The Babylonians were the first to develop actual "money" when they started to use gold and silver about 2500 B.C. The practice of using pieces of silver and gold as units of value gradually spread through much of the ancient world. In the following centuries, other items came to be used as money, for example, jewelry, land, and even cattle.

In the last two centuries, however, there has been a movement away from physical money and toward a more abstract system. One good example of an abstract type is fiat money, which is normally paper currency issued by a government. Fiat money isn't based on gold or silver; it has value only because the government says it does. Its value depends on trust in the government. Perhaps the most abstract type of money is electronic. E-money involves the electronic transfer of funds from one bank account to another. In such a financial transaction, no actual money is transferred. The balance in one account is simply increased, and the bal-

ance in the other account is correspondingly decreased.

Does this mean that there are no longer any advantages to cash? Not at all. Suppose, for example, that you're walking down a

(continued)

What's Happening to CA$H?

street and suddenly remember you need to buy some flowers. You see a flower vendor and decide this is the time to buy a dozen roses. What do you do? Write a check, or pull out your bank card? At this writing, few flower vendors take checks, and even fewer take plastic. Most of them prefer cash. If you've got some money, you simply pull out a few bills, hand them to the vendor, and happily walk away with your flowers. Pretty easy, huh? It wouldn't be that easy without cash.

Or suppose you'd like to give a little money as a gift. It's a lot more personal and pleasing to receive a few crisp bills in a birthday card than a check, which can seem rather cold and mechanical. Suppose you're at a food fair, and you feel like getting a couple of hot dogs. It's much easier to pull out cash to pay for them. In restaurants these days, it's become common to pay with a credit or debit card and to include the tip in the total amount. Sometimes, though, you might want to leave your server some actual money in appreciation of particularly good service. It seems to make a better emotional connection.

So cash has its advantages. Of course, it has a number of disadvantages as well. For example, you might be robbed. Also, cash can be heavy. Carrying a lot of coins can make holes in your pockets. It's inconvenient to take a great deal of money with you to pay for large purchases; imagine trying to carry enough cash to pay for a house or a car—or even a sofa. Besides that, cash has been handled by many different people and is covered with germs.

Then there's the matter of paying bills. Traditionally, most people in North America have paid their bills with checks, but the recent trend is to pay bills electronically. The Japanese, among others, have been doing this for years. In Japan, payment for such things as heat, electricity, and water is handled by automatic deduction from a bank account. It's much easier than writing out several checks to different agencies. And since it's automatic, people don't have to worry about whether they've forgotten to pay their bill.

There are a number of disadvantages to electronic money, however. Some people have little use for credit cards, saying that using them encourages us to live beyond our means. Others say that using electronic money places too much control of our personal finances in the hands of strangers. Mistakes are easily made and hard to correct.

The jury is still out on whether the trend toward less and less use of cash is good or bad. What seems clear is that it's definitely growing.

$

AFTER YOU READ

What does each sentence mean? Circle the correct answer.

1. Few flower vendors take checks.
   a. Some flower vendors take checks.
   b. Not many flower vendors take checks.

2. It's inconvenient to take a great deal of money with you.
   a. It's inconvenient to take a lot of money.
   b. It's inconvenient to take some money.

3. Some people have little use for credit cards.
   a. They like them.
   b. They don't like them very much.

Grammar Presentation

QUANTIFIERS

Quantifiers	With Count Nouns	With Non-Count Nouns
ONE EACH EVERY	**One store** is open. **Each coin** is valuable. **Every bank** is closed.	Ø* Ø Ø
TWO BOTH A COUPLE OF SEVERAL	**Two stores** are open. **Both stores** are nearby. She bought **a couple of gifts**. She bought **several gifts**.	Ø Ø Ø Ø
FEW A FEW MANY A GREAT MANY	They have **few investments**. She has **a few investments**. Does he own **many buildings**? He owns **a great many buildings**.	Ø Ø Ø Ø
LITTLE A LITTLE MUCH A GREAT DEAL OF	Ø Ø Ø Ø	They have **little money**. She has **a little money**. Does he have **much property**? He owns **a great deal of property**.
NO ANY SOME ENOUGH A LOT OF / LOTS OF PLENTY OF MOST ALL	They have **no bonds**. They don't have **any bonds**. They have **some stocks**. You have **enough stocks**. He has **a lot of / lots of clients**. He has **plenty of clients**. **Most banks** are safe. **All banks** are insured.	They have **no insurance**. They don't have **any insurance**. They have **some cash**. You have **enough cash**. He has **a lot of / lots of patience**. He has **plenty of patience**. **Most work** is useful. **All work** is tiring.

*Ø = quantifier not used

GRAMMAR NOTES

EXAMPLES

1. Quantifiers state the number or amount of something. Quantifiers can be single words or phrases.	• I bought **a dozen tulips**. • There's **some money** in my account.
Quantifiers are used with both nouns and pronouns.	• **A lot of people** vacation in the summer. • **Most of us** are going on the trip.
Quantifiers are often used alone if the noun or pronoun has just been mentioned, as in a question.	**A:** Have you made **many friends** here? **B:** Yes, I've made **a lot**.

2. Quantifiers are used with different types of nouns:	
a. with singular count nouns: *one, each, every*, etc.	• I took **each item** back to the store. • We were able to solve **every problem**.
b. with plural count nouns: *two, both, a couple of, a dozen, several, few, a few, many, a great many, a number of*, etc.	• We visited **a couple of countries**. • We bought **a few souvenirs**.
c. with non-count nouns: *a little, little, much, a great deal of, a great amount of*, etc.	• I only make **a little money** at that job. • She earns **a great deal of money**.
d. with both plural count nouns and non-count nouns: *no, any, some, enough, a lot of / lots of, plenty of, most, all*, etc.	• She has **no plans** to travel. • We took **no cash** on the trip.

3. Use *a few / few* with count nouns and *a little / little* with non-count nouns.	• Mary has **a few investments**. • She has saved **a little money**.
Note the difference between *a few* and *few* and between *a little* and *little*. Use *a few* and *a little* to make positive statements.	• I have **a few** good **friends**. • We have **a little food** at home.
Use *few* and *little* to make negative statements.	• Jerry has **few friends**. • Mary has **little self-confidence**.
▶ **BE CAREFUL!** In comparison, use *fewer* with count nouns and *less* with non-count nouns. Use *more* with both count and non-count nouns.	• I have **fewer problems** than I used to. • I also earn **less money**, though. • I have **more friends**. • I also have **more self-confidence**.

4. Use *many* with count nouns and *much* with non-count nouns.

In spoken affirmative statements, native speakers usually prefer *a lot of* or *lots of* to *much* and *many*, which sound more formal. This is especially true of *much*.

However, *much* and *many* are common in questions and negatives in spoken and written English.

Use *a great many* with count nouns and *a great deal of* with non-count nouns. These quantifiers are rather formal and found more in writing than in speech.

- He doesn't have **many friends**.
- I don't have **much trouble** getting to work.
- There are **a lot of accidents** on this road.
- There's **lots of construction** going on.
- Did they spend **much money**?
- She does not read **many magazines**.
- The government has **a great many responsibilities**.
- Presidents are under **a great deal of stress**.

5. Use *some* and *any* with count nouns and non-count nouns.

Use *some* in *affirmative* statements.

Use *any* in *negative* statements.

Use both *some* and *any* in questions. In general, use *some* in offers and *any* in negative questions.

- Did you make **some / any purchases**?
- Do you have **some / any cash** with you?
- Bill bought **some souvenirs**.
- He borrowed **some money** from me.
- Alice didn't take **any trips**.
- She didn't have **any money**.
- Did you buy **some / any clothes**?
- Would you like **some soda**?
- Didn't you send **any postcards**?

(continued)

6. Many **quantifiers** appear in phrases with the preposition *of*. Use *of* + *the* or another determiner when you are specifying particular persons, places, things, or groups.

- **Most of the EU countries** are using the euro.
- We saw **many of her films**.

We generally use quantifiers without *of* when we have no particular person, place, thing, or group in mind.

- **Most people** don't understand the economy.
- **Many restaurants** take credit cards.

▶ **BE CAREFUL!** Quantifiers with *of* can be used only with plural count nouns and non-count nouns.

- **Most of the coins** were very old.
- **Most of the gold** was pure.
- NOT ~~Most of the~~ coin was very old.

NOTE: Quantifiers like ***most of*** and ***many of*** can be followed by a singular or a plural verb, depending on the noun that follows *of*.

- Most of the **food has** been eaten. *(non-count noun + singular verb)*
- Most of the **people have** arrived. *(plural noun + plural verb)*

Reference Note
For more information on **count and non-count nouns,** see Unit 7.

Focused Practice

1 | DISCOVER THE GRAMMAR

Look at these sentences based on the opening reading. Could they be rewritten using the words in parentheses without changing the basic meaning or creating an incorrect sentence?

_____no_____ **1.** This is a trend that has been developing for *many* years now. (much)

_____ **2.** Are there still *any* advantages to cash? (some)

_____ **3.** You suddenly remember you need to buy *some* flowers. (any)

_____ **4.** At this writing, *few* flower vendors take checks. (a few)

_____ **5.** *Few* vendors take plastic. (little)

_____ **6.** Suppose you'd like to give *a little* money as a gift. (little)

_____ **7.** It's *much* easier to pull out cash to pay for them. (a lot)

_____ **8.** Cash has *some* disadvantages as well. (any)

_____ **9.** Cash has been handled by *many* different people. (a lot of)

_____**10.** *Most* people have paid their bills with checks. (a great deal of)

_____**11.** It's easier than writing out *several* checks. (a little)

_____**12.** Some people have *little* use for credit cards. (a little)

2 | OUR SECOND EUROPEAN TRIP
Grammar Notes 2–5

Complete the sentences by choosing the correct quantifier.

1. We just got back from our second trip to Europe. This time we visited _____*fewer*_____

    countries. (less / fewer)

2. We didn't visit _____ of the Scandinavian countries this time. (some / any)

3. We spent _____ money this time too. (less / fewer)

4. We did buy _____ wonderful souvenirs, though. (some / any)

5. Last time we rented a car and were amazed by the _____ cars on the

    roads. (amount of / number of)

6. This time we traveled by train. We expected _____

    people to be traveling that way. (much / a lot of)

7. However, there weren't very _____. (much / many)

8. We had _____ problems finding seats in the railroad cars. We never had

    to stand. (few / a few)

9. That's a good thing. My husband has _____ patience when it comes to

    competing with other passengers. (little / a little)

10. The trip was so economical that we had _____ extra money at the

    end. (little / a little).

3 | SAVING FOR A TRIP

Ron and Ashley Lamont are trying to save money for a trip to South America. They are examining their budget. Complete their conversation with quantifiers from the box, using each expression once.

a couple of	a few	~~a lot of~~	both of	enough
every	few	fewer	$40	less
more	most of	much	one of	some

ASHLEY: Ron, we're still spending _____*a lot of*_____ money on things we don't really need.
1.

   After I pay the bills this month, we're going to have _____ cash left over
   2.

   than we did last month. We're supposed to be saving for the trip to South America,

   remember? We're not saving _____ money. If we don't start saving
   3.

   _____, we won't be able to go.
   4.

RON: What have we bought that we don't need?

ASHLEY: That exercise machine, for one thing. We've only used it _____ times.
5.

   We could get a year's membership at the gym for what it cost and still have something

   left over.

RON: You mean _____ us could get a membership, don't you?
6.

ASHLEY: No, _____ us could. That's what I'm saying. The machine cost $500,
7.

   and memberships are $150 each. Let's sell the thing and go to the gym.

RON: Hmmm. Maybe you're right. What else?

ASHLEY: Well, we're spending about _____ extra a month on those premium
8.

   cable channels. We'd have _____ channels to choose from if we went
   9.

   back to the basic coverage, but we don't watch _____ TV anyway.
   10.

RON: Yeah, you're right . . . And you know, I'd say we could get rid of call waiting on the

   phone. We've used it very _____ times, and _____ my
   11.   12.

   friends say they hate it when they call, and then another call comes in while we're

   talking.

ASHLEY: Uh-huh. Let's cancel it, then. And here's one more suggestion. We should start taking a

sack lunch to work _____ times a week instead of going out at noon. If
13.

we did these four things, we'd have _____ money left over
14.

_____ month that could go into our trip fund.
15.

RON: Oh no! Not my lunches with the boys! Lunchtime is when I get to see them.

ASHLEY: Invite them over to play volleyball. Then think of Rio de Janeiro.

4 | WORLD NUMBERS   *Grammar Notes 4–6*

Look at the table. Then complete each sentence with the appropriate quantifier from the box. Use each quantifier once.

	The world in 1960	The world in 2000
Population	3,020,100,000	6,052,800,000
Birth rate per thousand people	31.2	21.5
Death rate per thousand people	17.7	9.0
Female life expectancy at birth	51.9 years	68.5 years
Male life expectancy at birth	48.6 years	64.6 years
Electricity use per person	1,445 kilowatt hours	2,175 kilowatt hours
Television sets per thousand people	112.8	272.4
Gross domestic product per person	$2,607	$5,666

a great deal of	a great many	few	fewer
less	many	more	much

1. ___A great many___ people were born between 1960 and 2000.

2. There were _____ births per thousand people in 2000 than in 1960.

3. There were _____ deaths per thousand people in 1960 than in 2000.

4. The life expectancy of men is _____ than that of women.

5. On the average, _____ females lived to be older than 52 or males older than 49 in 1960.

6. There was _____ growth in the use of electricity between 1960 and 2000.

7. There were more than twice as _____ TV sets in the world in 2000 as in 1960.

8. The gross domestic product was more than twice as _____ in 2000 as in 1960.

5 | A PERSONAL INVENTORY

Grammar Notes 5–6

Compare your life now to your life five years ago. Write eight sentences, using each of the quantifiers in the box.

a few	a little	a lot	fewer
less	many	more	much

Example: I have **more friends** now than I did five years ago.

6 | EDITING

Read this excerpt from a president's speech. There are 12 mistakes in the use of quantifiers. The first one is already corrected. Find and correct 11 more.

My fellow citizens: We are at a time in our history when we need to make some real

sacrifices. Recent presidents have made ~~a great deal of~~ *a great many* promises they didn't keep. You may

not like everything I tell you tonight, but you deserve to hear the truth. On the economy,

we've made little progress, but we still have a great many work to do, so there are several

measures I'm proposing. First, I want to raise taxes on the very wealthy because a few of

them are really paying their share. Second, many of members of the middle class are

carrying an unfair tax burden, so I'm asking for a tax cut for the middle class. If I'm

successful, most of you in the middle class will be paying 10 percent less in taxes next year,

though few of you in the higher-income group may see your taxes rise little.

How do I intend to make up the lost revenue? The problem with the national income

tax is that there are much loopholes in the current law which allow any people to avoid

paying any taxes at all; I want to close these loopholes. My additional plan is to replace the

lost revenue with a national sales tax, which is fairer because it applies to every people

equally. Third, we have no money to finance health care reform, and we've made a little

progress in reducing pollution and meeting clean air standards. Therefore, I am asking for

a 50-cent-a-gallon tax on gasoline, which will result in many more people using public

transportation and will create additional revenue. Thus, we will have enough of money to

finance our new health care program and will help the environment at the same time.

Communication Practice

7 | LISTENING

🎧 *Read the questions. Then listen to a conversation in a restaurant. Listen again and answer the questions.*

1. Which restaurant has fewer menu choices?
   a. this restaurant   **b.** the last restaurant

2. At which restaurant does the food cost less?
   a. this restaurant   **b.** the last restaurant

3. How much money does Bill have?
   a. none at all   **b.** a few dollars

4. Does Bill have enough money to pay the bill?
   a. yes   **b.** no

5. How much is the bill?
   a. $55   **b.** $15

6. How many credit cards does Bill have?
   a. one   **b.** none at all

7. Do Mary and Bill have enough money together to pay the bill?
   a. yes   **b.** no

8. Are there any ATM machines nearby?
   a. Yes, there are.   **b.** No, there aren't.

8 | THE QUANTIFIER GAME: WORLD FACTS

Form two teams. Each team uses its prompts to construct eight questions about world facts with quantifiers. Then each team creates two questions of its own, for a total of ten questions. The other team answers each question.

Example: country / more / people / China / India
   A: Which country has more people, China or India?
   B: China has more people.

Team A's Prompts

1. country / fewer / people / Canada / Mexico

2. country / more / land area / Canada / the United States

(continued)

3. country / produce / less / oil / Venezuela / Mexico

4. country / no / snowfall / Somalia / Tanzania

5. country / fewer / rivers / Libya / Nigeria

6. country / smaller number / people / Monaco / Cyprus

7. country / produce / large amount / gold / Nigeria / South Africa

8. city/ little / rainfall / Aswan, Egypt / Athens, Greece

Team B's Prompts

1. country / fewer / people / Great Britain / Spain

2. country / more / land area / Australia / Brazil

3. country / produce / less / oil / the United States / Saudi Arabia

4. country / no / military / Colombia / Costa Rica

5. country / fewer / rivers / Yemen / Turkey

6. country / smaller number / people / San Marino / Kuwait

7. country / use / larger amount / nuclear energy / the Netherlands / France

8. city / little / rainfall / Antofagasta, Chile / Nairobi, Kenya

9 | WRITING

Write about an interesting experience you have had with money. Choose one of these topics or create your own topic.

- a time when you ran out of money

- a time when you tipped too much or too little

- a time when you lost your wallet or purse

> **Example:** The most interesting experience I've ever had with money was three years ago when I was visiting New York City. I had gone to a restaurant and ordered a large, expensive meal. I thought I had more than enough money to pay for the meal, but I had a big surprise. Here's how it happened . . .

10 | ON THE INTERNET

Assume that you are going to take a trip to Europe. Use the Internet to compare the currency of your country to the euro. What is the current exchange rate? Find out if any members of the European Union are not using the euro. Also find out which European countries are not members of the EU. Report your findings to the class.

Modification of Nouns

Grammar in Context

BEFORE YOU READ

1 *What is the difference between hoping for something to happen and expecting it to happen? Discuss this with your classmates.*

2 *In your experience, does what you expect to happen usually happen? Give an example.*

3 *How can expectations be a negative force? How can they be a positive force?*

Read this article about expectations.

POCKET DIGEST

THE EXPECTATION SYNDROME
I Hope for It, but I Don't Expect It

by Jessica Taylor

Picture the scene: It's the fourteenth Winter Olympics in Lake Placid, New York. The U.S. team is playing the Soviet team in the men's semifinal ice hockey match. The supposedly unbeatable Soviet squad, winners of the last four gold medals in hockey, is so accomplished that it has already beaten a team of National Hockey League all-stars. The American team is a group of college players who weren't even expected to make it to the medal round, but here they are. Nearly everyone assumes the Soviet team will win and the American team will lose. Improbably, however, the Americans defeat the Soviets. They then go on to beat the Finnish team in the finals and win the gold medal. A sportscaster calling the match comes up with the famous line, "Do you believe in miracles?" Were the Americans a better team than the Soviets? Almost certainly not. Everyone (including the Soviet players themselves) expected the Soviets to win, and almost no one believed in the Americans, who had no expectations. They simply played spontaneously and energetically. The result: They won.

(continued)

━━━━━━━━━━━━━ **POCKET DIGEST** ━━━━━━━━━━━━━

THE EXPECTATION SYNDROME

Picture another situation: Your film-buff friends have seen all three parts of the Academy Award–winning *The Lord of the Rings*. They rave about its superb color photography, its fantastic computer-generated scenes of strange-looking creatures, and its awesome special effects. They praise its serious, profound, and heartwarming treatment of the age-old conflict between good and evil. They say it's the best English-language movie of the last decade. When you go to see one of the three parts, though, you're disappointed. You don't find it as excellent as everyone has been saying. In fact, you feel it's a tedious, boring movie and consider it basically just another special-effects fantasy film.

These situations illustrate what we might call "the expectation syndrome," a condition in which events do not turn out as we feel they will or ought to. Children often do not meet their parents' career expectations of them. Athletes do not always win the contests people expect them to win. Great literature doesn't always seem as good as it should. I asked psychiatrist Robert Stevens whether expectations can actually make things turn out negatively, or whether this is merely a philosophical question, an unpleasant, frustrating irony of the human condition.

RS: Well, what we're really talking about here, I think, is the immense power of the mind to control outcomes. For example, there's a medical condition called "focal dystonia," which is an abnormal muscle function caused by extreme concentration. Somehow, when athletes are concentrating too hard, it affects certain brain functions and they miss the basket, don't hit the ball, or lose the race. In effect, they're letting their expectations control them.

JT: Have you ever had any experience with this phenomenon in your personal everyday life?

RS: Yes, I certainly have. Let me give you an example from skiing that shows that the mind has immense power for both positive and negative things. There are days when, as a cautious skier, I stand at the top of a steep, icy slope, plotting my every move down the course, fearing that I'll fall. Sure enough, I do fall. Other days I feel different. My expectations are miles away. I forget about myself, ski well, and don't fall. When we focus excessively on goals, our expectations tend to take over, and our mind places us outside the process. On the other hand, when we concentrate on the process instead of the goal, we're often much more successful. Have you heard the phrase "trying too hard"? That's what people often do.

JT: Very interesting. What would be your recommendation about expectations, then?

RS: Well, all I've been able to come up with so far is that it's better to hope for things than to expect them.

AFTER YOU READ

Circle the letter of the choice that explains the meaning of the italicized phrase.

1. It's the best *English-language movie* of the last decade.

   a. It's a movie about language that was made in England.

   b. It's a movie in the English language.

2. Children often do not meet *their parents' career expectations* of them.

   a. The career expectations parents have

   b. The career expectations children have

3. Focal dystonia is an *abnormal muscle function* caused by extreme concentration.

    a. The function of a particular muscle is abnormal.

    b. A particular muscle is abnormal.

Grammar Presentation

MODIFICATION OF NOUNS

	Adjective Modifier	Noun Modifier	Head Noun
I remember the		Winter	Olympics.
	wonderful		athletes.
	amazing	hockey	games.
	unexpected	U.S.	victory.

Order of Adjective Modifiers								
	Opinion	Size	Age	Shape	Color	Origin	Material	
I saw a	great		new			French		movie.
I met its	fascinating		young			Chinese		director.
She had		large		round			jade	earrings.
She wore a		long			red		silk	dress.

Several Adjective Modifiers	
Different Modifier Categories	**Same Modifier Category**
A **great new epic** movie	A **serious, profound, and heartwarming** movie A **serious, profound, heartwarming** movie A **heartwarming, profound, serious** movie

Compound Modifiers		
The movie has lots of	computer-generated strange-looking	scenes. creatures.
The main character is a	10-year-old long-haired, short-legged	girl. boy.

GRAMMAR NOTES

EXAMPLES

1. Nouns can be modified both by adjectives and by other nouns. **Adjective** and **noun modifiers** usually come before the noun they modify. The noun that is modified is called the head noun.	adjective modifiers • Yao Ming is a **famous Chinese** noun modifier head noun **basketball player**.

2. Noun modifiers usually come directly before the nouns they modify. When there are both adjective and noun modifiers, the noun modifier comes closer to the head noun.	• **Milk chocolate** is chocolate made with milk. • **Chocolate milk** is milk that has chocolate in it. noun adj. mod. mod. head noun • Pelé is a **famous soccer player**.

3. Two common types of **adjective modifiers** are present participles and past participles (also called **participial adjectives**). Remember that participial adjectives that end in *-ing* describe someone or something that causes a feeling. Participial adjectives that end in *-ed* describe someone who experiences a feeling.	• It was a **boring** movie. • The **bored** viewers left. • The result of the game was **shocking**. • The news is **exciting**. • We were **shocked** by the result. • Everyone is **excited** by the news.

4. When there is **more than one modifier** of a noun, the modifiers generally occur in a **fixed order**. The following list shows the usual order of common adjective and noun modifiers. The order can be changed by the emphasis a speaker wants to give to a particular adjective.	

POSITION	CATEGORY OF MODIFIER	
1	Opinions	• ugly, beautiful, dull, interesting
2	Size	• big, tall, long, short
3	Age or temperature	• old, young, hot, cold
4	Shapes	• square, round, oval, diamond
5	Colors	• red, blue, pink, purple
6	Origins, nationalities, or social classes	• computer-generated, Brazilian, Chinese, middle-class
7	Materials	• wood, cotton, denim, silk, glass

5. When a noun has **two or more modifiers** in the same category, we separate the adjectives with a comma. If the modifiers are in different categories, do not separate the adjectives with a comma.

NOTE: The order of adjectives in the same category can vary.

- He is a **serious, hardworking** student.
- I bought a **beautiful denim** shirt.

- He is a **serious, hardworking** student.
- He is a **hardworking, serious** student.

6. Compound modifiers are constructed from more than one word. Here are four common kinds:

   a. number + noun

   b. noun + present participle

   c. noun + past participle

   d. adjective + past participle

When compound modifiers precede a noun, they are generally hyphenated.

▶ BE CAREFUL! Plural nouns used as modifiers become singular when they come before the noun.

- I work in a **10-story** building.
- It's a **prize-winning** film.
- It's a **crime-related** problem.
- The actor plays a **long-haired, one-armed** pirate in the movie.

- Her daughter is 10 years old.
- She has a **10-year-old** daughter.

  NOT She has a ~~10-years-old~~ daughter.

7. BE CAREFUL! In written English, avoid having more than two noun modifiers together. Using too many noun modifiers in sequence can be confusing. Look at the example: Is Jerry a student who won an award for painting portraits? Is Jerry a painter who won an award for painting students? Is the award given by the students?

To avoid confusing sentences like this, break up the string of noun modifiers with prepositional phrases or rearrange the modifiers in some other way.

There is no similar problem with adjective modifiers.

- Jerry Gonzales won the **student portrait painter** award.

- Jerry Gonzales won the award for painting portraits of students.

  OR

- Student Jerry Gonzales won the award for painting portraits.
- The **clever little brown-and-white** fox terrier impressed us all. (*All the adjectives clearly modify* fox terrier.)

Focused Practice

1 | DISCOVER THE GRAMMAR

Read these sentences based on the opening article. Circle all head nouns that have noun or adjective modifiers before them. Underline adjective modifiers once, noun modifiers twice, and compound modifiers three times.

1. It's the <u>fourteenth</u> <u><u>Winter</u></u> (Olympics.)

2. The U.S. team is playing the Soviet team in the men's semifinal ice hockey match.

3. The supposedly unbeatable Soviet squad, winners of the last four gold medals in hockey, is so good that it has already beaten a team of National Hockey League all-stars.

4. Your film-buff friends have seen the Academy Award–winning *The Lord of the Rings*.

5. They love its strange-looking creatures and awesome special effects.

6. They admire its serious, profound, and heartwarming treatment of the age-old conflict between good and evil.

7. Children often do not meet their parents' career expectations of them.

8. I asked Robert Stevens whether there is an actual scientific basis for the negativity of expectations.

9. There's a medical condition called "focal dystonia," which is an abnormal muscle function caused by extreme concentration.

10. I stand at the top of a steep, icy slope, plotting my every move down the course.

2 | PARTY EXPECTATIONS

Grammar Notes 4–5

Bill and Nancy are going to attend a party at the home of Nancy's new boss. They are trying to dress for the occasion and aren't sure what is expected. Nancy is very worried about making a good impression. Unscramble the modifiers in their conversation. Place commas where they are needed.

BILL: This is a _____*formal office*_____ party, isn't it? What if I wear my
        1. (office / formal)

_____ tie?
2. (silk / new)

NANCY: That's fine, but don't wear that _____ shirt with it. People will
        3. (purple / ugly / denim)

think you don't have any _____ clothes.
        4. (suitable / dress-up)

BILL: So what? Why should I pretend I like to dress up when I don't?

NANCY: Because there are going to be a lot of _____ businesspeople
                                                     5. (interesting / important)

there, and I want to make a _____ impression. It's my job,
                                    6. (memorable / good)

remember? I don't want people to think I have a _____
                                                        7. (unstylish / sloppy)

dresser for a husband, which of course you're not. Humor me just this once, OK

sweetie? Hmmm . . . I wonder if I should wear my _____
                                                        8. (round / sapphire / blue)

earrings or the _____ ones.
                      9. (green / oval / emerald)

[*Later, at the party.*]

NANCY: Hi, Paul. This is Bill, my husband.

PAUL: Welcome. Bill, I'm glad to know you. You two are our first guests to arrive. Help

yourselves to snacks. There are some _____ sandwiches.
                                            10. (excellent / tomato-and-cheese)

Please make yourselves at home. You know, Nancy, I'm sorry I didn't make it clear this

isn't a _____ party. You two look great, but I hope you won't
              11. (dress-up / fancy)

feel out of place.

BILL: Thanks. We'll be fine. By the way, Paul, I really like that _____
                                                                      12. (beautiful / denim / purple)

shirt you're wearing. Where did you get it?

3 | READING ALOUD

Grammar Note 6

Complete the sentences in this narrative with compound modifiers.

Pam and Allen Murray took their son Joshua to a reading specialist because Joshua could not

read aloud in class. Dr. Tanaka, the specialist, asked Joshua a number of questions about his

problems with reading. Joshua said that he got frustrated in his reading class, that even though it

was only a _____ *50-minute* _____ period, it seemed to him like a year. During this
                  1. (lasting 50 minutes)

particular semester, the teacher was giving the students oral reading assignments every day. At first

the teacher had called on Joshua to read aloud, and Joshua would panic every time, even if it was

only a _____ assignment. Now she was no longer calling on him.
            2. (one paragraph in length)

(continued)

Dr. Tanaka asked Joshua if he had any problem with silent reading. Joshua said he didn't, adding that he loved to read to himself and could finish a _____ book in
3. (300 pages in length)
a day or two. Pam, Joshua's mother, noted that his reading comprehension was excellent.

Dr. Tanaka asked Pam and Allen how long this problem had been going on. Allen said it had begun when Joshua was in the first grade. Since Joshua was now 12, the situation had been a

_____ ordeal. Dr. Tanaka wondered how the problem had started. Pam
4. (lasting six years)
replied that she felt it was definitely a _____ problem, for Joshua had
5. (related to stress)
lisped when he started school. Joshua added that he had felt bad when the other children would

laugh at him when he pronounced his "s" sounds as "th" sounds. The problem simply got worse

until Joshua was no longer able to read orally at all.

Dr. Tanaka agreed that teasing might have caused Joshua's problem but suggested another

possibility—that Joshua's inability to read aloud could be an _____
6. (related to eyesight)
problem. He asked if it would be all right to test Joshua's vision. When the Murrays agreed, Dr.

Tanaka asked Joshua to read two eye charts, which he was able to read perfectly. He then asked

Joshua to read a short passage that he held at a distance. The passage went like this:

"Night was falling in Dodge City. The gunfighter walked down the street wearing a

_____ hat."
7. (holding 10 gallons)
Joshua read the passage with no difficulty at all, and Dr. Tanaka said he felt he now

understood Joshua's problem well: He had _____ anxiety. He told the
8. (induced by performance)
Murrays he had distracted Joshua by referring to his vision. He then said he had a

_____ program that would have Joshua reading aloud proficiently if he
9. (lasting two months)
was willing to try it. Joshua was more than willing, so the Murrays made arrangements to start

the program soon.

4 | CREATIVE SENTENCES

Write a sentence for each of the following, changing the phrase so that the modifier appears before the head noun. Use correct punctuation.

1. a flight that takes 10 hours

   Last month I was on a 10-hour flight from Rio to Bogotá.

2. a cat that has long hair

_____

3. a jacket that is old and comfortable

_____

4. an experience that amuses and interests you

_____

5. a child who is 11 years old

_____

6. a movie that wins an award

_____

7. a table that has three legs

_____

8. people who look unusual

_____

9. a skirt that is made of cotton, is short, and is blue

_____

10. a bowl originating in China and made of jade

_____

11. a building that has 60 stories

_____

12. a bag that weighs 40 kilos

_____

5 | EDITING

Read this entry from medical student Jennifer Yu's computer journal. There are 11 mistakes in the use of modifiers. The first mistake is already corrected. Find and correct 10 more.

FRIDAY: It's midnight, the end of a long day. My first week of ~~school medical~~ *medical school* is over, and I'm exhausted but happy! I'm so glad I decided to go to the university. It was definitely a good decision. I'm not completely sure yet, but I think I want to go into child psychiatry because I love working with children—especially nine- and ten-years-old kids.

Yesterday our psychiatry class visited a new large hospital where many middle-class troubled children go for treatment. I expected to see a lot of boys and girls behaving badly, but most of them were pretty quiet and relaxed. They just looked like they needed some personal warm attention.

Today in our surgery class we had a bright hardworking teacher, a Brazilian young doctor who was substituting for our usual professor. We got a foreign helpful viewpoint on things.

The only thing I don't like about medical school is the cafeteria disgusting food. I'm going to have to start getting some hot tasty Chinese food from my local favorite place.

Well, it's time for me to get some sleep. I hope this computer new program works correctly.

Communication Practice

6 | LISTENING

🎧 **A** *Joshua Murray is working on his reading program with Dr. Tanaka. Read these questions. Then listen to their conversation. Check **True** or **False**.*

	True	False
1. The first session will last only 30 minutes.	☑	☐
2. Joshua likes his own voice.	☐	☐
3. A rapid growth period occurs during adolescence.	☐	☐

4. Joshua is 13 years old. ☐ ☐

5. Joshua is afraid of reading aloud. ☐ ☐

6. The phrase that Joshua will say to distract himself will not be
difficult to remember. ☐ ☐

7. The people in the story have three dogs. ☐ ☐

8. Large, warm, and furry dogs can keep you warm on a cold night. ☐ ☐

🎧 **B** *Now listen again and fill in the blanks. Place commas between adjectives when the speaker pauses, and be sure to hyphenate compound modifiers.*

1. Our first meeting is only going to be a _____ *30-minute session* _____ .

2. We don't want to make this a _____ .

3. I feel like a _____ .

4. And I feel like I have an _____ .

5. You're just going through a _____ .

6. It happens to a lot of _____ .

7. Now, the key to getting you over this _____ is to
distract you from thinking about how well you're doing.

8. Let's think of a _____ that you can keep in the
back of your mind.

9. "It was an _____ ."

10. "It promised to be one of those _____ ."

11. What's a _____ ?

12. It's a night that's so cold that you need _____ to
sleep with to keep you warm.

7 | GROUP DISCUSSION

Discuss these questions in small groups.

1. How does Joshua feel at the end of the session with Dr. Tanaka?

2. How can developmental problems like Joshua's affect a person's life? Do you know any examples you can share with the class?

3. If you had a friend with a similar problem, what advice would you give?

Example: **A:** Do you know anyone with stress-related problems like Joshua's?
B: Yes. My younger sister stuttered when she was a girl. It was definitely a stress-related problem. She . . .

8 | A STORY

A *Read a famous story.*

DEATH SPEAKS

There was a merchant in Baghdad who sent his servant to market to buy supplies. In a little while the servant came back, white and shaking, and said, "Master, just now when I was in the market I was bumped by a woman in the crowd, and when I turned I saw it was Death who had bumped me. She looked at me and made a threatening gesture. Now please lend me your horse, and I will ride away from this city and avoid my fate. I will go to Samarra, and there Death will not find me."

The merchant lent the servant his horse, and the servant mounted it. He rode away as fast as he could make the horse run. Then the merchant went down to the marketplace, and he saw me standing in the crowd. He came to me and said, "Why did you make a threatening gesture to my servant when you saw him this morning?"

"That was not a threatening gesture," I said. "It was only a gesture of surprise. I was amazed to see him in Baghdad, for I had an appointment with him tonight in Samarra."

B *Answer the questions. Then discuss your answers with a partner. Share your answers with the class. As a class, decide what the story shows about expectations.*

1. In the story, Death is _____.
   a. male
   b. female

2. In the last two paragraphs of the story, "I" and "me" refer to _____.
   a. the merchant
   b. Death

3. The servant expects to _____.
   a. escape from Death
   b. be captured by Death

4. The story suggests that _____.
   a. it's possible to escape fate
   b. it's not possible to escape fate

9 | PICTURE DISCUSSION

Form small groups. Look at this picture of the sinking of the Titanic *in April 1912.*

Describe what you see, using as many modifiers as possible. Share your sentences with other groups.

Example: The ship was sinking into the dark, icy ocean waters.

Then discuss what this painting suggests about expectations with the other groups.

Example: The builders of the *Titanic* didn't expect it to sink.

10 | WRITING

Have you ever expected something to happen that didn't turn out as you expected? For example, you didn't win a game, get an A, or win an election. Write two or three paragraphs telling what happened. Did it have anything to do with the expectation syndrome?

Example: A year ago our school basketball team was having a great year. In the regular season, we had a 19-1 record: 19 wins and one loss, and that one loss was in our first game. It seemed like we couldn't lose. When we got to the playoffs, however, things didn't turn out as we expected they would. In our first playoff game . . .

11 | ON THE INTERNET

Use the Internet to find out what was unexpected about one of the following topics. Share your findings with the class.

- the *Spruce Goose* of Howard Hughes
- the U.S. presidential election in 1948
- the reign of King Edward VIII of England

From **Grammar** to **Writing**
Agreement

There are two types of agreement: **subject-verb agreement** and **pronoun-antecedent agreement.**

Every sentence in English can be divided into two parts: the **subject** and the **predicate.** The subject is a person, place, or thing about which something is said. The predicate is what is said about the subject, and it always contains the principal verb. Subjects and verbs of English sentences must agree in person and number. In the following sentences, the complete subject is underlined once and the complete predicate twice.

Birds chirp.

Koalas live in Australia.

The men at Ron's office like to play volleyball.

Nadia and Phil Lopez are trying to save money.

The danger of credit cards is that they encourage us to live beyond our means.

To determine the **complete subject** of a sentence, ask a *who* or *what* question. The answer to that question will be the complete subject.

The man on the train reminded Penny of her father.

Who reminded Penny of her father? The man on the train. (complete subject)

The increasing extinction of plant and animal species is alarming.

What is alarming? The increasing extinction of plant and animal species. (complete subject)

1 | *Underline the complete subject in each of the sentences.*

1. Five of my best friends are coming over tonight to play cards.

2. The Siberian tiger and the blue whale are endangered species.

3. That man who is sitting at the mahogany desk is our loan officer.

4. Relatively few adults or teenagers are able to handle credit cards wisely.

5. The expectation that we will like well-known works of art, literature, or music can detract from our appreciation of them.

There is normally one word in the complete subject that controls the verb in the sentence. To determine this **main** (or **simple**) **subject**, find the word that the other words modify. In the following sentences, the main subject is underlined.

My blue silk <u>necktie</u> is gorgeous.

Our first three <u>attempts</u> were unsuccessful.

Notice that the main (simple) subject of a sentence is never located in a prepositional phrase (a phrase beginning with a preposition and ending with a noun or pronoun, for example, *on the table*). In the following sentences, the prepositional phrases are underlined, the main subject is circled, and an arrow is drawn between the main subject and the verb.

(One) <u>of my best friends</u> has nine credit cards.

(Both) <u>of my brothers</u> are behind on their car payments.

The (list) <u>on the bulletin board</u> is out of date.

(Either) <u>of the plans</u> is worthwhile.

The (man) <u>in the gray flannel suit</u> is a salesman.

(Neither) <u>of the skaters</u> is expected to win a gold medal.

2 | *Circle the main subject in each of the sentences, and draw an arrow between it and the verb.*

1. A (list) of available jobs was posted on the office bulletin board.

2. Much of what you were told was inaccurate.

3. Neither of those two politicians is in favor of cutting taxes.

4. None of the work has been completed successfully.

5. Very little of this work can be done by one person working alone.

6. The singing of that famous Australian opera star is uplifting.

Be careful with the word *there*. Even though *there* is often the grammatical subject of a sentence, it is linked to a word later in the sentence that controls the verb. In the following sentences, an arrow connects the word *there* and the noun it is linked to. Note the underlined verb.

There <u>are</u> numerous animals on the Endangered Species List.

There <u>have</u> been many environmental disasters in the last 20 years.

There <u>is</u> a large, fierce dog guarding the house.

BE CAREFUL! You will sometimes hear *there* used with a singular verb even though the noun that follows is plural. This occurs in conversation but is not correct in standard formal English.

Conversational:	**There's** some papers on my desk.
Standard:	**There are** some papers on my desk.

3 | *Choose the correct verb to complete each sentence.*

1. There _____*has*_____ never been an environmental disaster of this magnitude.
   (has / have)

2. There _____ many reasons why I am against the use of nuclear power.
   (is / are)

3. There _____ always a rational explanation for his behavior.
   (isn't / aren't)

4. There _____ been fewer business mergers this year than last.
   (has / have)

5. There _____ numerous demonstrators present at the environmental rally.
   (was / were)

6. There _____ any elegantly dressed people at the party. Everyone was
   (wasn't / weren't)
   wearing blue jeans.

Compound subjects are those in which the subject is composed of more than one item. The items are often connected by *and*.

Ron and Laurie are going to join a health club. (two subjects: *Ron, Laurie*)

The blue whale, the timber wolf, and **the whooping crane** need our protection. (three subjects: *whale, wolf, crane*)

Sometimes words appear to be compound subjects, but they really constitute a single phrase made up of two or more items acting as a unit. These take a **singular verb.**

Bacon and eggs is a high-cholesterol but nourishing meal. (*Bacon and eggs* is a single dish.)

The owner and manager of the bank is Mr. Bates. (*Mr. Bates* is one person who has two roles.)

4 | *Choose the correct verb to complete each sentence.*

1. Both the whale and the grizzly bear _____*need*_____ federal protection.
   (needs / need)

2. Bipolar disorder and schizophrenia _____ two serious mental disorders.
   (is / are)

3. The director and star of the film _____ Robert Redford.
   (was / were)

4. Liver and onions _____ a meal detested by many children.
   (is / are)

5. Mathematics and physics _____ often considered difficult subjects.
   (is / are)

Pronoun-antecedent agreement is similar to subject-verb agreement. In formal English, pronouns agree in person, number, and gender with their antecedents (words to which they refer).

All the **students** brought **their** books to class on the first day. (*Their* agrees with *students*.)

Jack ate **his** lunch quickly. (*His* agrees with *Jack*.)

Martha stopped by to see **her** mother after class. (*Her* agrees with *Martha*.)

Each of **us** needs to bring **our** own ideas to the meeting. (*Our* agrees with *us*.)

The pronouns *everyone / everybody*, *anyone / anybody*, *someone / somebody*, and *no one / nobody* are often treated differently in conversational and standard formal English. Look at these examples.

Formal	**Informal**
Everyone drove **his or her** own car to the picnic.	**Everyone** drove **their** own car to the picnic.
If you see **anyone** from our office, tell **him or her** to see me.	If you see **anyone** from our office, tell **them** to see me.
Everybody may leave when **he or she** wishes.	**Everybody** may leave when **they** wish.

BE CAREFUL! Use the forms on the right above only in informal (conversational) English. Use the correct singular forms in writing and formal speech.

Sometimes it is possible to make a sentence correct for formal English by changing the subject to a plural.

Informal: Everyone brought **their** own lunch.
Formal: All the employees brought **their** own lunch.

5 | *Complete each of these sentences with forms for formal and informal English.*

Formal	**Informal**
1. Does everyone have ___*his or her*___ book with him or her? a.	Does everyone have _____ book with them? b.
2. No one knows _____ own destiny. a.	No one knows _____ own destiny. b.
3. If anyone shows up, send _____ to my office. a.	If anyone shows up, send _____ to my office. b.
4. Everybody needs to have _____ priorities straight. a.	Everybody needs to have _____ priorities straight. b.

In formal English, subjects connected by **either / or** and **neither / nor** behave differently from compound subjects. The subject that is closer to the verb determines the agreement.

> Either the **president** or his cabinet **members are** responsible for this environmental policy. (two subjects: *president, members; members* is closer to the verb and requires the plural verb *are*)

> Neither the **members** of the city council nor the **mayor supports** more real estate development. (two subjects: *members, mayor; mayor* is closer to the verb and requires the singular verb *supports*)

Note that if we reverse the order of the subjects in the above sentences, the verb changes:

> Either the cabinet **members** or the **president is** responsible for this environmental policy.

> Neither the **mayor** nor the **members** of the city council **support** more real estate development.

Pronouns whose antecedents are nouns connected by *either / or* and *neither / nor* behave in the same way. The noun closer to the pronoun determines the correct pronoun.

> Neither **Susan** nor **the Johnsons** enrolled **their** children in that school. (*The Johnsons* is closer to the pronoun and requires *their*.)

6 | *Choose the correct verb or pronoun to complete the sentences.*

1. Either Bob Ashcroft or the Mendozas ___*are*___ going to host this year's party.
   (is / are)

2. Neither pollution nor other atmospheric factors _____ thought to be related to the
   (is / are)

   unusual weather we've been having.

3. Neither the local environmentalists nor the mayor _____ a plan that will satisfy everyone.
   (has / have)

4. Either major credit cards or a check _____ an acceptable means of payment.
   (is / are)

5. Neither Venus nor the outer planets _____ a breathable atmosphere.
   (has / have)

6. Neither my daughters nor my son owns _____ own car.
   (their / his)

7 | Read the letter to the editor of a newspaper. There are 12 mistakes in subject-verb agreement and pronoun-antecedent agreement. The first mistake is already corrected. Find and correct 11 more. Use forms that are correct for formal English.

Editor, The Times:

 Many parts of our once-beautiful city *are* ~~is~~ starting to look like mini garbage dumps. You will recall that legislation requiring recycling within the city limits were passed last year, and the mayor and other local politicians encourages us to recycle, but in my apartment complex there's no bins for recycling. The result is that people take no responsibility for his own actions, and everyone tosses their trash and recyclables (glass, plastic bottles, cans, etc.) right in with the food that is being thrown away. Neither the manager of the complex nor the owners of the building has bought any new containers for items that are supposed to be recycled. So what else can everybody do but mix his trash together? Either the manager or the owners is responsible for breaking the law here. Not us! Meanwhile, trash cans in the downtown area is overflowing with garbage, and vacant lots all around the city is littered with soda cans, broken glass, and paper. The owner and publisher of your newspaper, Stanford Black, have always been a supporter of a clean environment. I urge your paper to take leadership in solving this problem.

---

8 | Interview someone about his or her family or close friends. Ask about brothers, sisters, children, activities, and so on. Then write a paragraph of five or six sentences summarizing what you learned. Make sure that you have correct subject-verb and pronoun-antecedent agreement. Write the paragraph using the forms used in informal English. Exchange papers with a partner. Edit each other's paragraph. Then rewrite your paragraphs, if necessary, and submit them to your teacher.

Review Test

I *Fill in the blanks with **a / an** or **the**, or leave a blank if no article is needed.*

According to ___the___ National Weather Service, _____ cyclones are _____ areas of
1.   2.   3.
circulating winds that rotate counterclockwise in _____ Northern Hemisphere and clockwise
4.
in _____ Southern Hemisphere. They are generally accompanied by some kind of _____
5.   6.
precipitation and by _____ stormy weather. _____ tornadoes and _____ hurricanes
7.   8.   9.
are _____ types of cyclones, as are _____ typhoons, which are _____ storms that
10.   11.   12.
occur in _____ western Pacific Ocean.
13.

_____ hurricane is _____ cyclone that forms over _____ tropical oceans and seas
14.   15.   16.
and has _____ winds of at least 74 miles _____ hour. _____ hurricane rotates in
17.   18.   19.
_____ shape of _____ oval or _____ circle. _____ hurricanes can cause
20.   21.   22.   23.
_____ great environmental damage. _____ Hurricane Charley, which hit Jamaica, Cuba,
24.   25.
_____ west coast of Florida, and the Carolinas in August 2004, caused _____ extreme
26.   27.
devastation. In terms of _____ environmental damage, _____ Hurricane Charley is one of
28.   29.
_____ most destructive hurricanes ever to hit _____ United States. More than 20 people
30.   31.
died because of _____ Charley's effects.
32.

II *Each of the following sentences contains one mistake in the use of articles. Correct each sentence by rewriting the incorrect phrase.*

1. One of the best things we can do to help the environment is to encourage the recycling.

   to encourage recycling

2. Bats are mammals, not the birds.

   _____

3. An orangutan is humanlike ape living in the jungles of Borneo and Sumatra.

   _____

4. The Mesozoic era was third of the four major eras of geologic time.

   _____

5. Jurassic period was the period of the Mesozoic era when dinosaurs were present and birds first appeared.

   _____

6. The euro is official currency of the European Union.

   _____

7. The meltdown is an unplanned melting of a nuclear reactor's core.

   _____

8. Statues on Easter Island were apparently carved and erected by the Easter Islanders themselves.

   _____

9. Rain forests in South America are being cleared to make fields for raising the cattle.

   _____

10. Telephone was invented in 1876 by Alexander Graham Bell.

   _____

III *Look at the pictures here and on page 176. Write a sentence under each picture in which the noun in parentheses is used in a countable sense, either with **a / an** or in the plural.*

1. (soda)

_____She's drinking a soda._____

_____

2. (furniture)

_____

_____

3. (work)

_____

_____

4. (advice)

Here's what you should do.

_____

_____

5. (people)

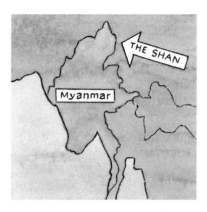

_____

_____

6. (spices)

_____

_____

(continued)

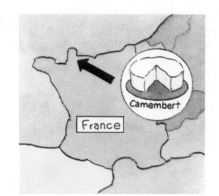

7. (lightning)

_____

_____

8. (cheese)

_____

_____

IV *Complete the conversations by putting the modifiers in the correct order.*

1. A: It feels like a _____ *sweltering summer* _____ day here, even though it's spring.
   a. (summer / sweltering)
   What's it like where you are?

   B: Here it feels like a _____ day. I envy you.
   b. (chilly / winter)

2. A: What do you think of my _____ tie?
   a. (silk / pink / new)
   B: It makes you look like a _____ businessman.
   b. (European / young / handsome)

3. A: We were finally able to build a _____ house. It's just
   a. (brick / new / beautiful)
   what we've always wanted.

   B: It sounds great. Maybe we could do the same. We feel like we're living in a

   _____ cabin.
   b. (little / dirty / old)

V *Complete the conversations with the correct quantifiers, choosing from the words in parentheses.*

1. A: Let's get off this freeway. There's just too _____ *much* _____ traffic.
   a. (much / many)

   B: Yeah, let's. The _____ *number* _____ of people driving is incredible. I've never seen this
   b. (amount / number)
   _____ *many* _____ cars.
   c. (much / many)

2. A: Can you bring soda to the picnic? I don't have _____.
   a. (some / any)
   B: Yes, I think I've got _____ left over from the party.
   b. (some / any)

3. **A:** How do you feel about your new job? Do you have as _____ responsibilities
                                                                a. **(much / many)**

   as you used to?

   B: The job is great. I have about the same _____ of work as before, but I have
                                                  b. **(amount / number)**

   _____ stress and _____ problems.
       c. **(less / fewer)**   d. **(less / fewer)**

4. **A:** How do you think you did on the test? I think I only missed _____
                                                      a. **(a few / a little)**

   questions. In fact, I hope I didn't miss _____ questions at all.
                                           b. **(some / any)**

   B: Well, I think I probably made _____ mistakes, but I have the feeling I did
                                      c. **(few / a few)**

   well overall.

5. **A:** Mr. President, do you believe _____ of your proposed legislation will be
                                           a. **(much / many)**

   passed by Congress during this session?

   B: Yes, I think _____ of our proposals will be approved. We're not making
                         b. **(a great deal / a great many)**

   _____ assumptions, though. We still have _____ work to
       c. **(no / any)**   d. **(a great deal of / a great many)**

   do.

   A: The polls say there's _____ support nationwide for your military program.
                         e. **(little / a little)**

   Isn't that going to hurt you?

   B: Not in the long run, no. _____ of the voters actually support the military
                         f. **(Few / A few)**

   system the way it is now. I think we'll be successful.

VI *Circle the letter of the one underlined word or phrase in each sentence that is not correct.*

1. <u>The journey</u> from Los Angeles to San Diego is <u>a</u> <u>three-hours</u>   **A B Ⓒ D**
       A   B   C
   trip if <u>the traffic</u> isn't heavy.
       D

2. <u>The chief executive officer</u> of <u>the company</u> I work for lives in   **A B C D**
       A   B
   <u>beautiful condominium</u> in <u>a 10-story building</u>.
       C   D

3. <u>Plan</u> to build <u>an extensive monorail system</u> is <u>a</u> <u>citizen-initiated proposal</u>.   **A B C D**
     A   B   C   D

4. One of <u>the most famous inventions</u> in <u>the history</u> of <u>humankind</u> is <u>a wheel</u>.   **A B C D**
            A   B   C   D

(continued)

5. The <u>two first</u> films shown in last weekend's film series were   **A B C D**
  A   B
  <u>the most popular ones</u> in <u>the series</u>.
  CD

6. <u>The extinction</u> of <u>the dinosaurs</u> is still <u>a matter</u> of debate   **A B C D**
  ABC
  in <u>scientific community</u>.
  D

7. Vancouver, <u>the largest city</u> in <u>Canadian Southwest</u>, is   **A B C D**
  AB
  <u>the closest major Canadian port</u> to <u>the Far East</u>.
  CD

8. When Sarah was a child, she disliked <u>cauliflower</u>, <u>carrots</u>, <u>bean</u>,   **A B C D**
  ABC
  and <u>most other vegetables</u>.
  D

9. <u>The Wheelers'</u> <u>10-years-old daughter</u>, Melanie, was born in   **A B C D**
  AB
  <u>the city of Rotterdam</u> in <u>the Netherlands</u>.
  CD

10. Ralph is in <u>the intensive care ward</u> of <u>the city hospital</u> after   **A B C D**
  AB
  being struck by <u>a lightning</u> on <u>a camping trip</u>.
  CD

VII   *Go back to your answers to Exercise VI. Write the correct form for each item that you believe is incorrect.*

1. _____ *three-hour* _____   6. _____

2. _____   7. _____

3. _____   8. _____

4. _____   9. _____

5. _____   10. _____

▶ *To check your answers, go to the Answer Key on page RT-2.*

PART
IV

Adjective Clauses

Grammar in Context

BEFORE YOU READ

1 *Complete this sentence with the one adjective that best describes your personality: "I am a person who is _____."*

2 *Is it helpful to classify people into personality types or to place yourself in a personality category? Why or why not?*

🎧 *Read this article about personality types.*

WHAT TYPE ARE YOU ?

Sunflowers

Four o'clocks

   Suppose you attend a party where there are several people you know well. The hosts have a new party game that involves asking everyone to compare each person to a flower. Which flower would you choose for each person and which flower for yourself? Are you the kind of person who resembles a sunflower, open to the world most of the time? Or are you more like a four o'clock, someone who opens up only at special moments?

   This may sound like just an amusing activity, but there is a science of personality identification that grew out of the work of Swiss psychologist Carl Jung and that of two American women, Katharine Briggs and her daughter, Isabel Briggs Myers. After studying Jung's work, Briggs and her daughter developed a system of 4 personality dimensions and 16 different personality types. Based on this system, they developed a test, which has been refined many times over the decades and has been taken by millions of people. Take a look at the following descriptions based on the Myers-Briggs test. Try to place people you know into one or more of the categories.* You may learn something about your co-workers, friends, loved ones, and yourself.

* To learn more about personality type and to determine your type, visit www.personality.type.com.

WHAT TYPE ARE YOU?

Category 1: extrovert or introvert. This category has to do with the way that people direct their energy. An extrovert is basically a person whose energies are activated by being with others. An introvert is essentially a person whose energies are activated by being alone. Mary is a good example of an extrovert. She's the kind of person whom others consider shy, but there's no correlation between shyness and either introversion or extroversion. At a party, Mary starts to open up and get energized once she meets some people who make her feel comfortable. Her friend Bill is the opposite. He isn't shy at all, but after he's been at a party for a while, he's tired and ready to go home. He finds the conversation interesting enough but is just as likely to be imagining a time when he was hiking alone in the mountains.

Category 2: sensor or intuitive. This category has to do with the kind of information we notice and remember easily. Sensors are practical people who notice what is going on around them and rely on past experiences to make conclusions. Intuitives are more interested in relationships between things or people, tending to focus on what *might* be. Consider Jack and Barbara, who have been married for years. At a party, Jack, whose parents own a sofa company, notices that their hosts have bought a new sofa and asks where they bought it. Barbara is less interested in the sofa and more interested in the tense way the hosts are talking with each other. Did they have a fight? Jack is the sensor and Barbara the intuitive.

Category 3: thinker or feeler. This category is about the way that we make conclusions. Thinkers are those who tend to make decisions objectively, on the basis of logic. Feelers make decisions based on their personal values and how they feel about choices. Helen and Gary are at a bank applying for a loan. The loan officer tells them they owe too much on their credit cards and will have to pay off their debt before they can borrow money. This makes perfect sense to Helen, which classifies her as a thinker. Gary's reaction is quite different. The loan officer, who makes Gary feel criticized, is only trying to do his job. However, Gary takes the loan officer's comments personally, which classifies him as a feeler.

Category 4: judger or perceiver. This dimension is about the kind of environment that makes us feel most comfortable. Judgers are people who prefer a predictable environment. They like to make decisions and have things settled. Perceivers are more interested in keeping their options open, preferring to experience as much of the world as possible. Consider Tim and Samantha. Tim, who always has a plan for everything, gets impatient with Samantha when he calls her to plan a time when they can get together. Tim wants things to be definite; Samantha wants to keep her options flexible.

So we're left with this question: What good is classifying people? It certainly doesn't give us any magic powers or tools for relationships. But it can give us insight. It can help us understand others better, and perhaps minimize or reduce conflict. Best of all, it can help us understand ourselves.

AFTER YOU READ

What does each sentence mean? Circle the correct answer.

1. An extrovert is basically a person whose energies are activated by being with others.
   a. Extroverts get energy from others.
   b. Others get energy from extroverts.

2. She's the kind of person whom others consider shy.
   a. She thinks others are shy.
   b. Others think she's shy.

3. Gary takes the loan officer's comments personally, which classifies him as a feeler.
   a. We classify Gary as a feeler.
   b. We classify the loan officer as a feeler.

Grammar Presentation

ADJECTIVE CLAUSES: REVIEW AND EXPANSION

ADJECTIVE CLAUSES: PLACEMENT

Main Clause		Adjective Clause	
	Noun / Pronoun	Relative Pronoun	
They met	a woman	**who**	**teaches psychology**.
I've read	everything	**that**	**discusses her work**.

Main . . .		Adjective Clause		. . . Clause
Noun / Pronoun	Relative Pronoun			
The woman	**who**	**teaches psychology**		is also a writer.
Everything	**that**	**discusses her work**		is very positive.

RELATIVE PRONOUNS: *WHO, WHOM, WHICH, THAT*

Subjects: *Who, Which, That*					
People			Things		
I have a friend	**who**	loves to talk.	This is a book	**which**	is useful.
I have friends	**that**	love to talk.	These are books	**that**	are useful.

Objects: *Who(m), Which, That, Ø**					
People			Things		
This is the doctor	**who(m)** **that** Ø	we consulted.	This is the test	**which** **that** Ø	he gave us.

*Ø = no pronoun

WHOSE TO INDICATE POSSESSION

Whose + Noun	
People	Things
She is the woman **whose son** is so famous.	It's the book **whose reviews** were so good.
She is the woman **whose son** I am tutoring.	It's the book **whose reviews** I have just read.

WHERE AND *WHEN* IN ADJECTIVE CLAUSES

Where		
Place		
I remember the café	**where**	we met.

When		
Time		
I remember the day	**(when)** **(that)** Ø	we parted.

ADJECTIVE CLAUSES: IDENTIFYING OR NONIDENTIFYING

Identifying Clause
No Commas
The woman **who / that created the test** studied psychology. The test **which / that / Ø she created** describes personality types.

Nonidentifying Clause
Commas
Katharine Briggs, **who created the test**, studied psychology. The Myers-Briggs test, **which she created**, describes personality types.

GRAMMAR NOTES	EXAMPLES
1. A sentence with an **adjective clause** can be seen as a combination of two sentences.	*John is a man. + He works hard.* = • John is a man **who works hard**. *Mary is interesting. + I like her a lot.* = • Mary, **whom I like a lot**, is interesting.
2. An adjective clause is a **dependent clause**. It modifies a noun or a pronoun in a main clause. An adjective clause often begins with a **relative pronoun**: *who*, *whom*, *which*, or *that*. It can also begin with *whose*, *when*, or *where*. The word that begins an adjective clause usually comes directly after the noun or pronoun that the clause modifies. An adjective clause can occur after a main clause or inside a main clause.	• Frank, **who is an introvert**, spends a lot of time alone. • Let's do something **that is fun**. • Toronto, **which is the largest city in Canada**, is a beautiful place. • Harriet is a woman **whom I respect**. • The house **that we bought** is in the suburbs.
3. To refer to people, use *who* and *that* as the subjects of verbs in adjective clauses. To refer to things, use *which* and *that* as the subjects of verbs in adjective clauses. **USAGE NOTE:** *That* is less formal than *who* or *which*. The verb in an adjective clause agrees with the noun or pronoun that the clause modifies. ▶ **BE CAREFUL!** Do not use a double subject in an adjective clause.	• The Ings are the **people who** bought the house. • Sam is the **man that** lives next door to me. • Math is the **subject which** is the easiest for me. • This is the **car that** is the nicest. • There are many **people who have taken** this personality test. • This test is the **one that is** the best known. • Extroverts are people **who like to be with others**. NOT Extroverts are people who ~~they~~ like to be with others.

4. To refer to people, use **whom**, **who**, and **that** as the **objects** of verbs in adjective clauses. *Whom* is very formal. *Who* and *that* are less formal and used in conversation and informal writing. *That* is the least formal.

- **Mr. Pitkin**, **whom** I mentioned yesterday, is my boss.
- Mr. Pitkin was the **person who** I mentioned.
- Mr. Pitkin was the **person that** I mentioned.

To refer to things, use **which** and **that** as the **objects** of verbs in adjective clauses. *Which* is a bit more formal.

- The **test which** I took was difficult.
- The **test that** I took was difficult.

In conversation and informal writing, you can sometimes omit the relative pronoun if it is an object. This is the most common spoken form. *(See note 8 for more information on omitting relative pronouns.)*

- Mr. Pitkin is the man **I mentioned.**
- The test **I took** was difficult.

The verb in an adjective clause agrees with the subject of the clause, not with the object.

- The Mendozas are the people **that Sally sees frequently**.

  NOT The Mendozas are the people that Sally ~~see~~ frequently.

5. Use **whose** to introduce an adjective clause that indicates **possession**. We use *whose* to replace *his / her / its / their* + noun. An adjective clause with *whose* can modify people or things.

Ken is the man + We met his wife. =
- Ken is the man **whose wife we met**.

It's a theory. + Its origins go back many years. =
- It's a theory **whose origins go back many years**.

▶ **BE CAREFUL!** *Whose* cannot be omitted.

- Harvey, **whose house we're renting**, is a lawyer.

  NOT Harvey, ~~house we're renting,~~ is a lawyer.

(continued)

6. You can use **where** to introduce an adjective clause that modifies a noun of **place**. *Where* replaces the word *there*.

This is the restaurant. + We ate there. =

- This is the restaurant **where we ate**.

▶ BE CAREFUL! Use an adjective clause with **where** only if you can restate the location with the word **there**. Do not use an adjective clause with *where* if the location cannot be stated in this way.

- Chihuahua is the town **where I was born**. = Chihuahua is the town. I was born **there**.

  NOT Rio de Janeiro is a city ~~where has beautiful scenery~~.

- Rio de Janeiro is a city **that has beautiful scenery**.

NOTE: *Where* can be replaced by *which* or *that* + a preposition, such as *in*, *at*, or *for*. In this type of adjective clause, *which / that* can be omitted.

- This is the building **where** she works.

- This is the building (**that**) she works **in**.

---

7. You can use **when** or **that** to begin an adjective clause that modifies a noun of **time**. You can omit *when* and *that* in this type of adjective clause. The sentence without *when* or *that* is informal.

- I can't think of a time **when / that I wasn't happy**.

- I can't think of a time **I wasn't happy**.

---

8. An adjective clause that distinguishes one person or thing from another is called **identifying** or essential. The clause is not enclosed in commas.

- The man **who delivers the mail** is friendly.

An adjective clause that adds extra information but does not distinguish one person or thing from another is called **nonidentifying** or nonessential. The clause is enclosed in commas.

- The man, **who delivers the mail**, is friendly.

▶ BE CAREFUL!

a. You can omit relative pronouns only in identifying adjective clauses. You cannot omit the relative pronoun in a nonidentifying adjective clause.

- The man **you met on Friday** is Tarik.
- That's Tarik, **who you met on Friday**.

  NOT That's Tarik, ~~you met on Friday~~.

b. Don't use **that** as a relative pronoun in a nonidentifying clause.

- The Myers-Briggs test, **which I took a long time ago**, has proved to be accurate.

  NOT The Myers-Briggs test, ~~that I took a long time ago~~, has proved to be accurate.

You can use **which** informally to refer to an entire previous idea.

- **Helen is hardworking, which** impresses me.

In formal writing and speech, use a noun at the beginning of a **which** clause.

- **Helen is hardworking, a characteristic which** impresses me.

Focused Practice

1 | DISCOVER THE GRAMMAR

A *Look at these sentences based on the opening reading. Could the relative pronoun be replaced by the relative pronoun in parentheses without creating a different meaning or making an incorrect sentence?*

yes **1.** Are you the kind of person **who** resembles a sunflower? (that)

_____ **2.** There is a science of personality identification **that** grew out of the work of Swiss psychologist Carl Jung. (which)

_____ **3.** Based on this system, they developed a test, **which** has been refined many times over the decades. (that)

_____ **4.** She's the kind of person **whom** others consider shy. (that)

_____ **5.** He is just as likely to be imagining a time **when** he was hiking alone in the mountains. (that)

_____ **6.** Jack and Barbara, **who** have been married for years, are good examples. (whom)

_____ **7.** The loan officer, **who** makes Gary feel criticized, is only trying to do his job. (that)

_____ **8.** Judgers are people **who** prefer a predictable environment. (which)

B *Find three sentences in the reading in which the relative pronoun has been omitted. Add a correct relative pronoun to each sentence.*

1. _____

_____

2. _____

_____

3. _____

_____

C *Look at these sentences based on the opening reading. Underline the adjective clause in each sentence. Then say whether the clause is identifying (**I**) or nonidentifying (**NI**).*

_____*I*_____ 1. Suppose you attend a party <u>where there are a lot of people</u>.

_____ 2. Are you the kind of person who resembles a sunflower?

_____ 3. They developed a test, which has been refined many times over the decades.

_____ 4. An introvert is a person whose energies are activated by being alone.

_____ 5. Mary starts to open up once she meets some people who make her feel comfortable.

_____ 6. He is imagining a time when he was hiking alone in the mountains.

_____ 7. Good examples are Jack and Barbara, who have been married for years.

_____ 8. Jack, whose parents own a sofa company, notices that their hosts have bought a new sofa.

_____ 9. The loan officer, who makes Gary feel criticized, is only trying to do his job.

_____ 10. However, Gary takes his comments personally, which classifies him a feeler.

2 | ABOUT MY FAMILY
Grammar Notes 3, 5–6, 8

Circle the correct relative pronoun in each sentence.

1. I come from a family ((that) / whom) has eight members.

2. I have three sisters and two brothers, (that / which) made things pretty crowded when we were growing up.

3. Our house, (which / that) is four stories high, has eight bedrooms.

4. The members of my family, (who / whom) are all interesting, fit nicely into the Meyers-Briggs personality categories.

5. My mother and father, (who / whom) both like to be with people a great deal, are extroverts.

6. My favorite brother, with (who / whom) I still spend a lot of time, is a perceiver and an introvert.

7. My other brother, (who / which) is a judger, is a great guy but always has to be right.

8. My favorite sister, (who / whose) fiancé is the same age as I am, is an intuitive.

9. Of my other two sisters, the one (no pronoun / which) I am closer to is a feeler.

10. I'm less close to the sister (who / no pronoun) is much older than I am. She's a thinker.

3 | PEOPLE IN THE WORKPLACE

Dolores Atwood, a personnel officer for a publishing company, is writing an evaluation of the employees in her department who are being considered for promotion. Complete her sentences using one of the pronouns in parentheses. Put the verbs in the correct form.

KIRBY, BROWN, AND EAGER

Confidential

Personnel Evaluation

Elaine Correa has only been with us for a year but is definitely ready for promotion,

_____which is not surprising_____ given the excellent recommendations
       1. (that / which) / not / be surprising

from the business _____ before.
      2. (which / where) / she / work

Burt Drysdale has proven himself to be a team player, amazingly. He had some prob-

lems at the company _____ previously, and
      3. (where / that) / he / work for

during the first month _____ here, he irritated
      4. (which / no pronoun) / he / work

everyone. I do recommend him for promotion.

Alice Anderdoff is not performing up to expectations, _____
      5. (that / which) / bother

_____ me because I was the one who recruited her. There was an early period

_____ excellent, but I don't believe she should
      6. (when / which) / her performance / be

be promoted at this time.

Mel Tualapa is an employee _____ because
      7. (which / no pronoun) / everyone / like

he's congenial and hardworking, but he can't be promoted yet because he's only been with us

for six months.

Tom Curran is an employee _____ often
      8. (that / no pronoun) / have

been ill and is consistently late to work. This is mystifying because at the time

_____ he seemed to be a model employee. I
      9. (when / which) / he / be hired

don't recommend him at this time.

4 | ABOUT MY JOB

Combine each pair of sentences into one sentence with an adjective clause, using the relative pronoun in parentheses. Use the first sentence in each pair as the main clause. Add commas where necessary.

1. The company makes computers. I work for the company. (that)

   The company that I work for makes computers.

2. The company has existed for 15 years. It is named Excelsior Computer. (which)

3. The building is located downtown. We do most of our work in the building. (where)

4. The office has been remodeled. I work in the office. (that)

5. Darren Corgatelli is the boss. His wife is my aunt. (whose)

6. Darren is an excellent boss. I've known Darren since I was a child. (whom)

7. Sarah Corgatelli keeps the company running smoothly. She is Darren's wife. (who)

8. I joined the company in 1995. I graduated from college then. (when)

9. I really admire my colleagues. Their advice has been invaluable. (whose)

10. Part of my job is telemarketing. I like telemarketing the least. (which)

5 | FORMAL AND INFORMAL

Read two reports by an attorney. Complete the spoken report with informal adjective clauses, omitting relative pronouns if possible and using contractions. Complete the formal written report with formal adjective clauses. Do not omit relative pronouns, and do not use contractions. Put all verbs in the correct forms.

Spoken Report

Our client is a guy _____*who's been in trouble*_____ for minor offenses, but I don't think
           1. (have / be / in trouble)

he's a murderer, _____ I feel comfortable defending him.
                        2. (be / why)

He did time in the penitentiary from 2002 to 2004, and according to all the reports he was

a person _____. Since he got out of jail in 2004, he's
              3. (the other prisoners / respected)

had a good employment record with Textrix, an electronics company

_____. The psychological reports on him show that
       4. (he / have / be working)

when he was in prison he was a person _____ well balanced
                                            5. (the psychiatrists / consider)

and even-tempered, _____ I don't think he's guilty.
                          6. (be / the reason)

Formal Written Report

Our client is a man _____ for minor offenses, but I do not
                          7. (have / be / in trouble)

believe that he is a murderer, _____ comfortable defending him.
                                      8. (an opinion / make me)

He served time in the penitentiary from 2002 to 2004, and according to all the reports he was a

person _____. Since he was released from prison in 2004, he
            9. (the other prisoners / respect)

has had a good employment record with Textrix, an electronics company

_____. His psychological profile suggests that when
        10. (he / have / be working)

he was in prison he was a person _____ well balanced and
                                        11. (the psychiatrists / consider)

even-tempered, _____ believe that he is not guilty.
                      12. (evidence / make me)

6 EDITING

Read the letter from a college student to his parents. There are eight mistakes in the use of adjective clauses. The first one is already corrected. Find and correct seven more.

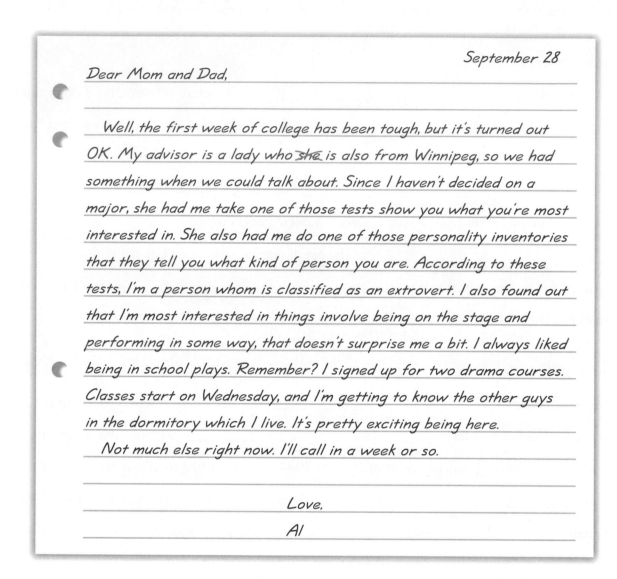

September 28

Dear Mom and Dad,

Well, the first week of college has been tough, but it's turned out OK. My advisor is a lady who ~~she~~ is also from Winnipeg, so we had something when we could talk about. Since I haven't decided on a major, she had me take one of those tests show you what you're most interested in. She also had me do one of those personality inventories that they tell you what kind of person you are. According to these tests, I'm a person whom is classified as an extrovert. I also found out that I'm most interested in things involve being on the stage and performing in some way, that doesn't surprise me a bit. I always liked being in school plays. Remember? I signed up for two drama courses. Classes start on Wednesday, and I'm getting to know the other guys in the dormitory which I live. It's pretty exciting being here.

Not much else right now. I'll call in a week or so.

Love,

Al

Communication Practice

7 | LISTENING 1

🎧 *Read the pairs of sentences. Listen to the conversation. Then listen again and circle the letter of the sentence in each pair that correctly describes what you heard.*

1. a. Bob took the job because it pays well.

　 b. Bob took the job because he likes the work.

2. a. Paperwork makes Bob angry.

　 b. Being assigned to do a lot of paperwork makes Bob angry.

3. a. Bob is irritated because of the kind of person his co-worker is.

　 b. Bob is irritated because he wasn't consulted before being assigned to his co-worker.

4. a. Jennifer is surprised that Bob is irritated.

　 b. Jennifer is surprised that Bob took the job.

5. a. Bob's feelings about his co-workers are making him wonder about himself.

　 b. Not investigating the company is making Bob wonder about himself.

8 | DISCUSSION

How can you deal with someone you are not getting along with? Talk with a partner. Then share your views with the class.

> **Example:** **A:** What do you do when you have someone you don't get along with?
> **B:** Well, when there's a problem with someone that I can't solve, I . . .

9 | LISTENING 2

🎧 *Read the pairs of sentences. Then read and listen to part of a telephone conversation that Al, a new college student, had with his parents. Circle the letter of the sentence in each pair that correctly describes what you heard.*

1. a. The dormitory has one supervisor.

　 b. The dormitory has more than one supervisor.

2. a. Both of Al's roommates are from Minnesota.

　 b. One of Al's roommates is from Minnesota.

3. a. Al has one English class.

　 b. Al has more than one English class.

(continued)

4. **a.** Al has one history class.

   b. Al has more than one history class.

5. **a.** There is one group of girls living in the dormitory.

   b. There is more than one group of girls living in the dormitory.

6. **a.** Al has one advisor.

   b. Al has more than one advisor.

10 | WRITING

Consider again the personality categories that have been mentioned in this unit, and choose the one which you believe fits you the best. Write two or three paragraphs showing why the category fits you. Include several examples from your own experience.

Example: No single personality type applies perfectly to a person, but for me one comes closer than all the others. The personality category that fits me most closely is "intuitive." First, intuitives are people who depend on their immediate feelings about something instead of their past experiences. For example, . . .

11 | ON THE INTERNET

Do a search on **online personality tests.** *Find a test you consider interesting and take it online. Study the results, and decide if they give an accurate description of your personality. Then report to the class. As a class, discuss how accurate you believe the tests are.*

Adjective Clauses with Prepositions; Adjective Phrases

Grammar in Context

BEFORE YOU READ

1 *Do you like movies? What do you look for in a movie? Do you see movies primarily for entertainment, or do you want a film to be something more?*

2 *Which kind of movie do you like better—one in which you already know what is going to happen, or one in which you don't know what is going to happen?*

Read this movie review.

At the Movies

Hobbits and Other Creatures
by Dartagnan Fletcher

Let me give it to you straight: I'm not a fan of fantasy or science fiction. It was Friday, and I was not looking forward to taking my children to *The Return of the King* that evening. In my day I've seen quite a few fantasy films, most of which bored me silly. Arriving home, I gave my wife several good reasons why she should take the kids and not I, all of which she dismissed quickly by saying, "You promised you'd take them, dear, and I made other plans." Once we were at the theater, I settled down for a boring evening, but you know how it goes: Sometimes you hate the things you expect to love and love the ones you expect to hate. Well, that's what happened: I loved this movie.

The Ring of Power

In case you haven't read J.R.R. Tolkien's *The Lord of the Rings* or seen either of the preceding two movies in the trilogy, you'll need a brief plot summary: At some time in the distant past, the evil Dark Lord made a number of Rings of Power. Unfortunately for him, he lost the most powerful ring, which causes anyone putting it on to become invisible, and which eventually corrupts anyone continuing to wear it. This addictive ring falls into the hands of the hobbits, small people who live in a tiny country called the Shire. The movie (and the book on which it is based) is about the struggle between the powers of good and evil. The forces of good, representatives of which are hobbits, men, a good wizard, an elf, and a dwarf, are trying to destroy the ring. The forces of evil, represented by the Dark Lord, orcs, and a bad wizard, must get the ring back if they are to have total control

(continued)

Hobbits and Other Creatures

over the world. A young hobbit named Frodo Baggins is appointed to destroy the ring by throwing it into the volcano where it was made. With him is his friend and gardener, Sam Gamgee. In *The Return of the King*, the last episode of the trilogy, Frodo and Sam are painfully nearing their goal. Will they make it?

If you're the type of person inclined to ask, "Why should I want to see a silly fantasy movie?" I would just say this: Anyone interested in cinema should see this film. It has good acting, awesome special effects, interesting characters, and a compelling story and theme. Let me make my case for each of these:

Acting: *The Return of the King* has many prominent actors, all of whom distinguish themselves: Elijah Wood plays Frodo, the hero; Viggo Mortensen stars as the king who "returns"; Ian McKellen is Gandalf, the good wizard; and Sean Astin is Frodo's loyal friend and servant Sam. For my money, Astin steals the show.

Special effects: Normally I'm not a fan of special effects since I usually view them as attempts to cover up a weak story. This time, however, they work. The world of Tolkien's book is so strange that it needs special effects to make the creatures and battle scenes seem real. The best special effect of all is the character Gollum, a miserable creature who once possessed the Ring of Power and now wants to

Gandalf, a wizard

Gollum

Orcs

get it back. Real-life actor Andy Serkis plays the prototype of Gollum, but Gollum in the film is a computer-generated character based on Serkis's prototype. It doesn't matter, though; he looks real.

Characters: Tolkien's characters, most of whom are interesting and believable, deal with the same struggles and insecurities that we all do, including greed, anger, bravery, and dishonesty. Let me just give you this challenge: Who is really the main character? Gandalf the wizard? Aragorn the king? Frodo? Or Sam? I'll leave it to you to decide for yourself.

Theme: Ultimately, what is more compelling than the struggle between good and evil, between right and wrong? Many, if not most, movies deal with this question in one form or another. *The Return of the King* (all three episodes, really) does so better than most.

By the way, I must assure my readers that I will not be a member of that group responsible for destroying your pleasure by revealing the ending—in particular, why Frodo ends up with only nine fingers. Find out for yourself by seeing the movie. There's a rumor that, with the reissue of *The Lord of the Rings*, the lines to get in will be long, which means you'd better take along a sleeping bag and a picnic lunch. The wait will be worth it. Rating: Four stars out of a possible four. ★★★★

AFTER YOU READ

What noun does the underlined word refer to? Circle the correct answer.

1. I gave my wife several good reasons why she should take the kids and not I, all of <u>which</u> she dismissed quickly.

   a. wife   **b.** reasons   **c.** kids

2. The movie (and the book on <u>which</u> it is based) is about the struggle between the powers of good and evil.

   a. movie   **b.** struggle   **c.** book

3. Tolkien's characters, most of <u>whom</u> are interesting and believable, deal with the same struggles and insecurities that we all do.

   a. characters   **b.** struggles   **c.** insecurities

Grammar Presentation

ADJECTIVE CLAUSES WITH PREPOSITIONS, QUANTIFIERS, OR NOUNS; ADJECTIVE PHRASES

ADJECTIVE CLAUSES WITH PREPOSITIONS

Main Clause	Adjective Clause			
People / Things	**Preposition**	**Relative Pronoun**		**Preposition**
	to	**whom**	she was talking.	
He's the actor		**who(m)** **that** **Ø***	she was talking	**to.**
	for	**which**	he works.	
It's the studio		**which** **that** **Ø**	he works	**for.**
That's the director		**whose**	movies I told you	**about.**
That's the movie			director I spoke	**of.**

*Ø = no pronoun

(continued)

ADJECTIVE CLAUSES WITH QUANTIFIERS

Main Clause	Adjective Clause			
People / Things	Quantifier	*Of*	Relative Pronoun	
I have many friends,	all most a number		**whom**	are actors.
I was in a lot of movies,	some a few several	**of**	**which**	were successes.
That's the director,	**a couple**		**whose**	movies are classics.
That's the movie,	**two**			actors got awards.

ADJECTIVE CLAUSES WITH NOUNS

Main Clause	Adjective Clause		
Things	Noun	*Of Which*	
He made comedies,	**an example**	**of which**	is *Some Like It Hot*.
I love that series,	**an episode**		she directed.

REDUCING ADJECTIVE CLAUSES TO ADJECTIVE PHRASES

	Adjective Clause
He's the actor	**who's from** the film school.
I saw the film	**which is based** on that book.
That's the man	**who was in charge** of lighting.
I read the scripts	**that are on my desk**.

	Adjective Phrase
He's the actor	**from** the film school.
I saw the film	**based** on that book.
That's the man	**in charge** of lighting.
I read the scripts	**on my desk**.

CHANGING ADJECTIVE CLAUSES TO ADJECTIVE PHRASES

	Adjective Clause
He's the actor	**who plays** the king.
Troy is an epic	**which stars** Brad Pitt.
It's a love story	**that takes** place in Rome.

	Adjective Phrase
He's the actor	**playing** the king.
Troy is an epic	**starring** Brad Pitt.
It's a love story	**taking** place in Rome.

GRAMMAR NOTES	EXAMPLES
1. The relative pronouns *who(m)*, *that*, *which*, and *whose* + noun can be used as **objects of prepositions** in adjective clauses.	• Bill is the man **to whom** I spoke. • That's the film **to which** I went.
Sentences with the preposition at the beginning of the clause are formal; sentences with the preposition at the end of the clause are informal.	• She's the director **to whom** I wrote. • She's the director **whom** I wrote **to**.
NOTE: A preposition can come at the beginning of the clause before *who(m)*, *which*, and *whose*. It cannot come at the beginning in a clause with *that*.	• It is the studio **for which** he works. • NOT It is the studio ~~for that~~ he works.
We can omit the relative pronouns *who(m)*, *that*, and *which* after a preposition. When we do this, the preposition moves to the end of the clause.	• She's the critic **we spoke of**. • That's the screenwriter **I read about**.
▶ **BE CAREFUL!** *Whose* cannot be omitted.	• He's the actor **whose** ~~films I go to~~. • NOT He's the actor ~~films I go to~~.
Remember that there are two types of adjective clauses: identifying (essential) and nonidentifying (nonessential).	• The film **to which I'm referring** is *Ran*. *(identifying)* • *Ran*, **to which I'm referring**, is good. *(nonidentifying)*
2. Some adjective clauses have the pattern **quantifier** + *of* + **relative pronoun**.	• The film has many stars, **few of whom** I recognized. • He made eight films, **all of which** I like.
Quantifiers occur only in clauses with *whom*, *which*, and *whose*. These clauses may refer to **people** or **things**. These clauses are formal.	
If a clause with a quantifier occurs within the main clause, it is enclosed in commas. If it occurs **after** the main clause, a comma precedes it.	• Her books, **most of which I've read**, are popular. • I like her books, **most of which I've read**.
3. Some adjective clauses have the pattern **noun** + *of which*. These clauses refer only to **things**.	• Musicals, **an example of which** is *Chicago*, are still popular. NOT Actors, ~~an example of which is Al Pacino,~~ are still popular.
If a clause with a noun + *of which* occurs within the main clause, it is enclosed in commas. If it occurs **after** the main clause, a comma precedes it.	• Strikes, **occurrences of which may delay filming**, are uncommon. • She has reviewed films, an **example of which is** *Tampopo*.

(continued)

4. We sometimes **shorten adjective clauses** to **adjective phrases** with the same meaning.

Remember that a clause is a group of words that has a subject and a verb. A phrase is a group of words that doesn't have both a subject and a verb.

- Anyone **who is interested in drama** should see this play. *(adjective clause)*
- Anyone **interested in drama** should see this play. *(adjective phrase)*

---

5. To shorten an adjective clause with a *be* verb, **reduce** the clause to an adjective phrase by deleting the relative pronoun and the *be* verb.

▶ BE CAREFUL! Adjective clauses with *be* verbs can be reduced only when *who*, *which*, or *that* is the subject pronoun of the clause

If an adjective clause needs commas, the corresponding phrase also needs commas.

- *Titanic*, **which was directed by James Cameron**, won many awards.
- *Titanic*, **directed by James Cameron**, won many awards.
- I met Chris Rock, **whose latest film is a hit.**

  NOT I met Chris Rock, ~~latest film is a hit~~.
- Cher starred in *Moonstruck*, **which was released in 1987**.
- Cher starred in *Moonstruck*, **released in 1987**.

---

6. If there is no *be* verb in the adjective clause, it is often possible to **change** the clause to an adjective phrase. Do this by deleting the relative pronoun and changing the verb to its *-ing* form. You can do this only when *who*, *which*, or *that* is the subject pronoun of the clause.

- *Titanic*, **which stars Leonardo DiCaprio**, is the top-earning film.
- *Titanic*, **starring Leonardo DiCaprio**, is the top-earning film.
- I like any movie **that features Helen Hunt**.
- I like any movie **featuring Helen Hunt**.

Focused Practice

1 | DISCOVER THE GRAMMAR

A *Look again at the opening reading. Find four adjective clauses containing prepositions plus **which** and two containing prepositions plus **whom**. Underline them. Then circle the head noun referred to by each relative pronoun and draw a line between it and the clause.*

(films) . . . <u>most of which bored me silly</u>

B *Look at eight adjective phrases that have been reduced from clauses. Make each adjective phrase a clause by adding a relative pronoun and a verb.*

1. which causes anyone <u>putting it on</u> to become invisible

   who / that puts it on _____

2. which eventually corrupts anyone <u>continuing to wear it</u>

   _____

3. small people who live in a tiny country <u>called the Shire</u>

   _____

4. the forces of evil, <u>represented by</u> the Dark Lord, orcs, and a bad wizard

   _____

5. if you're the type of person <u>inclined to ask</u>

   _____

6. anyone <u>interested in cinema</u>

   _____

7. many prominent actors, <u>including</u> Elijah Wood playing Frodo

   _____

8. a computer-generated character <u>based on</u> Serkis's prototype

   _____

2 | FILM TRIVIA
Grammar Note 2

Complete the following statements about movies using adjective clauses in the form of quantifier + preposition + relative pronoun.

1. Walt Disney's animated productions, _____*most of which are loved by children*_____, are
   (most / be loved by children)

   known all over the world.

2. *Saving Private Ryan* and *Schindler's List*, _____,
   (both / be directed by Steven Spielberg)

   are critical and commercial successes.

3. Roberto Benigni, Wim Wenders, and Lina Wertmüller, _____
   (all / be / highly regarded European directors)

   _____, are not too well known in the United States.

   (continued)

4. *Star Wars, The Empire Strikes Back,* and *Return of the Jedi,* _____
(all / have / earn a great deal of money)

_____, are the middle three films in a nine-part series.

5. Sean Connery and Roger Moore, _____, are from
(both / have / play the role of James Bond)

Britain, while Pierce Brosnan, a more recent Bond, is from Ireland.

6. Richard Gere, Catherine Zeta-Jones, and Renée Zellweger, _____
(none / be known as singers)

_____, surprised everyone with their singing in *Chicago.*

3 | POPULAR MOVIES
Grammar Notes 5–6

Combine each pair of sentences into one sentence with an adjective phrase. Note that in sentence 4, the adjective phrase will come from the second sentence; in all other cases, the adjective phrase will come from the first sentence.

1. *E.T.* was directed by Steven Spielberg. It was the top-earning film until it was passed by *Titanic* and the reissued *Star Wars.*

E.T., directed by Steven Spielberg, was the top-earning film until it was passed by Titanic and the

reissued Star Wars.

2. *Spider-Man* is based on the popular comic book. It is the fifth-highest-earning movie of all time.

_____

_____

3. *The Matrix* and *The Matrix: Reloaded* star Keanu Reeves. They are both very popular.

_____

_____

4. James Cameron has directed many big movies. These include *Titanic, True Lies,* and the *Terminator* films.

_____

_____

5. The Harry Potter novels were written by J. K. Rowling. They have translated well to the screen.

_____

_____

6. *Star Wars, The Empire Strikes Back,* and *Return of the Jedi* feature Harrison Ford, Carrie Fisher, and Mark Hamill. They were conceived, written, and directed by George Lucas.

_____

_____

4 | MOVIE TYPES

Each of these sentences about types of films contains an adjective clause or phrase. Imagine that each sentence was formed from an original pair of sentences. Write the original pairs.

1. Comedies, examples of which are *Legally Blonde*, *Barbershop*, and *Johnny English*, have continued to be popular and successful.

   Comedies have continued to be popular and successful. Examples of these are Legally Blonde, Barbershop, and Johnny English.

2. Many recent science fiction films have been financially successful, including *The Phantom Menace*, *Independence Day*, and *Spider-Man I and II*.

   _____

   _____

3. The top-earning animated films, both of which I've seen, are *The Lion King* and *Shrek*.

   _____

   _____

4. *Chicago*, featuring three well-known actors, was the best picture of 2002.

   _____

   _____

5. Sequels to big movie hits may lose their appeal, causing filmmakers to become more creative.

   _____

   _____

5 | MY MOVIES

Use the items in the box to describe movies you have seen or that you know about. Write a sentence for each item.

directed by	examples of which	featuring
including	quantifier + *of which*	starring

Examples: I've seen a lot of Arnold Schwarzenegger's movies, **including** *Terminator I*, *II*, and *III* and *True Lies*.

Dances with Wolves and *Unforgiven*, **both of which I've seen**, made westerns more popular.

6 | EDITING

Read this letter. There are ten mistakes in the use of adjective clauses and phrases. The first mistake is already corrected. Find and correct nine more. Delete verbs or change pronouns where necessary, but do not change punctuation or add relative pronouns.

Venice Beach Rialto

July 28

Dear Brent,

   Sarah and I are having a great time in Los Angeles. We spent the first day at the beach in Venice and saw where The Sting was filmed— you know, that famous movie ~~starred~~ starring Paul Newman and Robert Redford? Yesterday we went to Universal Studios and learned about all the cinematic tricks, most of that I wasn't aware of. Amazing! The funny thing is that even though you know the illusion presenting on the screen is just an illusion, you still believe it's real when you see the movie. Then we took the tram tour around the premises and saw several actors working, some which I recognized. I felt like jumping off the tram and shouting, "Would everyone is famous please give me your autograph?" In the evening we went to a party at the home of one of Diana's friends, many of them are connected with the movie business. I had a really interesting conversation with a fellow works in the industry who claims that a lot of movies making these days are modeled conceptually after amusement park rides. Just like the rides, the movies start slowly and easily, then they have a lot of twists and turns are calculated to scare you to death, and they end happily. Maybe Pirates of the Caribbean is an example. Pretty fascinating, huh? What next?

   Sorry to spend so much time talking about movies, but you know what an addict I am. Anyway, I'll let you know my arrival time, that I'm not sure of yet, so that you can pick me up at the airport.

                                        Love you lots,

                                        Amanda

Communication Practice

7 | LISTENING

🎧 *Listen to the TV film reviewer give her weekly review. Then listen again to certain of the reviewer's sentences. Write **T** (true) or **F** (false) to indicate if each item correctly restates the sentence that you hear.*

___T___ 1. The film festival can be seen this holiday weekend.

_____ 2. None of these great movies has been shown in more than a decade.

_____ 3. *A Beautiful Mind* is about a character created by director Ron Howard.

_____ 4. Jennifer Connelly won an Oscar for her portrayal of Nash's wife.

_____ 5. *Saving Private Ryan* is about an army captain who is rescued by a soldier in World War II.

_____ 6. *Saving Private Ryan* makes the reviewer cry.

_____ 7. *Chicago* has only one main star.

_____ 8. Michael J. Fox was responsible for launching *Back to the Future*.

_____ 9. All who regard themselves as serious movie buffs must see *Casablanca*.

_____ 10. The reviewer says black-and-white movies are not pretty.

8 | INFORMATION GAP: A MOVIE REVIEW

Work with a partner. Each of you will read a version of a review of the film A Beautiful Mind. *Each version is missing some information. Take turns asking your partner questions to get the missing information.*

Student A, read the review of A Beautiful Mind. *Ask questions and fill in the missing information. Then answer Student B's questions.*

Student B, turn to the Information Gap on page 209 and follow the instructions there.

Example: **A:** What is the movie inspired by?
   B: It is inspired by incidents in the life of John Nash. What was Nash's occupation?
   A: Nash was . . .

(continued)

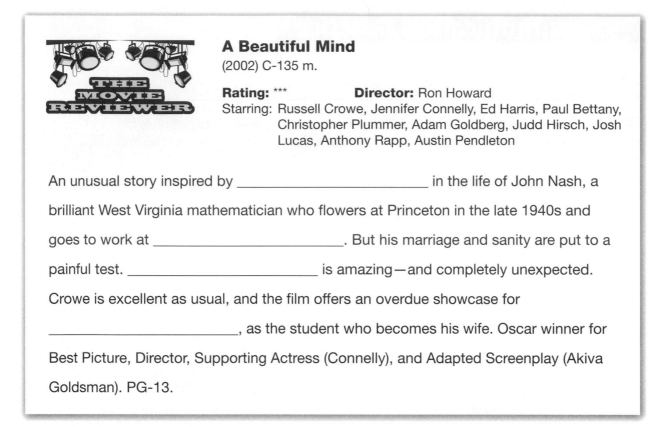

A Beautiful Mind
(2002) C-135 m.

Rating: ***   **Director:** Ron Howard
Starring: Russell Crowe, Jennifer Connelly, Ed Harris, Paul Bettany, Christopher Plummer, Adam Goldberg, Judd Hirsch, Josh Lucas, Anthony Rapp, Austin Pendleton

An unusual story inspired by _____ in the life of John Nash, a brilliant West Virginia mathematician who flowers at Princeton in the late 1940s and goes to work at _____. But his marriage and sanity are put to a painful test. _____ is amazing—and completely unexpected. Crowe is excellent as usual, and the film offers an overdue showcase for _____, as the student who becomes his wife. Oscar winner for Best Picture, Director, Supporting Actress (Connelly), and Adapted Screenplay (Akiva Goldsman). PG-13.

9 | GROUP DISCUSSION: MOVIE RATINGS

*Look at the chart describing the current movie rating system. Then complete the following questionnaire for yourself; circle **yes** or **no**. Discuss your answers with a partner. Then discuss your answers with the class as a whole.*

Example: **A:** I think many movies are too violent today.
             B: I disagree. Sometimes violence is necessary for the director to make the point.

Movie Ratings	Description
G	Suitable for general audiences, all ages.
PG	Parental guidance is suggested; some material may not be appropriate for children.
PG-13	Parents strongly cautioned; some material may not be appropriate for children under 13.
R	Restricted; anyone under 17 must be accompanied by a parent or adult guardian.
NC-17	No one under 17 is admitted.

Movies and Rating Systems		
Movie rating systems are a good idea.	yes	no
Rating systems are enforced in my area.	yes	no
If I want to see a movie, I don't pay attention to the rating.	yes	no
Many movies today are too violent.	yes	no
Movie rating systems should be made stronger.	yes	no

10 | PICTURE DISCUSSION

A *Discuss the picture with a partner, using adjective clauses or phrases whenever possible.*

> **Example:** **A:** In the theater there are a lot of people trying to concentrate on the movie.
> **B:** One woman is talking on her cell phone, annoying the people near her.

B *What is proper behavior at movie theaters? Discuss these points with the class as a whole.*

- Should cell phones be allowed in movie theaters?

- Should moviegoers have to pick up their own trash?

- Should small children be allowed at movies?

- Should people be allowed to talk during showings of movies?

> **Example:** **A:** I don't think cell phones should be allowed in movie theaters.
> **B:** Why not?
> **A:** It's inconsiderate to other people because . . .

11 | WRITING

Write your own movie review in three or more paragraphs. Choose a film that you liked or disliked, but try to be objective in your review. Read your review to the class, and answer any questions your classmates might ask about the movie. Use adjective clauses and phrases as appropriate.

Example: One of the best movies I've seen recently is *Super Size Me*, directed by Morgan Spurlock. Spurlock, fascinated by the recent court case in which two American women sued McDonald's for serving food that was less than healthy, decided to find out whether or not fast food is really unhealthy. His plan was simple: eat nothing but McDonald's food for a month. The film is about his month-long adventure. It's humorous and interesting, and . . .

12 | ON THE INTERNET

Use the Internet to find out the answers to these questions. Report your findings to the class.

- Who has won the most Academy Awards for best actor?
- Who has won the most Academy Awards for best actress?
- What is the all-time top moneymaking film?
- What are the three most expensive movies ever made?
- What male director has made the most films?
- What female director has made the most films?

INFORMATION GAP FOR STUDENT B

Student B, read the review of A Beautiful Mind. *Answer Student A's questions. Then ask your own questions and fill in the missing information.*

Example: **A:** What is the movie inspired by?

B: It is inspired by incidents in the life of John Nash. What was Nash's occupation?

A: Nash was . . .

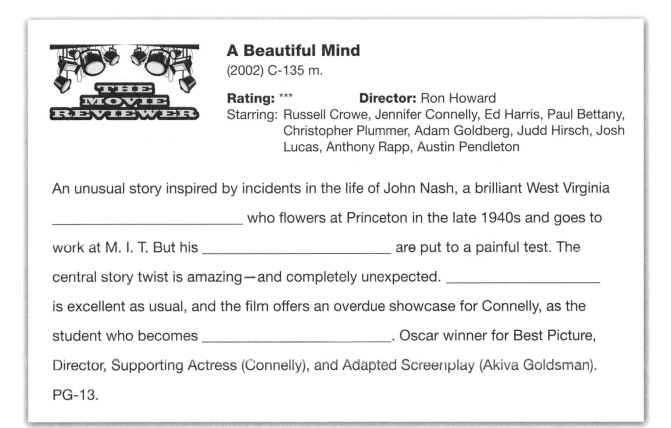

A Beautiful Mind
(2002) C-135 m.

Rating: ***   **Director:** Ron Howard
Starring: Russell Crowe, Jennifer Connelly, Ed Harris, Paul Bettany, Christopher Plummer, Adam Goldberg, Judd Hirsch, Josh Lucas, Anthony Rapp, Austin Pendleton

An unusual story inspired by incidents in the life of John Nash, a brilliant West Virginia

_____ who flowers at Princeton in the late 1940s and goes to

work at M. I. T. But his _____ are put to a painful test. The

central story twist is amazing—and completely unexpected. _____

is excellent as usual, and the film offers an overdue showcase for Connelly, as the

student who becomes _____. Oscar winner for Best Picture,

Director, Supporting Actress (Connelly), and Adapted Screenplay (Akiva Goldsman).

PG-13.

From **Grammar** to **Writing**
Punctuation of Adjective Clauses and Phrases

Remember that the two types of adjective clauses are **identifying** and **nonidentifying**. Identifiying adjective clauses give information essential for distinguishing one person or thing from another. Nonidentifying clauses give additional (= nonessential) information that doesn't identify.

> **Example:** I saw three movies last week. The movie **that I liked best** was *Vanity Fair.*

The adjective clause *that I liked best* is identifying because it says which movie I am talking about. If the clause were removed, the sentence would not make complete sense:

The movie was *Vanity Fair.*

Therefore, the clause is essential for the sentence's meaning.

> *Casablanca,* **which contains the famous song "As Time Goes By,"** is considered a film classic.

The nonidentifying clause *which contains the famous song "As Time Goes By"* adds information about *Casablanca*; however, it is not used to identify. If it were removed, the sentence would still make sense:

Casablanca is considered a film classic.

In speech, identifying clauses have no pauses before or after them and are not enclosed in commas when written. Nonidentifying clauses, on the other hand, do have pauses before and after them when spoken and are enclosed in commas when written.

> **Examples:** A person who needs others to become energized is an extrovert. (identifying; no commas)
>
> James, who comes alive in the presence of friends, is an extrovert. (nonidentifying; commas)

1 Punctuate the following sentences containing adjective clauses. They form a narration.

1. Tom and Sandra, who have been married for more than 30 years, are both outgoing people.^

2. Tom who is clearly an extrovert loves meeting new people.

3. Sandra who is very quick to make friends loves to have friends over for dinner.

4. Tom and Sandra have two married sons both of whom live abroad.

5. The son who is older lives with his family in Britain.

6. The son who is younger lives with his family in southern Italy.

7. Tom and Sandra own a house in the city and one in the country. The one where they spend most of their time is in the city.

8. The house that they spend summers in is located in New Hampshire.

One way to decide whether a clause is identifying or nonidentifying is to ask whether (1) it refers to a unique person or thing or (2) it refers to all the members of a group. If it is either type, it is a nonidentifying clause and needs commas.

My eldest brother, **whose name is Jim**, is a businessman. (refers to my eldest brother, a unique individual; needs commas)

Bats, **which are actually mammals**, are active mostly at night. (refers to all the members of the group—all bats; needs commas)

In contrast, a clause that refers to one or more but not all the members of a group is identifying.

The bats **that live in Carlsbad Caverns** are seen nightly by visiting tourists. (refers to some of the members of the group—a particular group of bats; identifying)

2 | *Punctuate the following pairs of sentences containing adjective clauses. One sentence in each pair is identifying, and one is nonidentifying.*

1. **a.** College students who live close to campuses spend less money on gas.
   b. College students who are expected to study hard have to become responsible for themselves.

2. **a.** People who are the only animals with a capacity for creative language have highly developed brains.
   b. People who live in glass houses shouldn't throw stones.

3. **a.** The car which was invented in the late 19th century has revolutionized modern life.
   b. The car which I would really like to buy is the one in the far corner of the lot.

4. **a.** Science fiction movies which have become extremely popular in the last two decades often earn hundreds of millions of dollars for their studios.
   b. The science fiction movies which have earned the most money collectively are the *Star Wars* films.

5. **a.** The panda that was given to the National Zoo died recently.
   b. The panda which is native only to China is on the Endangered Species List.

Like adjective clauses, adjective phrases are also identifying or nonidentifying, depending on whether they add essential or extra information.

Examples: The postwar director **most responsible for putting Italian cinema on the map** is Federico Fellini. (identifying; no commas)

Federico Fellini, **the director of such classics as 8½,** died in 1993. (nonidentifying; commas)

3 | *Punctuate these sentences containing adjective phrases.*

1. A film produced by George Lucas is almost a guaranteed success.

2. A film directed by Steven Spielberg is likely to be a blockbuster.

3. *A Beautiful Mind* directed by Ron Howard won the Academy Award for best picture.

4. Many Canadians including Donald Sutherland and Michael J. Fox are major international film stars.

5. The Universal Studios facility located in California was established decades ago.

6. The Cineplex theater complex near our neighborhood has 12 separate theaters.

4 | *Complete the punctuation of this letter containing adjective phrases and clauses.*

September 30

Dear Mom and Dad,

Thanks again for bringing me down here to the university last weekend. Classes didn't start until Wednesday, so I had a few days to get adjusted. I'm signed up for five classes: zoology, calculus, English, and two history sections. It's a heavy load, but they're all courses that will count for my degree. The zoology class, which meets at 8:00 every morning is going to be my hardest subject. The history class that I have in the morning is on Western civilization; the one that I have in the afternoon is on early U.S. history. Calculus which I have at noon every day looks like it's going to be relatively easy. Besides zoology, the other class that's going to be hard is English which we have to write a composition a week for.

I like all of my roommates but one. There are four of us in our suite including two girls from Texas and a girl from Manitoba. Sally who is from San Antonio is great; I feel like I've known her all my life. I also really like Anne the girl from Manitoba. But Heather the other girl from Texas is kind of a pain. She's one of those types of people who never tell you what's bothering them and then get hostile. All in all, though, it looks like it's going to be a great year. I'll write again in a week or so.

Love,
Vicky

5 | *Bring to class a detailed photograph from a magazine, a newspaper, or your own collection. In class, write a paragraph of eight to ten sentences describing the picture. Include a number of adjective clauses in your paragraph, making sure to use at least one identifying and one nonidentifying adjective clause. Exchange your paper with a partner. Read each other's paragraph and make suggestions or corrections if necessary. Check for correct punctuation.*

Review Test

I *Read the composition and underline all of the adjective clauses. Write **I** (identifying) or **NI** (nonidentifying) above each clause.*

We've all heard it said that "Things may not be what they seem." Recently at work I had an experience <u>that proved to me the truth of that saying</u>. The experience involved two people I work with in my secretarial job. The first, whom I'll call "Jennifer," is one of those sunny types who always greet you in a friendly manner and never have an unkind word to say. The second, whom I'll call "Myrtle," is the type who rarely gives compliments and can sometimes be critical. Between the two of them, I thought Jennifer was the one who was my friend. Myrtle never seemed to care much for me, which is why I didn't seek out her friendship. I learned, though, that I had been reading them wrong.

About two months ago, some money was stolen from someone's purse in the office. It happened on an afternoon when all three of us, Jennifer, Myrtle, and I, were working together. Our boss, who tends to jump to conclusions, questioned the three of us and said that someone whose name he wouldn't reveal had implicated me in the theft. Jennifer, whom I expected to stand up for me, said she didn't know where I'd been at the time of the theft, which was a lie. Myrtle, however, spoke up and said she knew I couldn't have been the one who had stolen the money because she and I had been working together all afternoon. The boss accepted her statement, and that ended the unpleasantness and my friendship with Jennifer as well. I found out later that she wanted my job. I don't know whether or not she was the one who took the money, but I do know that the old proverb that tells us not to judge a book by its cover has some truth in it. Myrtle and I have been friends ever since.

II *Read the sentences, which form a narration. Circle the correct relative pronoun for each sentence.*

1. Jerry and Sue Carter, (that / (who)) got married about a year ago, recently bought a new house.

2. The neighborhood (where / which) they had been living is a somewhat dangerous one.

3. The neighborhood (that / whose) they are moving into is much safer.

4. Their new house, (that / which) they bought quite cheaply, does need some fixing up.

5. However, they will be receiving some help from their neighbors, most of (who / whom) they like.

6. The Ingrams, (who / whom) live next door to them, have volunteered to lend their tools.

7. The Thomases, (which / whose) house is across the street from Jerry and Sue's, have promised to help them put in a new lawn.

8. The Ingrams, (who / whose) daughter is the same age as Laura, Jerry and Sue's daughter, are helping Laura make new friends.

9. Sue, (that / who) works for a county hospital, will still have to commute to work.

10. Jerry, (whom / whose) company is nearby, will be able to walk to work.

III *Read the sentences, which form a narration. Put parentheses around each relative pronoun that can be omitted. Do not put relative pronouns in parentheses if they are subjects.*

1. On our trip to Europe last summer, we met a lot of people (whom) we liked.

2. One of the most interesting was Cosimo, a young Italian man who picked us up when we were hitchhiking outside Florence.

3. Cosimo, who was on his way home to Pisa, was driving so slowly that it was easy for him to stop.

4. The car that he was driving was a 1986 Volkswagen.

5. We were afraid that the car, which looked like a lemon, wouldn't make it to Pisa, but it did.

6. Cosimo took us to the house that he and his family lived in and invited us to stay for a few days.

7. The house, which was not far from downtown Pisa, was charming.

8. He also introduced us to a group of people that we felt very comfortable with.

9. We were scheduled to go to Switzerland next, so Cosimo gave us the address of a cousin of his who lived in Bern.

10. We had such a wonderful time in Italy and Switzerland that we decided to go back next year, which will cost money but will be worth it.

IV *Rewrite these sentences, reducing or changing the adjective clauses to adjective phrases.*

1. A movie that is directed by Peter Jackson is likely to be successful.

   A movie directed by Peter Jackson is likely to be successful.

2. A film that stars Jamie Foxx will probably be a blockbuster.

   _____

3. *Seabiscuit*, which features Chris Cooper in a supporting role, is a heartwarming movie.

_____

4. *Cats*, which was written by Andrew Lloyd Webber and Tim Rice, was a long-running Broadway musical.

_____

5. Several James Cameron films, which include the *Terminator* movies and *Titanic*, have earned a great deal of money.

_____

V *Write sentences containing an adjective clause describing the people or things indicated. Punctuate the clauses correctly, paying attention to whether the clauses are identifying or nonidentifying. Use* **who**, **whom**, **whose**, **that**, *or* **which**.

1. The man *who is talking with the receptionist has brought his daughter to the dentist.*

2. The man _____

3. The girl _____

4. The boy _____

5. The poster _____

6. The poster _____

7. The woman _____

8. The woman _____

VI *Circle the letter of the one underlined word or phrase in each sentence that is not correct.*

1. George Lucas, <u>whose</u> work <u>including</u> *Star Wars*, *The Empire Strikes*   **A** **Ⓑ** **C** **D**
    _A   _B
Back, and *Return of the Jedi* and <u>who</u> <u>has become</u> a world-famous
    _C _D
movie director and producer, has been directing more *Star Wars* films.

2. Previously married couple Kenneth Branagh and Emma Thompson,   **A** **B** **C** **D**
<u>both</u> <u>of which</u> are well known internationally, appeared together
 _A _B
while still married in films <u>directed</u> by Branagh, <u>including</u> *Henry V*
              _C   _D
and *Peter's Friends*.

3. Police <u>in Charleston</u> are investigating a crime <u>that</u> was <u>committing</u>   **A** **B** **C** **D**
     _A   _B   _C
yesterday evening between 11:00 P.M. and midnight at the city art
museum, <u>which</u> is located on Fifth Avenue.
       _D

4. Detective Amanda Reynolds, <u>who</u> is the chief investigating officer   **A** **B** **C** **D**
                     _A
in the case, says <u>that</u> the police have no suspects yet but are focusing
           _B
on tips <u>suggest</u> <u>that</u> the theft may have been an inside job.
    _C   _D

5. Al, <u>whom</u> is a freshman at the university, is pleased with his college   **A** **B** **C** **D**
   _A
living situation because he likes <u>the people</u> <u>he</u> is rooming <u>with</u>.
                          _B   _C   _D

6. His courses, <u>none</u> of <u>which</u> are easy, are all classes <u>requiring</u> a   **A** **B** **C** **D**
          _A   _B   _C
considerable amount of study, <u>that</u> is why he has joined a study group.
                       _D

7. Textrix, <u>the company</u> for <u>that</u> Alex works part-time, tends to employ   **A** **B** **C** **D**
        _A   _B
people <u>who are</u> highly motivated and <u>who have</u> at least 10 years
     _C   _D
of experience in the field.

8. Alicia, <u>an extrovert loves</u> working with people and <u>who can</u> also work   **A** **B** **C** **D**
        _A   _B
independently, accomplished a great deal in her last job, <u>which</u> is why
                                     _C
I think she's <u>the person we should hire</u>.
         _D

(continued)

9. The lines <u>to get into</u> the remake of *King Kong*, <u>a movie</u> <u>directed</u>
        A   B   C
   by Peter Jackson, may be long, <u>in that case</u> I would recommend
                                          D
   going to a matinee screening.

               A B C D

10. Jaime, <u>who</u> has been employed for ten years at a company <u>that</u>
         A   B
    stresses team-building and cooperative effort, is a person <u>who</u> has
                                                             C
    learned to value <u>the people with he works</u>.
                             D

               A B C D

VII   *Go back to your answers to Exercise VI. Write the correct form for each item that you believe is incorrect.*

1. _____ *includes* _____   6. _____

2. _____   7. _____

3. _____   8. _____

4. _____   9. _____

5. _____   10. _____

▶ *To check your answers, go to the Answer Key on page RT-3.*

APPENDICES

1 | Irregular Verbs

Base Form	Simple Past	Past Participle
arise	arose	arisen
awake	awoke/awaked	awaked/awoken
be	was/were	been
bear	bore	borne/born
beat	beat	beaten/beat
become	became	become
begin	began	begun
bend	bent	bent
bet	bet	bet
bite	bit	bitten
bleed	bled	bled
blow	blew	blown
break	broke	broken
bring	brought	brought
broadcast	broadcast/broadcasted	broadcast/broadcasted
build	built	built
burn	burned/burnt	burned/burnt
burst	burst	burst
buy	bought	bought
cast	cast	cast
catch	caught	caught
choose	chose	chosen
cling	clung	clung
come	came	come
cost	cost	cost
creep	crept	crept
cut	cut	cut
deal	dealt	dealt
dig	dug	dug
dive	dived/dove	dived
do	did	done
draw	drew	drawn
dream	dreamed/dreamt	dreamed/dreamt
drink	drank	drunk
drive	drove	driven
eat	ate	eaten
fall	fell	fallen
feed	fed	fed
feel	felt	felt
fight	fought	fought
find	found	found
fit	fitted/fit	fitted/fit
flee	fled	fled
fling	flung	flung
fly	flew	flown
forbid	forbade/forbad	forbidden
forget	forgot	forgotten
forgive	forgave	forgiven

Base Form	Simple Past	Past Participle
forgo	forwent	forgone
freeze	froze	frozen
get	got	gotten/got
give	gave	given
go	went	gone
grind	ground	ground
grow	grew	grown
hang	hung/hanged*	hung/hanged*
have	had	had
hear	heard	heard
hide	hid	hidden
hit	hit	hit
hold	held	held
hurt	hurt	hurt
keep	kept	kept
kneel	knelt/kneeled	knelt/kneeled
knit	knit/knitted	knit/knitted
know	knew	known
lay	laid	laid
lead	led	led
leap	leaped/leapt	leaped/leapt
learn	learned/learnt	learned/learnt
leave	left	left
lend	lent	lent
let	let	let
lie (down)	lay	lain
light	lit/lighted	lit/lighted
lose	lost	lost
make	made	made
mean	meant	meant
meet	met	met
pay	paid	paid
prove	proved	proved/proven
put	put	put
quit	quit	quit
read	read	read
rid	rid	rid
ride	rode	ridden
ring	rang	rung
rise	rose	risen
run	ran	run
saw	sawed	sawed/sawn
say	said	said

*hung = hung an object
  hanged = executed by hanging

(continued)

Base Form	Simple Past	Past Participle		Base Form	Simple Past	Past Participle
see	saw	seen		stick	stuck	stuck
seek	sought	sought		sting	stung	stung
sell	sold	sold		stink	stank/stunk	stunk
send	sent	sent		strew	strewed	strewn
set	set	set		stride	strode	stridden
sew	sewed	sewn/sewed		strike	struck	struck/stricken
shake	shook	shaken		swear	swore	sworn
shave	shaved	shaved/shaven		sweep	swept	swept
shear	sheared	sheared/shorn		swell	swelled	swelled/swollen
shine	shone/shined*	shone/shined*		swim	swam	swum
shoot	shot	shot		swing	swung	swung
show	showed	shown/showed		take	took	taken
shrink	shrank/shrunk	shrunk/shrunken		teach	taught	taught
shut	shut	shut		tear	tore	torn
sing	sang	sung		tell	told	told
sink	sank/sunk	sunk		think	thought	thought
sit	sat	sat		throw	threw	thrown
slay	slew/slayed	slain/slayed		undergo	underwent	undergone
sleep	slept	slept		understand	understood	understood
slide	slid	slid		upset	upset	upset
sneak	sneaked/snuck	sneaked/snuck		wake	woke/waked	woken/waked
speak	spoke	spoken		wear	wore	worn
speed	sped/speeded	sped/speeded		weave	wove/weaved	woven/weaved
spend	spent	spent		weep	wept	wept
spill	spilled/spilt	spilled/spilt		wet	wet/wetted	wet/wetted
spin	spun	spun		win	won	won
spit	spit/spat	spit/spat		wind	wound	wound
split	split	split		withdraw	withdrew	withdrawn
spread	spread	spread		wring	wrung	wrung
spring	sprang	sprung		write	wrote	written
stand	stood	stood				
steal	stole	stolen				

*shone = intransitive: *The sun shone brightly.*
 shined = transitive: *He shined his shoes.*

2 | Non-Action Verbs

EXAMPLES: She **seems** happy in her new job.
I **have** a terrible headache.
The food **smells** good.
Mary **owes** me money.

APPEARANCES	EMOTIONS	MENTAL STATES		PERCEPTION AND THE SENSES	POSSESSION	WANTS AND PREFERENCES
appear	abhor	agree	favor	ache	belong	desire
be	admire	amaze	feel (= believe)	feel	contain	need
concern	adore	amuse	figure (= assume)	hear	have	prefer
indicate	appreciate	annoy	find (= believe)	hurt	own	want
look	care	assume	guess	notice	pertain	wish
mean (= signify)	desire	astonish	hesitate	observe	possess	
parallel	detest	believe	hope	perceive		**OTHER**
represent	dislike	bore	imagine	see		cost
resemble	doubt	care	imply	sense		include
seem	empathize	consider	impress	smart		lack
signify (= mean)	envy	deem	infer	smell		matter
	fear	deny	know	sound		owe
	hate	disagree	mean	taste		refuse
	hope	disbelieve	mind			suffice
	like	entertain (= amuse)	presume			weigh
	love	estimate	realize			
	regret	expect	recognize			
	respect	fancy	recollect			

APPEARANCES	EMOTIONS	MENTAL STATES		PERCEPTION AND THE SENSES	POSSESSION	OTHER
	sympathize	remember	suspect			
	trust	revere	think (= believe)			
		see (= understand)	tire			
		suit	understand			
		suppose	wonder			

3 | Non-Action Verbs Sometimes Used in the Progressive

EXAMPLES: The students **are being** silly today.
We**'re having** dinner right now. Can I call you back?
Mary **is smelling** the roses.
The cook **is tasting** the soup.

ache	bore	expect	hear	include	perceive	sense
admire	consider	favor	hesitate	indicate	presume	smell
agree	deny	feel	hope	lack	realize	sympathize
amuse	disagree	figure	hurt	look	refuse	taste
annoy	doubt	find	imagine	notice	represent	think
assume	empathize	guess	imply	observe	see	wonder
be	entertain	have	impress			

4 | Irregular Noun Plurals

SINGULAR FORM	PLURAL FORM	SINGULAR FORM	PLURAL FORM	SINGULAR FORM	PLURAL FORM
alumna	alumnae	fish	fish/fishes*	paramecium	paramecia
alumnus	alumni	foot	feet	person	people
amoeba	amoebas/amoebae	genus	genera	people**	peoples
analysis	analyses	goose	geese	phenomenon	phenomena
antenna	antennae/antennas	half	halves	—	police
appendix	appendixes/appendices	index	indexes/indices	policeman	policemen
axis	axes	knife	knives	policewoman	policewomen
basis	bases	leaf	leaves	protozoan	protozoa/protozoans
businessman	businessmen	life	lives	radius	radii
businesswoman	businesswomen	loaf	loaves	series	series
calf	calves	louse	lice	sheaf	sheaves
—	cattle	man	men	sheep	sheep
child	children	millennium	millennia/millenniums	shelf	shelves
crisis	crises	money	monies/moneys	species	species
criterion	criteria	moose	moose	thesis	theses
datum	data	mouse	mice	tooth	teeth
deer	deer	octopus	octopuses/octopi	vertebra	vertebrae/vertebras
dwarf	dwarfs/dwarves	ox	oxen	wife	wives
elf	elves			woman	women

* fishes = different species of fish

** a people = an ethnic group

ABSTRACTIONS

advice
anarchy
behavior
chance
decay
democracy
energy
entertainment
evil
freedom
fun
good
happiness
hate
hatred
honesty
inertia
integrity
love
luck
momentum
oppression
peace
pollution
responsibility
slavery
socialism
spontaneity
stupidity
time
totalitarianism
truth
violence

ACTIVITIES

badminton
baseball
basketball
biking
billiards
bowling
boxing
canoeing
cards
conversation
cycling
dancing
football
golf
hiking
hockey
judo
karate
reading
sailing
singing
skating
soccer
surfing
tae kwon do
talking
tennis
volleyball
wrestling

DISEASES

AIDS
appendicitis
bronchitis
cancer
chicken pox
cholera
diabetes
diphtheria
flu (influenza)
heart disease
malaria
measles
mumps
pneumonia
polio
smallpox
strep throat
tuberculosis (TB)

FOODS

barley
beef
bread
broccoli
cake
candy
chicken
corn
fish
meat
oats
pie
rice
wheat

GASES

carbon dioxide
helium
hydrogen
neon
nitrogen
oxygen

LIQUIDS

coffee
gasoline
juice
milk
oil
soda
tea
water

NATURAL PHENOMENA

air
cold
electricity
fog
hail
heat
ice
lightning
mist
rain
sleet
slush
smog
smoke
snow
steam
thunder
warmth
wind

OCCUPATIONS

banking
computer
  technology
construction
dentistry
engineering
farming
fishing
law
manufacturing
medicine
nursing
retail
sales
teaching
writing
work

PARTICLES

dust
gravel
pepper
salt
sand
spice
sugar

SOLID ELEMENTS

calcium
carbon
copper
gold
iron
lead
magnesium
platinum
plutonium
radium
silver
tin
titanium
uranium

SUBJECTS

accounting
art
astronomy
biology
business
chemistry
civics
computer science
economics
geography
history
linguistics
literature
mathematics
music
physics
psychology
science
sociology
speech
writing

OTHER

clothing
equipment
film
furniture
news

6 | Ways of Making Non-Count Nouns Countable

ABSTRACTIONS
a piece of advice
a matter of choice
a unit of energy
a type/form of entertainment
a piece/bit of luck

ACTIVITIES
a game of badminton/baseball/basketball/
   cards/football/golf/soccer/tennis, etc.
a badminton game/a baseball game, etc.

FOODS
a grain of barley
a cut/piece/slice of beef
a loaf of bread
a piece of cake
a piece/wedge of pie
a grain of rice
a portion/serving of . . .

LIQUIDS
a cup of coffee, tea, cocoa
a gallon/liter of gasoline
a can of oil
a glass of milk, water, juice
a can/glass of soda

NATURAL PHENOMENA
a bolt/current of electricity
a bolt/flash of lightning
a drop of rain
a clap of thunder

PARTICLES
a speck of dust
a grain of pepper, salt, sand, sugar

SUBJECTS
a branch of accounting/art/
   astronomy/biology/chemistry/
   economics/geography/literature/
   linguistics/mathematics/music/
   physics/psychology/sociology, etc.

MISCELLANEOUS
an article of clothing
a piece of equipment
a piece/article of furniture
a piece of news/a news item/an item of
   news
a period of time

7 | Nouns Often Used with the Definite Article

the air
the atmosphere
the authorities
the Bhagavad Gita
the Bible
the cosmos
the Creator

the earth
the economy
the Empire State
   Building
the environment
the flu

the gross national
   product (GNP)
the Internet
the Koran
the measles
the Milky Way
   (galaxy)

the moon
the movies
the mumps
the ocean
the police
the Queen Mary

the radio
the sky
the solar system
the stock market
the stratosphere
the sun

the Taj Mahal
the Titanic
the United Nations
the universe
the Vatican
the world

8 | Countries Whose Names Contain the Definite Article

the Bahamas
the Cayman Islands
the Central African Republic
the Channel Islands
the Comoros
the Czech Republic

the Dominican Republic
the Falkland Islands
the Gambia
the Isle of Man
the Ivory Coast
the Leeward Islands

the Maldives (the Maldive Islands)
the Marshall Islands
the Netherlands
the Netherlands Antilles
the Philippines
the Solomon Islands

the Turks and Caicos Islands
the United Arab Emirates
the United Kingdom (of Great
   Britain and Northern Ireland)
the United States (of America)
the Virgin Islands

GULFS, OCEANS, SEAS, AND STRAITS

the Adriatic Sea	the Indian Ocean
the Aegean Sea	the Mediterranean (Sea)
the Arabian Sea	the North Sea
the Arctic Ocean	the Pacific (Ocean)
the Atlantic (Ocean)	the Persian Gulf
the Baltic (Sea)	the Philippine Sea
the Black Sea	the Red Sea
the Caribbean (Sea)	the Sea of Japan
the Caspian (Sea)	the South China Sea
the Coral Sea	the Strait of Gibraltar
the Gulf of Aden	the Strait of Magellan
the Gulf of Mexico	the Yellow Sea
the Gulf of Oman	

MOUNTAIN RANGES

the Alps	the Himalayas
the Andes	the Pyrenees
the Appalachians	the Rockies (the Rocky
the Atlas Mountains	Mountains)
the Caucasus	the Urals

RIVERS

(all of the following can contain the word *River*)

the Amazon	the Nile
the Colorado	the Ob
the Columbia	the Ohio
the Danube	the Orinoco
the Don	the Po
the Euphrates	the Rhine
the Ganges	the Rhone
the Huang	the Rio Grande
the Hudson	the St. Lawrence
the Indus	the Seine
the Jordan	the Tagus
the Lena	the Thames
the Mackenzie	the Tiber
the Mekong	the Tigris
the Mississippi	the Volga
the Missouri	the Yangtze
the Niger	

OTHER FEATURES

- the equator
- the Far East
- the Gobi (Desert)
- the Kalahari (Desert)
- the Middle East
- the Near East
- the North Pole
- the Occident
- the Orient
- the Panama Canal
- the Sahara (Desert)
- the South Pole
- the Suez Canal
- the Tropic of Cancer
- the Tropic of Capricorn

---

10 | **Verbs Used in the Passive Followed by a *That* Clause**

EXAMPLE: It is alleged **that** he committed the crime.

allege	believe	fear	hold	predict	theorize
assume	claim	feel	postulate	say	think

---

11 | **Stative Passive Verbs + Prepositions**

EXAMPLE: The island of Hispaniola **is divided into** two separate nations.

be bordered by	be divided into/by	be known as	be measured by
be composed of	be filled with	be listed in/as	be placed near/in
be comprised of	be found in/on, etc.	be located in/on, etc.	be positioned near/in
be connected to/with/by	be intended	be made (out) of	be related to
be covered by/with	be joined to	be made up of	be surrounded by

12 | Verbs Followed by the Gerund

EXAMPLE: Jane enjoys **playing** tennis and **gardening**.

abhor	confess	endure	give up (= stop)	postpone	resume
acknowledge	consider	enjoy	imagine	practice	risk
admit	defend	escape	keep (= continue)	prevent	shirk
advise	delay	evade	keep on	put off	shun
allow	deny	explain	mention	recall	suggest
anticipate	detest	fancy	mind (= object to)	recollect	support
appreciate	discontinue	fear	miss	recommend	tolerate
avoid	discuss	feel like	necessitate	report	understand
be worth	dislike	feign	omit	resent	urge
can't help	dispute	finish	permit	resist	warrant
celebrate	dread	forgive	picture		

13 | Adjective + Preposition Combinations

These expressions are followed by nouns, pronouns, or gerunds.

EXAMPLES: I'm not **familiar with** that writer.
I'm **amazed at** her.
We're **excited about** going.

accustomed to	capable of	fascinated with/by	intent on	ready for	suited to
afraid of	careful of	fed up with	interested in	responsible for	surprised at/about/
amazed at/by	concerned with/	fond of	intrigued by/at	sad about	by
angry at/with	about	furious with/at	mad at (=angry at/	safe from	terrible at
ashamed of	content with	glad about	with)	satisfied with	tired from
astonished at/by	curious about	good at	nervous about	shocked at/by	tired of
aware of	different from	good with	obsessed with/about	sick of	used to
awful at	excellent at	guilty of	opposed to	slow at	weary of
bad at	excited about	happy about	pleased about/with	sorry for/about	worried about
bored with/by	famous for	incapable of	poor at		

14 | Verbs Followed by the Infinitive

EXAMPLE: The Baxters **decided to sell** their house.

agree	care	determine	hurry	plan	say	swear	wait
appear	chance	elect	incline	prepare	seek	tend	want
arrange	choose	endeavor	learn	pretend	seem	threaten	wish
ask	claim	expect	manage	profess	shudder	turn out	would like
attempt	come	fail	mean (=	promise	strive	venture	yearn
beg	consent	get	intend)	prove	struggle	volunteer	
can/cannot	dare	grow (up)	need	refuse			
afford	decide	guarantee	neglect	remain			
can/cannot	demand	hesitate	offer	request			
wait	deserve	hope	pay	resolve			

15 | Verbs Followed by the Gerund or Infinitive Without a Significant Change in Meaning

EXAMPLES: Martha hates **to go** to bed early.
Martha hates **going** to bed early.

begin	can't stand	hate	love	propose
can't bear	continue	like	prefer	start

16 | Verbs Followed by the Gerund or the Infinitive with a Significant Change in Meaning

forget
I've almost **forgotten meeting** him. (= At present, I can hardly remember.)
I almost **forgot to meet** him. (= I almost didn't remember to meet him.)

go on
Jack **went on writing** novels. (= Jack continued to write novels.)
Carrie **went on to write** novels. (= Carrie ended some other activity and began to write novels.)

quit
Ella **quit working** at Sloan's. (= She isn't working there anymore.)
Frank **quit to work** at Sloan's. (= He quit another job in order to work at Sloan's.)

regret
I **regret telling** you I'd take the job. (= I'm sorry that I said I would take it.)
I **regret to tell** you that I can't take the job. (= I'm telling you now that I can't take the job, and I'm sorry I can't take it.)

remember
Velma **remembered writing** to Bill. (= Velma remembered the previous activity of writing to Bill.)
Melissa **remembered to write** to Bill. (= Melissa didn't forget to write to Bill. She wrote him.)

stop
Hank **stopped eating**. (= He stopped the activity of eating.)
Bruce **stopped to eat**. (= He stopped doing something else in order to eat.)

try
Martin **tried skiing**. (= Martin sampled the activity of skiing.)
Helen **tried to ski**. (= Helen attempted to ski but didn't succeed.)

17 | Verbs Followed by Noun / Pronoun + Infinitive

EXAMPLE: I asked Sally **to lend** me her car.

advise	choose*	forbid	invite	pay*	remind	tell	warn
allow	convince	force	need*	permit	require	urge	would like*
ask*	encourage	get*	order	persuade	teach	want*	
cause	expect*	hire					

*These verbs can also be followed by the infinitive without an object:

EXAMPLES: I **want to go**.
I **want Jerry to go**.

EXAMPLE: I was **glad to hear** about that.

advisable*	careful	disappointed	essential*	happy	lucky	proud	sorry
afraid	crucial*	distressed	excited	hard	mandatory*	ready	surprised
alarmed	curious	disturbed	fascinated	hesitant	necessary*	relieved	touched
amazed	delighted	eager	fortunate	important*	nice	reluctant	unlikely
angry	depressed	easy	frightened	impossible	obligatory*	right	unnecessary*
anxious	desirable*	ecstatic	furious	interested	pleased	sad	upset
ashamed	determined*	embarrassed	glad	intrigued	possible	scared	willing
astonished	difficult	encouraged	good	likely	prepared	shocked	wrong

* These adjectives can also be followed with a noun clause containing a subjunctive verb form.

EXAMPLES: It's essential **to communicate**.
It's essential **that she communicate with her parents**.

actually	clearly	frankly	importantly	possibly	surprisingly
amazingly	definitely	generally	mainly	probably	thankfully
apparently	essentially	happily	maybe	significantly	understandably
basically	evidently	honestly	mercifully	surely	unfortunately
certainly	fortunately	hopefully	perhaps		

SUBORDINATING CONJUNCTIONS (TO INTRODUCE ADVERB CLAUSES)		RELATIVE PRONOUNS (TO INTRODUCE ADJECTIVE CLAUSES)	OTHERS (TO INTRODUCE NOUN CLAUSES)
after	no matter if	that	how
although	no matter whether	when	how far
anywhere	now that	where	how long
as	on account of the fact that	which	how many
as if	once	who	how much
as long as	only if	whom	however (= the way in which)
as many as	plus the fact that	whose	if
as much as	provided (that)		that
as soon as	providing (that)		the fact that
as though	since		what
because	so that		what color
because of the fact that	so . . . that (= in order to)		whatever
before	such . . . that		what time
despite the fact that	though		when
due to the fact that	till		where
even if	unless		whether (or not)
even though	until		whichever (one)
even when	when		why
everywhere	whenever		
if	where		
if only	whereas		
inasmuch as	wherever		
in case	whether (or not)		
in spite of the fact that	while		

21 | Transitions: Sentence Connectors

TO SHOW ADDITION
additionally
along with this/that
also
alternatively
as a matter of fact
besides
furthermore
in addition
indeed
in fact
in other words
in the same way
likewise
moreover
plus

TO SHOW A CONTRAST
actually
anyhow
anyway
as a matter of fact
at any rate
despite this/that
even so
however
in any case
in contrast
in either case
in fact
in spite of this/that
instead (of this/that)
nevertheless
nonetheless
on the contrary
on the other hand
rather
still
though

TO SHOW AN EFFECT/ RESULT
accordingly
as a result
because of this/that
consequently
for this/that reason
hence
in consequence
on account of this/that
otherwise
then
therefore
this/that being so
thus
to this end

TO SHOW TIME AND SEQUENCE
after this/that
afterwards
an hour later (several hours later, etc.)
at last
at this moment
before this/that
from now on
henceforth
hitherto
in the meantime
just then
meanwhile
next
on another occasion
previously
then
under the circumstances
until then
up to now

22 | Transitions: Blocks of Text

all in all
nother reason/point, etc.
finally
first(ly)
in conclusion

in short
in sum
in summary
last(ly)
most importantly

second(ly)
the most important reason/factor, etc.
third(ly)

to conclude
to resume
to return to the point
to summarize

23 | Reporting Verbs

EXAMPLE: "This is the best course of action," Jack **maintained**.

add
allege
allow
ask

claim
comment
confess
exclaim

maintain
murmur
note
observe

point out
query
report

respond
say
shout

tell
wonder
yell

EXAMPLES: We **demand (that)** he **do** it.
It is **essential (that)** he **do** it.
The professor **suggested (that)** we **buy** his book.

AFTER SINGLE VERBS

ask*
demand
insist
move (= formally propose something in a meeting)
order*
prefer*
propose
recommend
request*
require*
suggest
urge*

AFTER *IT* + ADJECTIVE + NOUN CLAUSE

it is advisable that
it is crucial that
it is desirable that
it is essential that
it is important that
it is mandatory that
it is necessary that
it is obligatory that
it is reasonable that
it is required that
it is unnecessary that
it is unreasonable that

* These verbs also take the form verb + object pronoun + infinitive.

EXAMPLE: We **asked** that she **be** present.
We **asked her to be** present.

GLOSSARY OF GRAMMAR TERMS

action verb   A verb that describes an action.

- *The tourist **finds** a beautiful rug.*

active sentence   A sentence in which the subject acts upon the object.

- ***William Shakespeare** wrote <u>Hamlet</u>.*

adjective   A part of speech modifying a noun or pronoun.

- *The **blue** sofa is **beautiful**, but it's also **expensive**.*

adjective clause   A clause that identifies or gives additional information about a noun.

- *The man **who directed the film** won an Oscar.*

adjective phrase   A phrase that identifies or gives additional information about a noun.

- *The actress **playing the Queen** is Glenn Close.*

adverb   A part of speech modifying a verb, an adjective, another adverb, or an entire sentence.

- *Ben drives his **incredibly** valuable car **very carefully**.*

adverb clause   A dependent clause that indicates how, when, where, why, or under what conditions things happen; or which establishes a contrast. An adverb clause begins with a subordinating conjunction and modifies an independent clause.

- *We're going to leave for the airport **as soon as Jack gets home**.*

adverb/adverbial phrase   A phrase that indicates how, when, where, why, or under what conditions things happen. An adverb phrase modifies an independent clause.

- *We learned a great deal of Spanish **while traveling in Mexico**.*

An adverbial phrase performs the same functions as an adverb phrase but does not contain a subordinating conjunction.

- ***Having had the professor for a previous class,** I knew what to expect.*

auxiliary (helping) verb   A verb that occurs with and "helps" a main verb.

- ***Did** Mary contact you? No. She **should have** called at least.*

base form   The form of a verb listed in a dictionary. It has no endings (-s, -ed, etc.).

- *It is mandatory that Sally **be** there and **participate** in the discussion.*

causative   A verb construction showing that someone arranges for or causes something to happen. ***Get*** and ***have*** are the two most common causative verbs.

- *We **got** Martha to help us when we **had** the house remodeled.*

clause   A group of words with a subject and a verb that shows time. An **independent clause** can stand by itself. A **dependent clause** needs to be attached to an independent clause to be understood fully.

  independent   dependent

- *We'll go out for dinner as soon as I get back from the bank.*

comma splice   An error resulting from joining two independent clauses with only a comma.

- *I understand the point he made, however, I don't agree with it. (comma splice)*

- *I understand the point he made; however, I don't agree with it. (correction)*

common noun   A noun that does not name a particular thing or individual.

- *We bought a **turkey**, cranberry **sauce**, mashed **potatoes**, and **rolls** for the **dinner**.*

complement   A noun or adjective (phrase) that describes or explains a subject or direct object.

- *Hal is **a man with unusual tastes**. He painted his house **orange**.*

compound modifier   A modifier of a noun that is composed of more than one word. A compound modifier is usually hyphenated when it precedes a noun.

- *My **five-year-old** daughter can already read.*

conditional sentence   A sentence containing a dependent clause showing a condition and an independent clause showing a result. The condition may or may not be fulfilled.

   condition   result
- *If I had enough time, I would visit Morocco.*

coordinating conjunction   A word connecting independent clauses or items in a series. The seven coordinating conjunctions are ***and**, **but**, **for**, **nor**, **or**, **so**,* and ***yet**.*

- *Mom had forgotten to buy groceries, **so** we had a supper of cold pizza, salad, **and** water.*

count noun   A noun that can be counted in its basic sense. Count nouns have plural forms.

- *The **students** in my **class** all have at least one **sibling**.*

definite article   The article ***the**;* it indicates that the person or thing being talked about is unique or is known or identified to the speaker and listener.

- *China is **the** most populous nation in **the** world.*

definite past   The simple past form; it shows an action, state, or event at a particular time or period in the past.

- *I **lived** in Spain in the '70s and **visited** there again last year.*

dependent clause   A dependent clause cannot stand alone as a sentence: it requires a main clause for its meaning.

   main clause   dependent clause
- *They saw the bandit, who was wearing a bandanna.*

direct object   A noun or pronoun that receives the action of a verb.

- *Martin discovered an autographed **copy** of the novel.*

direct speech   The exact words (or thoughts) of a speaker, which are enclosed in quotation marks.

- *"**Barry,**" Phyllis said, "**I want you to tell me the truth.**"*

embedded question   A question that is inside another sentence.

- *He didn't know **what to buy his mother**.*

focus adverb   An adverb that focuses attention on a word or phrase. Focus adverbs come before the word or phrase they focus on.

- ***Even** I don't support that idea. It's too radical.*

fragment   A group of words that is not a complete sentence. It is often considered an error.

- *Because he doesn't know what to do about the situation. (fragment)*
- *He's asking for our help because he doesn't know what to do about the situation. (correction)*

future in the past   A verb construction showing a state, action, or event now past but future from some point of time in the past.

- *We **were going to help** Tim move but couldn't. Sam said he **would help** instead.*

generic   Referred to in general; including all the members of the class to which something belongs.

- ***The computer** has become essential in today's world.*
- ***Whales** are endangered.*
- ***An orangutan** is a primate living in Borneo and Sumatra.*

gerund   A verbal noun made by adding ***-ing*** to a verb.

- *Dad loves **cooking**, and we love **eating** what he cooks.*

identifying (essential) clauses and phrases   Clauses and phrases that distinguish one person or thing from others. They are not enclosed in commas.

- *The student **who is sitting at the end of the second row** is my niece.*
- *The film **starring Johnny Depp** is the one I want to see.*

***if* clause**   The clause in a conditional sentence that states the condition.

- ***If it rains,** they will cancel the picnic.*

implied condition   A condition that is suggested or implied but not stated fully. Implied conditional sentences use expressions such as *if so*, *if not*, *otherwise*, *with*, and *without*.

- *You may be able to get the item for half price.* ***If so,*** *please buy one for me as well.* (= if you are able to get the item for half price)

indefinite article   The articles *a* and *an*; they occur with count nouns and indicate that what is referred to is not a particular or identified person or thing.

- *In the last year I have bought* ***an*** *old* ***house*** *and* ***a*** *new* ***car***.

indefinite past   The present perfect; it shows a past action, event, or state not occurring at any particular or identified time.

- *We* ***have seen*** *that movie several times.*

indirect object   A noun or pronoun that shows the person or thing that receives something as a result of the action of the verb.

- *Martin gave* ***Priscilla*** *an autographed copy of his new novel.*

indirect (reported) speech   A report of the words of a speaker. Indirect speech does not include all of a speaker's exact words and is not enclosed in quotation marks.

- *Phyllis told Barry* ***that she wanted him to tell her the truth***.

infinitive   ***To*** + the base form of a verb.

- *Frank Jones is said* ***to be*** *the author of that article.*

inverted condition   The condition of a conditional sentence, stated without the word *if*. Inverted conditions occur with the verbs *had*, *were*, and *should*, which come first in the sentence and are followed by the subject.

- ***Had I*** *known that would happen, I never would have agreed.*

main clause   A main clause can stand alone as a sentence.

   main clause   dependent clause
- *They saw the bandit, who was wearing a bandanna.*

mixed conditional   A conditional sentence which shows the hypothetical present result of a past unreal situation or the hypothetical past result of a present unreal situation.

- *If I had taken that job, I would be living in Bucharest now.*
- *Sam would have arrived by now if he were planning to come.*

modal (auxiliary)   A type of helping verb. The modals are ***can***, ***could***, ***had better***, ***may***, ***might***, ***must***, ***ought to***, ***shall***, ***should***, ***will***, and ***would***. They each have one form and no endings.

- *You certainly* ***can*** *do that; the question is whether you* ***should*** *do it.*

modal-like expression   An expression with a meaning similar to that of a modal. Modal-like expressions have endings and show time.

- *Russell* ***has to*** *find a new job.*

non-action (stative) verb   A verb that in its basic sense does not show action.

- *It* ***seems*** *to me that Joe* ***has*** *a problem.*

non-count noun   A noun that in its basic sense cannot be counted.

- ***Smoke*** *from the* ***fire*** *filled the* ***air***.

nonidentifying (nonessential) clauses and phrases   Clauses and phrases that add extra information but do not distinguish one person or thing from others. They are enclosed in commas.

- *Henry,* ***who is a member of the hockey team,*** *is also a star basketball player.*

noun clause   A dependent clause that performs the same function as a noun. Noun clauses function as subjects, objects, objects of prepositions, and complements.

- ***What I want to do*** *is spend a week relaxing on the beach.*

noun modifier   A noun that modifies another noun.

- *What did you buy,* ***milk*** *chocolate or* ***chocolate*** *milk?*

parallelism (parallel structure)   The placing of items in a series in the same grammatical form.

- *Marie loves* ***hiking***, ***riding*** *horses, and* ***collecting*** *artifacts.*

participial adjective An adjective formed from present and past participial forms of verbs.

- The **bored** students were not paying attention to the **boring** speaker.

passive causative A verb structure formed with **have** or **get** + **object** + **past participle**. It is used to talk about services that you arrange for someone to do for you.

- I usually **have my dresses made** by Chantal.

passive sentence A sentence that shows the subject being acted upon by the object.

- <u>Hamlet</u> was written by **William Shakespeare**.

perfect forms Verb constructions formed with the auxiliary verbs **had**, **has**, and **have**, and a past participle. They include the **past perfect**, **present perfect**, and **future perfect**.

- I **had** never **been** to Brazil before 1990. Since then **I've been** there eight times. By this time next year, **I'll have been** there ten times.

phrase A group of related words without a subject or a verb showing time.

- **Relaxing in the hammock,** I pondered my future.

proper noun The name of a particular individual or thing. Proper nouns are capitalized.

- **Stella** and I both think that **Rio de Janeiro** and **Paris** are the world's two most beautiful cities.

quantifier A word or phrase showing the amount or number of something.

- Ken earned **a lot of** money selling vacuum cleaners.

relative pronoun A pronoun used to form adjective clauses. The relative pronouns are **that**, **when**, **where**, **which**, **who**, **whom**, and **whose**.

- The fairy tale **that** always scared me when I was a child was Rumpelstiltskin.

reporting verb A verb such as **said**, **told**, or **asked**, which introduces both direct and indirect speech. It can also come after the quotation in direct speech.

- The mayor **said**, "I've read the report." OR "I've read the report," the mayor **said**.

result clause The clause in a conditional sentence that indicates what happens if the condition occurs.

- If it rains, **they'll cancel the picnic.**

run-on sentence An error resulting from the joining of two independent clauses with no punctuation.

- I think therefore, I am. (run-on sentence)
- I think; therefore, I am. (correction)

sentence adverb An adverb that modifies an entire sentence. It can occur at the beginning, in the middle, or at the end of a sentence.

- **Fortunately,** Sarah was not hurt badly in the accident.

stative passive A passive form used to describe situations or states.

- North and South America **are connected** by the Isthmus of Panama.

subjunctive A verb form using the base form of a verb and normally following a verb or expression showing advice, necessity, or urgency. The verb *be* has the special subjunctive form *were* used for all persons.

- We always **insist** that our daughter **do** her homework before watching TV.
- If I **were** you, I would pay off my mortgage as soon as possible.

subordinating conjunction A connecting word used to begin an adverb clause.

- We were relieved **when** Jack finally called at 1 A.M.

tag question A statement + tag. The **tag** is a short question that follows the statement. Tag questions are used to check information or comment on a situation.

- She's an actor, **isn't she?**

transition A word or phrase showing a connection between sentences or between larger blocks of text.

- Global warming is a serious problem. **However,** it is not as serious as the problem of poverty.

unreal conditional sentence A sentence that talks about untrue, imagined, or impossible conditions and their results.

- If I were you, I would study a lot harder.

zero article The absence of a definite or indefinite article. The zero article occurs before unidentified plurals or non-count nouns.

- **Whales** are endangered. **Water** is necessary for survival.

REVIEW TESTS ANSWER KEY

Note: In this answer key, where the contracted verb form is given, it is the preferred form, though the full form is also acceptable. Where the full verb form is given, it is the preferred form, though the contracted form is also acceptable.

PART I

I (Units 1 and 2)
2. was going to
3. 're going to
4. he was going to
5. we'll eat, we're going to eat
6. Weren't you going to turn over
7. we'd try
8. he'll take

II (Unit 2)
1. **b.** 'd smoke
   c. used to smoke
   d. 'd smoke
2. **e.** would take
   f. 'd go
   g. used to own
   h. 'd spend
   i. used to be
3. **j.** used to be
   k. used to live
   l. would go
   m. 'd have
   n. used to be
   o. would start
   p. 'd feel

III (Units 1 and 2)
2. stayed
3. toured
4. 've seen
5. 've been walking
6. haven't gone
7. 're taking
8. 'll be arriving / 'll arrive
9. 're spending / 're going to spend / 'll be spending
10. 'll have returned
11. fly /'re flying

IV (Unit 3)
1. **a.** are   **b.** 're being
2. **a.** has written **b.** has been writing
3. **a.** are having   **b.** have
4. **a.** has been   **b.** has developed
   developing

V (Units 1–3)
2. A   7. B
3. C   8. A
4. D   9. B
5. D   10. B
6. C

VI (Units 1–3)
2. isn't going   6. did
   (to go)   7. terrible
3. you   8. had
4. was taking   9. didn't use to
5. It smells   10. visited

PART II

I (Unit 4)
1. **c.** 'm
   d. 'm not
   e. am
2. **a.** didn't earn
   b. did earn
3. **a.** haven't lived
   b. have traveled
4. **a.** isn't
   b. is
   c. does have
   d. would like

II (Unit 4)
2. So did   6. Neither would
3. hasn't either   7. hadn't either
4. Neither will   8. So does
5. am too

III (Unit 5)
2. 're supposed to
3. shouldn't have
4. aren't supposed to
5. 're supposed to
6. should have
7. should have brought
8. don't have to
9. must
10. shouldn't
11. is supposed to do

IV (Units 5 and 6)
Possible answers:

2.	could	8.	can't
3.	must have	9.	might
4.	may have	10.	should have
5.	might have	11.	could have
6.	should	12.	may
7.	's got		

V (Units 5 and 6)
Possible answers:

2. They must have forgotten to put gas in the tank.
3. They'd better slow down.
4. Drivers are supposed to carry their driver's license with them.
5. Jerry might have missed his flight. / Jerry might have decided to take a different flight.
6. Jerry could have called his parents to tell them what he was going to do.
7. It may rain.
8. They should have brought their umbrellas. / They shouldn't have tried to play tennis today.

VI (Units 4–6)

2.	B	7.	C
3.	B	8.	C
4.	C	9.	D
5.	A	10.	C
6.	D		

VII (Units 4–6)

2.	too	7.	mustn't / can't
3.	set	8.	should
4.	be	9.	won't
5.	are	10.	neither
6.	have		

PART III

I (Unit 8)

2.	no article	18.	an
3.	no article	19.	a
4.	the	20.	the
5.	the	21.	an
6.	no article	22.	a
7.	no article	23.	no article
8.	no article	24.	no article
9.	no article	25.	no article
10.	no article	26.	the
11.	no article	27.	no article
12.	no article	28.	no article
13.	the	29.	no article
14.	A	30.	the
15.	a	31.	the
16.	no article	32.	no article
17.	no article		

II (Unit 8)

2. . . . not birds . . .
3. . . . a humanlike ape . . .
4. . . . was the third of . . .
5. The Jurassic period . . .
6. . . . the official currency . . .
7. A meltdown is . . .
8. The statues on Easter Island
9. . . . for raising cattle.
10. The telephone . . .

III (Unit 7)
Possible answers:

2. Several pieces of furniture are for sale.
3. *Gabriela, Clove* and *Cinnamon* is a literary work by Jorge Amado.
4. Let me give you a piece of advice.
5. The Shan are a people of northern Myanmar.
6. There are several spices on the rack.
7. The tree was hit by a bolt of lightning.
8. Camembert is a cheese produced in France.

IV (Unit 10)

1. **b.** chilly winter
2. **a.** new pink silk
   b. handsome, young European
3. **a.** beautiful new brick
   b. dirty little old

V (Unit 9)

2. **a.** any
   b. some
3. **a.** many
   b. amount
   c. less
   d. fewer
4. **a.** a few
   b. any
   c. a few
5. **a.** much
   b. a great many
   c. any
   d. a great deal of
   e. little
   f. Few

VI (Units 7–10)

2.	C	7.	B
3.	A	8.	C
4.	D	9.	B
5.	B	10.	C
6.	D		

VII (Units 7–10)

2. a beautiful condominium
3. The plan
4. the wheel

5. first two
6. the scientific community
7. the Canadian Southwest
8. beans
9. 10-year-old
10. lightning / a bolt of lightning

PART IV

I (Unit 11)

I   I work with in my secretarial job
NI whom I'll call "Jennifer"
I   who always greet you in a friendly manner and never have an unkind word to say
NI whom I'll call "Myrtle"
I   who rarely gives compliments and can sometimes be critical
I   who was my friend
NI which is why I didn't seek out her friendship
I   when all three of us, Jennifer, Myrtle, and I, were working together
NI who tends to jump to conclusions
I   whose name he wouldn't reveal
NI whom I expected to stand up for me
NI which was a lie
I   who had stolen the money
I   who took the money
I   that tells us not to judge a book by its cover

II (Unit 11)

2.	where	7.	whose
3.	that	8.	whose
4.	which	9.	who
5.	whom	10.	whose
6.	who		

III (Unit 11)

2.	no omission	7.	no omission
3.	no omission	8.	(that)
4.	(that)	9.	no omission
5.	no omission	10.	no omission
6.	(that)		

IV (Unit 12)

2. A film starring Jamie Foxx will probably be a blockbuster.
3. *Seabiscuit*, featuring Chris Cooper in a supporting role, is a heartwarming movie.
4. *Cats*, written by Andrew Lloyd Webber and Tim Rice, was a long-running Broadway musical.
5. Several James Cameron films, including the *Terminator* movies and *Titanic*, have earned a great deal of money.

V (Unit 11)

Possible answers:

2. The man who is looking at one of the posters has a toothache.
3. The girl, whose father is talking to the receptionist, doesn't want to visit her dentist.
4. The boy, whose mother is reading him a story, is named Jerry.
5. The poster that is to the left of the receptionist is about gum disease.
6. The poster that is to the left of the door is about brushing properly.
7. The woman who is reading a story to her son is wearing a big hat.
8. The woman who is reading a magazine has her dog with her.

VI (Units 11 and 12)

2.	B	7.	B
3.	C	8.	A
4.	C	9.	D
5.	A	10.	D
6.	D		

VII (Units 11 and 12)

2. of whom
3. committed
4. suggesting
5. who
6. which
7. which
8. an extrovert who loves
9. in which case
10. the people with whom he works / the people he works with

PART V

I (Unit 13)

1. **b.** was discovered
2.   will get beaten
3.   got hit
4. **a.** we've been getting overcharged
   b. have the company investigated
5. **a.** Aren't they cleaned
   b. didn't get done
6. **a.** are fed
   b. Are they being fed
   c. won't be fed

II (Unit 13)

2. he has learned his lesson
3. He parked his motorcycle
4. he discovered
5. his motorcycle had been removed
6. It had been placed
7. No one had been noticed
8. Mason commented

III **(Unit 14)**
2. was located
3. were found
4. are assumed
5. is believed
6. should not be considered

IV **(Units 13 and 14)**
Suggested answers:
2. Mrs. Riley just got stopped.
3. Two months ago a building was being torn down.
4. Now a new building is being built.
5. Mrs. Platt is going to have her toaster repaired.
6. Once a month, Mr. Platt gets his hair and beard cut and trimmed.
7. The yeti is thought to live in the Himalayas.
8. The lost continent of Atlantis is said to have been located in the Atlantic Ocean.

V **(Units 13 and 14)**
2. A
3. B
4. C
5. B
6. B
7. D
8. C
9. D
10. C

VI **(Units 13 and 14)**
2. was
3. said
4. reported
5. being
6. suspended
7. started
8. are being / are to be / are going to be
9. be launched
10. staffed

PART **VI**

I **(Units 15 and 16)**
1. b. going
2. a. to tell
   b. lying
3. a. to defend
   b. defending
4. a. to major
   b. being / to be
   c. doing

II **(Unit 15)**
2. Seward's having perceived
3. Court's having outlawed
4. Parks's deciding
5. her refusing
6. John F. Kennedy's having agreed
7. his having been warned
8. The reformers' having misjudged
9. protesters' seizing the moment and demanding

III **(Units 15 and 16)**
2. using
3. slowing
4. to have been completed
5. causing / having caused
6. to be finished
7. to be cleared
8. taking
9. switching

IV **(Unit 16)**
2. was supposed to
3. planning to
4. ought to
5. didn't have time to
6. don't want to

V **(Units 15 and 16)**
Possible answers:
1. (second verb) to read
2. driving, getting
3. working / to work
4. staying
5. working
6. reading

VI **(Units 15 and 16)**
2. C
3. A
4. A
5. B
6. D
7. B
8. C
9. D
10. C

PART **VII**

I **(Unit 18)**
1. B: OK. We can leave <u>as soon as you back the car out of the garage</u>.
2. A: Harry is a lot more responsible <u>since he's been class president</u>.
   B: Yes, I know. He never used to do his chores <u>unless I threatened him</u>.
3. A: I'll call you <u>when the plane gets in</u>.
   B: OK, but you'd better take down Harriet's number <u>in case I'm not home</u>.
4. A: Wasn't that a great dinner? It won't surprise me <u>if I'm five pounds heavier tomorrow</u>.
   B: Yeah. <u>Whenever I come home to visit</u>, I gain weight. Mom is a such a great cook.
5. A: There were better TV shows <u>before there were so many channels</u>.
   B: I don't agree. <u>Now that cable is available</u>, we have access to some impressive programming.

6. A: Joe, <u>since you didn't turn in your term paper</u>, you didn't pass the course—<u>even though you did well on the tests</u>.

B: Yes, I know. I didn't do the term paper <u>because I couldn't think of anything to write about</u>.

7. A: Is your new house going to be finished <u>by the time you leave on your big trip</u>?

B: I think so. <u>Once they've laid the foundation</u>, they can start building.

II (Unit 20)

2. However
3. therefore
4. otherwise
5. on the contrary
6. Moreover

III (Unit 18)

Suggested answers:

2. Though they had been leaving the children with Sarah's mother, this wasn't a satisfactory solution. OR They had been leaving the children with Sarah's mother, though this wasn't a satisfactory solution.
3. One of them was going to have to quit working unless they could find a solution to the problem.
4. When one of their neighbors proposed the creation of a daycare co-op involving five families, their problem was solved.
5. Each day, one of the parents in the co-op cares for all the children while the other parents are working.

IV (Unit 17)

Dear Samantha,

I wanted to thank you again for your hospitality while we were in Vancouver. Not only *did you and Michael show* ~~you and Michael showed~~ us a wonderful time, but we also got to reestablish the close ties we used to have. *Even the kids* ~~The even kids~~ enjoyed the trip, and you know how kids are on vacations. *I only hope* ~~Only I hope~~ that Dan and I can reciprocate sometime.

The drive back to Edmonton was something else; *we almost didn't* ~~almost we didn't~~ make it back in one piece. About 4:30 on the day we left, there was an ice storm near Calgary that turned the highway into a sheet of ice. Little did we know that it would take us four hours to get through the city. Rarely *have I* ~~I have~~ been in such an awful traffic jam. By the time we got off the freeway, it was 11:30 at night, and the kids were crying. We stopped at a motel to try to get a room; they were full up, but when we asked the proprietors if *we could just* ~~just we could~~ spend the night in their lobby, they took pity on us and made us up a bed in their living room. People can be so kind sometimes. Never again *will I* ~~I will~~ think twice about helping people when they need it. By the next morning, the roads had been cleared, and we made it safely back to Edmonton.

Well, here *come the kids* ~~the kids come~~ to get their afternoon snack. Please write soon. Thanks again.

Love,
Barb

V (Units 18 and 20)

2. They tried combinations of threats, punishments, and rewards; however, nothing seemed to work.
3. Tim and Zeya both got home about 5:30 P.M., and they needed to occupy the children's attention while they were fixing dinner.
4. Though they felt so much TV watching wasn't good, they allowed it because they had no alternative.
5. Their children weren't getting enough exercise; in addition, they weren't interacting with the other children in the neighborhood.
6. Since a lot of their neighbors were having similar problems with their children, someone came up with the idea of starting a neighborhood activity club.
7. The club met every afternoon from 5:00 until 6:30, and two parents from different families supervised activities.
8. The club has been a big success; none of the children have watched very much television lately.

VI (Units 17–20)

2. A
3. D
4. C
5. B
6. B
7. C
8. A
9. D
10. D

VII (Units 17–20)

2. Feeling
3. even if
4. is capital punishment
5. but
6. clearly
7. obviously
8. Having landed
9. he doesn't even
10. he comes

PART VIII

I (Unit 21)

1. **A:** I don't know what we should do tonight.
   B: <u>Whatever you want to do</u> is fine with me.
2. **A:** We haven't decided <u>where we want to go on vacation</u>.
   B: Don't you think <u>Hawaii would be nice</u>?
3. **A:** How do we decide <u>who wins the prize</u>?
   B: Give it to <u>whoever gets the most points</u>.
4. **A:** Do you think <u>she's guilty</u>?
   B: Well, <u>the fact that she waited so long to contact the police</u> doesn't help her case.
5. **A:** I can't believe <u>what I'm seeing</u>. The Bengals might even win this game.
   B: Yeah, I know. I'm amazed <u>that they're doing this well</u>.
6. **A:** Mr. Brown, I'm sorry to report <u>that I need more time to complete the assignment</u>.
   B: That's all right. Take <u>whatever time you need</u>. I want the job done well.
7. **A:** As for the problem of stopping violence in schools, I don't know <u>what the answer is</u>.
   B: I think <u>that we need to ban weapons of all kinds</u>.
8. **A:** Do you know <u>what Samantha's problem is</u>?
   B: No, but it's clear <u>that she's very unhappy</u>.

II (Unit 21)

November 28
Dear Manny,

Well, my first month as a literacy volunteer is over, and I feel exhilarated!

What

~~The fact that~~ I like best is the chance to work

what's

with real people. In the mornings I report to ~~it's~~ called "Open Classroom." I'm assigned to tutor

whoever

~~whomever~~ comes in and asks for help. Most of the students are wonderful; sometimes I'm amazed

[that]

~~what~~ they're so motivated to learn. In the afternoons I tutor my regular students. I often work with a lady from Vietnam named Mrs. Tranh. When I started working with her, she could hardly read at all. Now I'm really impressed by

what

~~whichever~~ she's learned. At first I chose the

whatever / what

assignments, but now we work on ~~whomever~~ Mrs. Tranh chooses. If she wants to practice oral

what

reading, that's ~~which~~ we do. If she wants to work on comprehension, we do that for as long as she likes. Sometimes we spend all afternoon on one

the fact that / that

thing, but that's OK; ~~what~~ she's so motivated is very rewarding.

Well, that's all for now. Write soon, and I'll do the same.

Best,
Diane

III (Unit 21)

2. where she is
3. a. that Bill is
   b. the fact that he is ill a great deal
4. a. that we need to do
   b. whatever is necessary
5. a. whoever it is
   b. that it isn't
6. a. how far it is
   b. that it's

IV (Units 21 and 22)
Possible answers:

2. The Martins wondered if they could afford a bigger house.
3. Mrs. Martin's father asked where the house was located.
4. Mrs. Martin's mother said it was important that they have the house they needed.
5. Mrs. Martin's father told them that they would help them with the down payment.
6. The Martins were thrilled that they got their new house.

V (Unit 21)

2. C	7. A
3. A	8. D
4. C	9. D
5. A	10. B
6. B	

PART IX

I (Units 23 and 24)

2. F	7. P
3. F	8. PR
4. PR	9. F
5. P	10. PR
6. PR	

II (Unit 23)

2. If he had changed the oil, the engine wouldn't have seized.
3. If the engine hadn't seized, the other car wouldn't have rear-ended him.
4. He wouldn't have had to pay a towing bill.
5. He wouldn't have had to replace the engine.
6. He could have made it to the job interview if all this hadn't happened.
7. If he had made it to the interview, he might have a job now.
8. Brandon wishes he had listened to his inner voice.

III (Unit 24)

2. that Mary not lose her temper
3. that her neighbor keep the dog in at night
4. that the neighbor get rid of the animal
5. that Mary call the animal control bureau

IV (Unit 23)

2. we'd realized
3. he keeps
4. there were
5. we could contact
6. it weren't
7. we had
8. this isn't / this won't be
9. we knew
10. it is

V (Units 23 and 24)

Possible answers:

2. Karen insisted that they leave.
3. If they hadn't stayed up late, Sam wouldn't have overslept.
4. If Sam had already gotten some gas, he wouldn't have run out.
5. If he had taken a taxi, he could have made it to the interview.
6. If he had listened to Karen's advice, he might have gotten the job / he might have a job now.

VI (Units 23 and 24)

2. B
3. A
4. A
5. B
6. C
7. A
8. D
9. C
10. D

INDEX

This Index is for the full and split editions. All entries are in the full book. Entries for Volume A of the split edition are in black. Entries for Volume B are in color.